Sunset

Seafood
COOKBOOK

By the Editors of Sunset Books and Sunset Magazine

For elegance with ease, serve Grilled Salmon on Wilted Chicory Salad (page 113).

Sunset Publishing Corporation ■ *Menlo Park, California*

The Fish Market Revolution

Book Editor
Phyllis Elving

Research & Text
Annabel Post

Contributing Editors
Tori Bunting
Cynthia Scheer

Coordinating Editor
Deborah Thomas Kramer

Design
Joe di Chiarro

Illustrations
Lois Lovejoy

Photography by Darrow Watt

Additional photography: Glenn Christiansen: 12, 19, 114; Norman A. Plate: 6, 44, 116; Tom Wyatt: 107; Nikolay Zurek: 55, 108.

Photo styling by Susan Massey-Weil: 4, 10, 14, 25, 28, 39, 78, 79, 80, 81, 83, 86, 90, 92, 93, 94, 95, 96, 98, 118, 123, 125.

Cover: Broiled fillet of king salmon (page 53) served with roasted potatoes and fresh asparagus. Photography by Noel Barnhurst, art direction by Vasken Guiragossian, food styling by Kim Konecny and Erin Quon.

About the Recipes

All of the recipes in this book were tested and develped in the *Sunset* test kitchens.

Food and Entertaining Editor, *Sunset* Magazine
Jerry Anne Di Vecchio

Until recently, when you asked for the "catch of the day" at a restaurant, you were served something that you recognized—perhaps a fillet of sole. Even at the fish market, you found the same selection week after week. Fish was sometimes called brain food, but few appreciated its nutritional value.

Times have changed. Today's catch is prized as both a gourmet delicacy and a source of high-quality protein, along with important vitamins and minerals. Expanded and ever changing, the catch now includes such fish as orange roughy, flown in from New Zealand, or papio from Hawaii. A seafood salad, once built around canned tuna, is likely to feature morsels of monkfish instead.

Newly discovered species are brought up from ocean depths never before plumbed; at the same time, old favorites—including catfish, salmon, trout, mussels, and shrimp—are grown by aquaculture, both onshore and offshore. Improved air transport rushes seafood to markets across the world, and new technology allows fresher-than-ever frozen fish.

For the shopper, cook, and diner, all this amounts to nothing less than a seafood revolution—raising not only expectations of good eating habits but also many questions. Within the pages of this book, you'll find these questions explored and answered in detail.

With the comprehensive A-to-Z buyer's guide, you'll be able to identify, prepare, and cook nearly any fish or shellfish on the market today. Whether you like seafood baked, grilled, fried, or steamed, you're sure to find a technique or recipe that will satisfy from among the 150 presented here.

For our recipes, we provide a nutritional analysis prepared by Hill Nutrition Associates, Inc., of New York (for details, see page 13).

For her thorough and careful editing of the manuscript, we extend a very special thank you to Fran Feldman.

We also with to extend our gratitude to all those who assisted us in our research or helped locate fish for our testing. For sharing his expertise on fish and shellfish, we thank Jon Rowley of Fish Works!, Seattle. We also thank Susan Asanovic, M.S., Nutrition Consultant, Wilton, Connecticut; The Berelson Company, San Francisco; Jim Brooker, National Marine Fisheries, Washington, D.C.; Drs. Mel Ecklund and Jack Wakell, Northwest and Alaska Fishery Center, Seattle; Linda Foley, Foley Seafoods, Boston.

Also, Mark Goforth, Goforth and Fish, Palo Alto, California; Intersea Fisheries, Ltd., Seattle; Paul Johnson, Monterey Fish, Berkeley, California; Ken Oliveira, H. & N. Fish Co., San Francisco; Gina Paladini, Paladini Seafood, San Francisco; Robert J. Price, Ph.D, University of California, Davis; Curt Sinclair, Sun Coast Seafoods, St. Petersburg, Florida; and Steven T. Wright, Signal Crayfish, Inc., Sacramento.

Finally, we acknowledge Williams & Ziller Design for their initial book design work.

VP, Editorial Director, Sunset Books:
Bob Doyle

3 4 5 6 7 8 9   QPD   04 03

Previously published as
Fish & Shellfish - A to Z.

Contents

Fresh from Sea & Stream 5

A Buyer's Guide to Seafood 15

Basic Techniques 79

Cleaning Whole Fish ■ Cutting Fish
■ Baking ■ Barbecuing ■ Broiling ■
Deep-frying ■ Pan-frying ■ Poaching,
Steaming & Steeping ■ Stir-frying

A Repertoire of Recipes 99

Appetizers ■ Soups & Stews ■ Salads ■
Main Dishes ■ Sauces & Butters

Index 126

Special Features

Cooking Characteristics of Fish 8
Caviar—A Choice of Luxuries 19
Rediscovering Salt Cod 25
Gravlax—More than Just Salmon 47
Sushi Made Simple 54
Surimi: Shellfish Look-Alikes 69
Smoking Fish on the Barbecue 84
Bastes & Marinades 87
Parchment Packets of Flavor 91
Fish & Shellfish in the Microwave 96
Quick Ways with Smoked Seafood 116

Fresh from Sea & Stream

*An introduction to seafood—
guidelines to selecting, storing,
and understanding how to use
fresh fish and shellfish*

Seafood, unlike our other basic food-stuffs, is still mainly a wild harvest. Working against the uncertainties of fish runs and weather, most fishermen today go to sea in small boats just as they have for centuries. Their success largely determines what markets have for sale.

But as a visit to your neighborhood fish market will tell you, some things have actually changed a great deal. Once a simple matter of choosing among a half-dozen familiar species, shopping for seafood has now become a new and sometimes bewildering experience.

Today, thanks mainly to the use of wide-body jets, fresh fish and shellfish from halfway around the world can reach U.S. markets in little more time than it takes a local fisherman to deliver his catch. Never before has the consumer been confronted with a greater selection of familiar—and not so familiar—fish and shellfish. And the trend is certain to continue.

The Changing Seafood Industry

Seafood has become an international business as demand for it has increased all over the world. Because the United States now depends on imports for

nearly two-thirds of its seafood supply, both world trade practices and the dollar's value in relation to other currencies affect what's available in local markets, and at what price.

The decreasing supply of some traditionally popular species—among them striped bass, red drum, pompano, and abalone—because of overfishing and pollution has caused prices for them to soar. At the same time, once-overlooked species, such as Pacific cod, cusk, shark, skate, squid, and mussels, are now being harvested by commercial fishermen in order to meet the increasing demand.

The methods of catching fish have also changed. Newer and larger boats, equipped with the latest sounding instruments, can now locate and identify schools of fish in midwater. Fishing at greater depths than possible in the past, fishermen are catching fish, such as orange roughy, seldom seen just a few years ago.

In many areas of the world, large vessels called factory ships are processing and freezing fish and shellfish at sea, which enables them to harvest species that were too perishable to get to market in the past. They're also helping to change the image of frozen fish: freshly caught fish that are filleted and then individually quick-frozen with a protective glaze (called IQF in the trade) are often superior to all but truly fresh fish.

Moreover, increasing amounts of live shellfish are being shipped to market today. Holding tanks have developed into sophisticated life-support systems, enabling even supermarkets to sell live fish as well as shellfish.

Aquaculture, the science of breeding and raising fish in captivity, now accounts for a sizable, consistent supply of trout and catfish—and has significantly increased the world's supply of salmon, scallops, and shrimp. In the United States and abroad, a new breed of farmers is producing exquisite oysters, mussels, and clams; even abalone may be easier to buy in a few years, thanks to aquaculture.

Sorting Out Your Choices

The many new seafood varieties and constantly changing selection in markets today make it difficult for consumers to know what to buy. If the fish or shellfish is unfamiliar, how should it be prepared and cooked? More importantly, how will it taste? What sauces or accompaniments will best complement the fish?

To add to the difficulty, market names for fish have traditionally been confusing, overlapping, and sometimes downright incorrect. Often, the same fish will go by a variety of names from region to

A delicious meal served from the grill demonstrate's seafood's versatility. For appetizers, start with shrimp and scallop kebabs in Lemon-Butter Baste and skewered garden-fresh vegetables. Swordfish soaked in Italian-style Marinade is ready to be cooked for the main course. For barbecuing techniques and recipes, see pages 86–88.

region and sometimes from one market to another.

When a new species is introduced, the tendency has been for markets to give it a familiar-sounding name that customers will understand and buy. As a result, some fish with very different characteristics have acquired similar common names. Some markets have even adopted fanciful names, such as "blue scrod" for Atlantic pollock and "silverbrite salmon" for chum salmon, in order to sell less popular species.

To answer all these questions and concerns, this book offers a comprehensive buyer's guide (pages 15–77) to fish and shellfish, organized in alphabetical order for easy reference.

A San Diego fisherman proudly displays his catches: a 220-pound common thresher shark and a 20-pound grouper. Regardless of size, fish must be handled with care from the moment they're landed to ensure top quality for market.

Pertinent information about each of the commonly available species is presented so you can identify the one you're buying and determine the best ways to cook and serve it.

For example, the many kinds of bass and sea bass range in texture from soft and flaky to dense and meaty, calling for quite different cooking techniques. The buyer's guide will help you find out which bass you're buying by giving you the information you need in order to question the fishmonger on the fish's origin or its other common names. (You can often judge the quality of a fish market by how well informed they are about the seafood they sell.)

In addition, the guide also describes in detail any special preparation needed for a particular fish or shellfish, which basic cooking methods give the best results, and any special handling required to cook it that way. Any cooking methods unique to a particular species are included in the guide. It also directs you to appropriate recipes in the recipe section beginning on page 99. And finally, it suggests simple serving ideas and complementary sauces to enhance the fish or shellfish after it's cooked.

The section called Basic Techniques, beginning on page 79, gives step-by-step directions for the best and simplest ways to cook fish and shellfish. And for those who catch their own fish or buy one whole, there are complete instructions for scaling, cleaning, and cutting it up.

Use the techniques section and the recipes in conjunction with the chart of fish groupings on pages 8–9. This chart classifies fish according to cooking characteristics, helping you to make your selection at the fish market and decide how to prepare your purchase. It will also help you make substitutions if the fish you planned to buy is unavailable.

Fish Forms & Anatomy

In today's fish markets, most fish is sold ready to cook. Usually, it's conveniently cut into *fillets,* the fleshy sides of fish cut away from the backbone and ribs (with or without the skin), or *steaks,* cross-section slices.

Whole fish may be cleaned, or dressed, which means the fish has been eviscerated, often with the gills removed. The term "pan-dressed" is sometimes used to indicate the fish is ready to cook; it may have the head and scales removed, and sometimes the fins and tail are trimmed.

There are advantages to buying fish whole. Some fish are sold only in that form, so you'll have a wider selection if you're willing to buy a whole fish. With the head and skin intact, fish tend to stay fresh longer; also, it's easier to judge the freshness of a whole fish. As a bonus, you'll have the fish trimmings for making Fish Stock (page 93).

In an increasing number of markets, you can even select your fish live; the fishmonger will kill and clean it for you.

Whether you buy it at the market or catch it yourself, handling a whole fish is easier if you understand its anatomy. Knowing where the bones are hiding also makes it easier to avoid them. Most species fall into one of three categories based on their bone structure: flatfish, round fish, or tunas.

All *flatfish* (shown on facing page) have a row of bones attached to each side of a flat center bone, like a comb with teeth on both sides. Flatfish are easy fish to fillet either before or after cooking. Trimming deeply on both edges removes all the fin bones, so flatfish fillets are boneless. Except for halibut and some large flounders, flatfish (soles and flounders) are too thin to cut into steaks.

Round fish have a more complex bone structure. Their fillets and steaks usually have some pinbones; however, before cooking them, you can run your fingers over the surface to locate small bones and then pluck them out with tweezers or pliers.

Many of the small bones on round fish are attached to fins. Before cooking a whole fish, you can cut the flesh on both sides of the dorsal and anal fins and simply pull them out with the bones attached. If you plan to cook round fish whole, however, leave the fins in—they help hold the fish's shape and are easy to pull out of the cooked fish before serving.

The tail section of a round fish usually has the fewest small bones; the collar area has the most. Round fish have thick bodies that can be either filleted or, if large enough, cut crosswise into steaks.

Fish in the *tuna* family have a unique bone structure. Four rows of bones radiate like spokes from a thick bone running through the center of their submarine-shaped bodies, dividing the flesh into four triangular, boneless sections called loins (see illustration on page 75). Tuna loins may be cut into chunks or slices, usually called steaks.

The largest fish tend to have the fewest bothersome small bones. Swordfish and tunas are almost free of them. Shark and sturgeon skeletons are cartilage rather than bone.

Shopping for Seafood

Freshness is the key to quality in seafood. But the way fish or shellfish is caught and how it's handled from the moment it comes out of the water affect freshness far more than the actual time it takes it to reach the market. If landed alive and unbruised, and then immediately bled, cleaned, packed in ice, and held at close to 32°F, some kinds of fish will stay fresh for 10 days. Improperly handled and allowed to stand on a boat deck or dock, fish can spoil within a few hours.

■ **Judging freshness of fish.** Your nose is the most reliable gauge of freshness, and you should trust your first impression when you sniff a fish or first walk into a fish market (it's a fact that your nose doesn't register odors as well on a second sniff).

Fish should smell like a fresh ocean breeze. Any disagreeable, sweet, or ammonialike odor is caused by bacteria that proliferate as seafood deteriorates. It's more difficult to determine the freshness of packaged fish, but sometimes you can detect a strong odor by smelling the package.

Check appearance, too. Fresh fillets and steaks look moist and lustrous, an appearance called "bloom" in the trade. They should appear cleanly cut, as if just placed in the case or tray. Avoid packages of fish in which liquid has accumulated, especially if it's cloudy or off-white in appearance. Always check packaged frozen fish for signs of mishandling, such as a buildup of ice crystals, discoloration, or drying, especially around the edges.

The gills of whole fish should be clean and red, not sticky and gray. The scales should be shiny and hold tightly to the skin. When you press the flesh

Anatomy of Two Fish

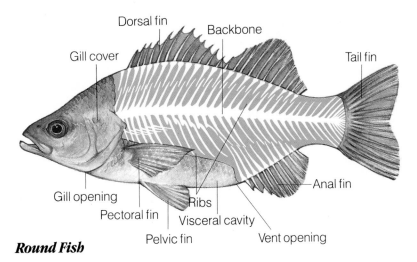

Round Fish

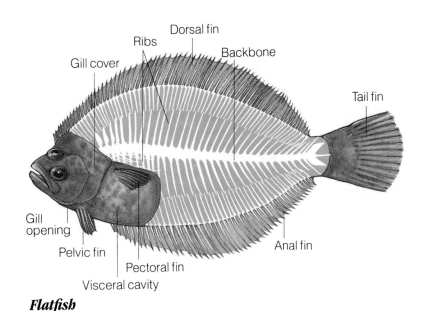

Flatfish

with your finger, it should feel firm and elastic.

Next to truly fresh fish, frozen is best. Most markets thaw frozen fish before putting it out in the cases, so you may have to ask your dealer for fish that has not been thawed.

■ **Choosing fresh shellfish.** You know shellfish is fresh if it's alive and vigorous. With hard-shell clams, oysters, and mussels, a tightly closed shell is the best indication of freshness. If a shell is slightly open, it should close when

gently tapped. Touch the neck of a soft-shell clam to see if it twitches. The foot an an abalone should feel hard and should wiggle when tickled.

Live crabs, lobsters, and crayfish move their legs. A live lobster's tail curls under the body rather than hanging down when the lobster is picked up.

If shellfish die naturally, they won't necessarily make you sick, but their meat spoils so rapidly that it's wise to discard them. The enzymes in a dead crab work especially fast to make it unfit to eat.

(Continued on page 10)

Cooking Characteristics of Fish

Atlantic cod

Size, texture, taste, and fat content are the factors that determine to a large extent what cooking methods will be most successful for a particular type of fish. This chart shows you at a glance which fish have similar characteristics and what methods are best for cooking them. Fish within each group may vary widely in quality, but usually they can be substituted for one another in recipes. A few fish, such as eel, monkfish, ocean pout, skate, and smelt, are not included because they're one of a kind and don't fit into the groups. For details on the suggested cooking methods, see pages 82–95.

Winter flounder

Group I: *Thin & Delicate*

Small flatfish yielding fillets less than ½ inch thick and flexible (can be rolled). Whole fish are too thin to cut into steaks. Smallest species (rex sole and sanddab) are sold whole or deeply trimmed (pan-ready). Meat is tender and delicate to mild in flavor. All are lean*. Dusting with flour aids browning when pan-frying.

- All the small flounders and soles, including American plaice, gray sole, winter flounder, and yellowtail flounder on the Atlantic coast; English sole, petrale sole, rex sole, and sanddab on the Pacific coast.

▨ Best ways to cook

Fillets: Pan-fry or pan-poach; roll fillets to poach the classic way or to steep.

Small whole fish: Oven-brown, pan-fry, pan-poach, poach the classic way, or steep.

---

*Lean: Less than 2.5 percent fat
*Moderately lean: Less than 5 percent fat
*Oilier: More than 5 percent fat
 These small differences in oiliness are not significant nutritionally.

Group II: *Medium-dense, Flaky*

Small to medium-size fish with moist, tender meat. Steaks and fillets are usually ½ to 1 inch thick and sturdier than fish in Group I, but they need to be supported on foil or in a hinged wire broiler if grilled. Crumb coatings usually add flavor and texture. Group includes small, pan-size fish and larger fish sold whole. Fish vary in oiliness and flavor.

II a: Lean, mild in flavor*

- Bass, striped and white (freshwater)
- Cods and related fish, including Antarctic queen, Atlantic whiting, haddock, hake (white and red), hoki, and pollock
- Flounder (large), including arrowtooth, southern, and summer
- Halibut, California
- John Dory
- Kingklip
- Lingcod
- Perch, walleye and yellow (freshwater)
- Pike, northern (freshwater)
- Rockfish, including Atlantic and Pacific ocean perch and Pacific snapper
- Snapper, red and others, including Hawaiian ta'ape
- Tilapia (freshwater)
- Tilefish
- Wolffish

▨ Best ways to cook

Steaks and fillets: Bake in sauce or with a creamy topping, oven-brown, broil with moist heat or with a crumb coating, deep-fry, pan-fry, pan-poach, steep, foil-steam, or steam Chinese-style.

Small whole fish: Bake in sauce or with a stuffing, oven-brown, broil with moist heat, pan-fry, pan-poach, poach the classic way, steep, foil-steam, or steam Chinese-style.

Larger whole fish: Bake in sauce or with a stuffing, poach the classic way, or foil-steam.

II b: Moderately lean, mild in flavor*

- Catfish (freshwater)
- Croaker and spot
- Salmon, chum and pink
- Sea bream, including porgy, scup, and sheepshead
- Seatrout, spotted, and gray weakfish
- Trout, rainbow (freshwater)

▨ Best ways to cook

Steaks and fillets: Bake in sauce, oven-brown, barbecue, broil with dry or moist heat or with a crumb coating, deep-fry, pan-fry, pan-poach, poach the classic way, steep, or steam Chinese-style.

Small whole fish: Bake in sauce or with a stuffing, oven-brown, barbecue, broil with dry or moist heat, pan-fry, pan-poach, poach the classic way, foil-steam, or steam Chinese-style.

Larger whole fish: Bake in sauce or with a stuffing, barbecue, poach the classic way, or foil-steam.

II c: Oilier* or distinctively flavored

Oilier* and mild in flavor:
- Buffalo (freshwater)
- Butterfish, Atlantic and Pacific
- Carp (freshwater)
- Greenland turbot (halibut)
- Sablefish (black cod, butterfish)
- Sea bass, Chilean
- Shad (freshwater)
- Trout, lake (freshwater)
- Whitefish, lake (freshwater)

Distinctively flavored:
- Barracuda, California
- Bluefish
- Herring, including freshwater alewife
- Mackerel, Atlantic, cero, jack, Pacific, and Spanish
- Mullet, striped
- Pompano, Florida
- Salmon, Atlantic, king (Chinook), silver (coho), and sockeye

■ Best ways to cook

Steaks and fillets: Bake in sauce, oven-brown, barbecue, smoke, broil with dry heat or with a crumb coating, pan-fry, pan-poach, poach the classic way, or steam Chinese-style.

Small whole fish: Bake in sauce, oven-brown, barbecue, smoke, broil with dry heat, pan-fry, pan-poach, poach the classic way, or steam Chinese-style.

Larger whole fish: Bake in sauce or with a stuffing, barbecue, smoke, or poach the classic way.

Red drum

Group III: Medium-dense with Extra-firm Flakes

Medium-size to large fish with firm, compact flakes. Thick cuts are sturdy enough to put directly on a greased grill. Fish hold their shape well when cooked. Steaks and fillets are generally at least ¾ inch thick; they usually don't need a coating for good browning. Some species are sold whole. As a group, they're lean* (except orange roughy) and light to moderately pronounced in flavor.

- Drum, black and red
- Grouper, Atlantic black and red
- Mahi mahi (dolphin)
- Orange roughy
- Papio (Hawaiian jack)
- Sea bass, black (Atlantic) and white (croaker)
- Snook
- Tautog (blackfish)

■ Best ways to cook

Steaks and fillets: Bake in sauce or with a creamy topping, oven-brown, barbecue, broil with moist heat or with a crumb coating, deep-fry, pan-fry, pan-poach, poach the classic way, steep, foil-steam, steam Chinese-style, or stir-fry.

Larger whole fish: Bake in sauce or with a stuffing, barbecue, poach the classic way, or foil-steam.

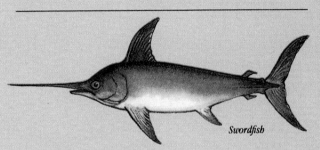

Swordfish

Group IV: Dense & Meaty

Large fish with the fewest small bones of all fish. Meat holds its shape very well, so these are the best choices for skewer-cooking. Fish are usually cut into thick steaks, fillets, or boneless pieces at least 1 inch thick; they brown well without a coating when pan-fried. Fish range from lean and mild tasting to oily and rich tasting.

IV a: Lean*, mild in flavor

- Halibut, Atlantic and Pacific
- Grouper, large species such as giant, Nassau, and Warsaw
- Sea bass, baquetta, bluenose (New Zealand), and Hawaiian
- Shark

■ Best ways to cook

Steaks and fillets: Bake in sauce or with a creamy topping, barbecue, cook on skewers, broil with moist heat, pan-fry, pan-poach, poach the classic way, foil-steam, or stir-fry.

IV b: Moderately lean* to oilier*, distinctively flavored

- Cobia
- Jack, amberjack, California yellowtail, Hawaiian ulua, jack cravelle, and travalle
- Mackerel, king and wahoo
- Opah (moonfish)
- Sturgeon
- Swordfish
- Tuna, including albacore

■ Best ways to cook

Steaks and fillets (boneless slices): Bake in sauce, barbecue, smoke, cook on skewers, broil with dry or moist heat, pan-fry, pan-poach, poach the classic way, foil-steam, or stir-fry.

Fresh fish is sold at market in a variety of forms. At top (from left) are a whole flatfish (gray sole), a pan-ready cleaned trout, and a whole round fish (freshwater drum). Cuts of fish include fillets (middle row), here orange roughy and rockfish; steaks (bottom row), swordfish and salmon; and chunks (tuna, far right). Follow the guidelines on page 7 for selecting fresh fish.

Shopping (cont'd)

If you purchase cooked crab or lobster, it should have a bright red shell and be free of any noticeable odor of ammonia. Shucked oysters and clams should be plump and free of any sour aroma. The liquid inside a jar of oysters should be clear, not cloudy or pink.

Fresh scallops should have a slightly sweet aroma and, when packaged, be practically free of liquid. Scallop meat can vary in color from creamy white to tan or orange; color is not an indication of quality.

Fresh shrimp are firm and have a mild, faintly sweet smell (as they deteriorate, you'll notice an ammonialike odor). Signs of mishandling are black legs, slippery shells, and dry-looking patches or dark spots on shells. When you buy frozen shrimp, crab, or lobster tail, make sure any exposed meat is well glazed and not dried out; the meat should be white with no yellowing.

■ **How much to buy.** Depending on appetites and when in the meal the seafood is being served, the following are estimated amounts of fish or shellfish you'll need to buy per person:

Fish, fillets or steaks, ⅓ to ½ pound
Fish, whole or cleaned, ½ to 1 pound
Abalone steaks, about ¼ pound
Clams, shucked, about ¼ pound
Clams in the shell, about 1½ pounds
Crab or lobster, whole or live,
   1 to 2 pounds
Crabmeat, about ¼ pound
Crayfish, 10 to 12
Mussels in the shell, about 1 pound
Oysters, shucked, 4 or 5 ounces
Oysters in the shell, 6 to 9
Scallops, about ¼ pound
Shrimp, peeled, about ¼ pound
Shrimp, unpeeled, ¼ to ½ pound
Squid, cleaned, about ¼ pound
Squid, whole, about ½ pound

Guidelines for Storing Seafood

Once you leave the market, keep your fish or shellfish purchases as cool as possible and refrigerate them as soon as you can. If you think you may be delayed getting home, it's a good idea to carry an ice chest when you shop. For longer storage, you can freeze most seafood.

■ **Storing seafood purchases.** At home, fish should be unwrapped, rinsed under cool running water, placed in a container, and covered with wet paper towels. Store it in the coldest part of your refrigerator, ideally at 32° to 35°F. Use the fish the day you purchase it, if possible, or within 2 days at most.

Store oysters cup sides down in the refrigerator so the juices won't leak out. Refrigerate live oysters, clams, and mussels covered with wet paper towels; never store them in water or in an airtight container—that will kill them. Use them as soon as possible after purchase; they should stay alive for about a week after harvest.

Shucked oysters that are refrigerated in the original container should stay fresh for a week after shucking.

Shrimp are usually shipped to market in frozen blocks and then thawed before being displayed or packaged at the market. Unwrap, cover with wet paper towels, and refrigerate; cook them the day of purchase. Scallops should be treated the same way.

Store live crab, lobster, or crayfish in the refrigerator, covered with wet paper towels, and use within 12 hours of purchase. It's best to eat fresh-cooked crab or lobster the day you buy it, but in any case, don't keep it for more than 2 days.

■ **Storing frozen seafood.** Date commercially packaged frozen seafood and store it in your freezer at 0°F or colder; plan to use it within 2 months for best flavor. For freshest flavor, cook frozen fish without thawing (the techniques chapter tells you how).

When thawing is required for a particular preparation, defrost fish slowly in the refrigerator (allow about 18 hours per pound). You can thaw it more quickly under cool running water (allow about 30 minutes per pound) or in a microwave oven using the defrost cycle (follow the manufacturer's directions). Don't thaw frozen fish at room temperature or in warm water.

■ **Home freezing of fish and shellfish.** If you have more fish on hand than you can eat fresh, freezing it may be your best option.

Freezing, even at 0°F, doesn't completely prevent deterioration; chemical and physical changes during freezer storage eventually cause fish to lose moisture and even become unpalatable. This happens more quickly if fish is frozen slowly and stored above 0°F. For best results, freeze only very fresh, high-quality fish or shellfish.

In general, lean fish can be stored in the freezer longer than oilier species. With a good protective coating, moderately fat to fat fish, as well as crab and lobster, should keep well for up to 3 months. Lean fish and other shellfish (shells removed) can remain frozen for 6 months.

Before freezing, fish must be eviscerated. Freeze small fish whole; cut large fish into steaks, fillets, or chunks. To prevent oily fish, such as tuna and salmon, from darkening and becoming rancid, dip pieces in an ascorbic acid solution (made with 2 tablespoons ascorbic acid to 1 quart water) for 20 seconds.

If seafood is to be frozen no longer than 2 months, wrap meal-size portions (separating pieces with freezer wrap) in moisture-proof, vapor-proof paper or in foil or plastic wrap overwrapped with freezer paper or a heavy plastic bag. Exclude as much air as possible. Seal and date the package. Freeze as quickly as possible (don't overload the freezer) and store at 0°F or lower.

For longer storage (up to 6 months), place small fish or pieces in plastic freezer containers or empty milk cartons. Fill each container with water to within ½ inch of the top; close tightly and freeze.

Using this Book

You make your menu decisions for a number of different reasons—sometimes planning a meal around a favorite recipe or a special ingredient, sometimes gearing it to a particular occasion. To give you maximum flexibility when you plan seafood menus, this book is designed to be approached in any of the following ways.

■ *Start with a recipe.* Turn to "A Repertoire of Recipes," pages 99–125, to choose a recipe that's right for the occasion or the meal course you're planning. The recipe may offer a choice of seafood—for example, "rockfish or other Group IIa fish." This enables you to pick what looks best at the market, or what's the best buy.

Use the chart on pages 8–9 to find Group IIa fish; then double-check that a particular fish in that group is suitable for your recipe by consulting "A Buyer's Guide to Seafood," starting on page 15. The buyer's guide lists the recipes considered best for each fish. Sometimes, a fish may have the right cooking characteristics for a recipe but still not be especially recommended—perhaps because it's difficult to fillet, or too expensive to be used in a way that doesn't show off its special character.

■ *Start with a fish or shellfish.* If someone brings you a fresh-caught salmon, or if black sea bass is today's featured item at the market, that might be your starting point. Turn to "A Buyer's Guide to Seafood," starting on page 15; the listing for your fish or shellfish will tell you all the different ways you can prepare it, from basic cooking methods to specific recipes. You'll also find instructions for any special preparation needed for the fish or shellfish.

■ *Start with a cooking method.* Perhaps you want to barbecue, or to stuff a whole fish. Turn to "Basic Techniques," pages 79–97, for detailed instructions on nearly two dozen different ways of cooking seafood—and the categories of fish or shellfish that work best for each. Use the chart on pages 8–9 to find which fish are recommended for the cooking method you've chosen. The buyer's guide starting on page 15 also tells which cooking methods can be used for each kind of seafood.

■ *Start with a general category of fish.* Turn to the chart on pages 8–9 to find which fish share characteristics of texture, fat content, and flavor. If you know you like a particular fish, you may want to try others in the same group. Or if the fish you'd planned to use isn't available, you can find a substitute by studying the chart.

Seafood & Your Health

Consumers today are becoming increasingly aware of the important role fish and shellfish play in good nutrition. This awareness accounts in large part for the rising popularity of seafood. But if you're planning to use fish raw, in sushi, for example, or if you gather your own fresh shellfish, it's very important to take adequate precautions to ensure that the seafood you consume is healthful.

■ Nutritional benefits of seafood.

Seafood supplies high-quality protein for a generally low number of calories. A 3-ounce serving of most fish or shellfish provides at least a third of the U.S. recommended daily allowance (RDA) of protein—at fewer than 100 calories for many lean fish (cod, sole, halibut, and rockfish, for example) and most shellfish. Even oil-rich fish, such as salmon, tuna, and mackerel, generally come in at under 200 calories for a 3-ounce serving, making them comparable to lean meats.

The fat in all fish and shellfish is mainly polyunsaturated and mono-unsaturated rather than saturated. And some fish have a unique polyunsaturated fatty acid called omega-3, believed to have a beneficial effect in reducing blood clots, lowering blood cholesterol levels, and preventing heart disease. Fish richest in oil—salmon, tuna, mackerel, sardines, trout, herring, lake whitefish, and sablefish—have the highest levels of omega-3.

All shellfish were once considered high in cholesterol, but new research has shown that although shrimp and squid have quite high levels of cholesterol, other shellfish—clams, mussels, oysters, scallops, crab, and lobster—actually have amounts comparable to most finfish. Most fish have levels

Shellfish lovers will rejoice when presented with this menu of oysters on the half shell, Dungeness crab, lobster, and steamed mussels and clams. Handle shellfish with care to maintain freshness; see page 10 for tips on storing seafood purchases.

of cholesterol about the same as white meat of poultry and lean, well-trimmed meat.

In general, fish are low in sodium, similar to meat and chicken. Though most shellfish contain more sodium than finfish, their levels are moderate compared to many commercially processed foods. Those on low-sodium diets, however, should limit their intake of salted or dried fish, pickled herring, smoked fish and shellfish, sardines, surimi products, and anchovies.

Fish and shellfish also contain important vitamins and minerals, especially some of the B vitamins, iron, potassium, magnesium, and phosphorus. Saltwater fish and shellfish supply iodine; oysters are a rich source of copper, zinc, selenium, and iron, as well as iodine. If you eat canned salmon, sardines, and herring with their soft bones, you'll also get calcium.

■**Using raw fish.** The increasing popularity of Japanese sashimi (raw fish, served at sushi bars) and seviche (fish marinated in an acid such as citrus juice) has led people to question the safety of eating raw fish.

The fact is that many fish do carry parasites, such as roundworm and tapeworm, and some of them can make you sick if they're ingested in raw fish. They present no danger if fish is adequately cooked or if it's been hot-smoked or frozen—either commercially or in a home freezer below 0°F for at least 3 days. (Some authorities advise freezing for at least 7 days at −10°F to be absolutely sure.)

Be especially cautious when using certain kinds of fish. Tuna, popular at sushi bars, is relatively free of parasites, but freshwater fish and fish like salmon that spend part of their life cycles in fresh water almost invariably have some (reputable sushi bars that serve raw salmon use frozen fish). Worms are generally more prevalent in inshore species (for example, rockfish and sole) than in deep-sea species, such as tilefish and mahi mahi. The buyer's guide beginning on page 15 points out those fish that should never be eaten raw.

Though dealers make every effort to remove any worms from fish before it's sold, some invariably get through. Finding worms in fresh fish can be alarming, but the problem is mainly an aesthetic one. At home, you can hold pieces of fish up to the light to inspect for parasites; most, but not all, are visible. If you find any, simply cut them out.

Typically, roundworms are about the thickness of a pencil lead and 1½ to 3 inches long. They don't live long in the human body, but they can make you sick. Tapeworms, most common in salmon and freshwater fish, can grow in the human intestines for years, so it's risky to eat these fish raw unless they've been frozen first.

Some fish from the Gulf of Mexico and other warm waters around the world contain spaghetti worms that resemble spaghetti in color and size; they're unsightly but harmless.

In making sashimi, fish is generally cut very thin, making it unlikely a worm would go undetected; worms can more easily escape detection in chunks of fish used in seviche. It's best to be cautious in choosing any fish to eat raw; if you're ever in doubt, use fish that's been commercially frozen or frozen at home below 0°F for at least 3 days.

■**Seafood and safety.** At certain times and in certain places, clams, oysters, mussels, and scallops become unsafe to eat because they contain a poison that's harmless to them but very harmful to humans. This poison is the result of the shellfish consuming large amounts of a microscopic organism during a condition referred to as a "red tide."

People who eat tainted shellfish can develop paralytic shellfish poisoning (PSP), the symptoms of which are tingling of lips and tongue, progressing to tingling of fingers and toes and then loss of control of arms and legs, followed by difficulty in breathing. Some cases result in death, so it's imperative to get medical attention at once.

The old axiom that oysters, clams, and mussels should only be eaten in months containing the letter "r" is no longer true. Nowadays, just about any shellfish can be purchased at any time, since commercial beds are inspected regularly and must be certified safe for the shellfish to be shipped interstate. If you gather your own shellfish, check with your county or state department of health to be sure an area is safe to harvest shellfish.

As more imported tropical fish have begun to be sold in the United States, a few cases of ciguatera poisoning have occurred. This poisoning results from fish eating certain microorganisms (harmless to the fish) found at times in some tropical reefs; most cases occur on islands in the Caribbean and South Pacific. The poison cannot be detected by taste, smell, or looks.

From time to time, incidents of scombroid fish poisoning have resulted from fish that haven't been adequately refrigerated after being caught. Once the toxin is formed, it's not destroyed by either cooking or freezing. Dark-meat fish, such as bluefish, tuna, mahi mahi, mackerel, and jack, are the most susceptible to the toxin. Avoid any fish that have a strong smell or show signs of mishandling.

Symptoms of scombroid poisoning include headache, dizziness, burning of the mouth and throat, abdominal cramps, nausea, vomiting, and diarrhea. In severe cases, respiratory distress may develop. Symptoms usually begin within a few minutes to a few hours after eating the toxic fish and usually end after about 4 hours.

Unlike meat, seafood is not subject to mandatory federal inspection. Though the Food and Drug Administration (FDA) is responsible for the wholesomeness and proper labeling of seafood products, enforcement is largely up to individual states.

The FDA does monitor levels of toxic substances such as PCBs and mercury and inspects products in interstate commerce; it also inspects imported products for excessive levels of additives, toxic substances, or bacteria.

Your best assurance of getting fresh or well-frozen seafood that's good tasting and safe to eat is to buy it only from a reliable, high-quality market.

A Word About Our Nutritional Data

For our recipes, we provide a nutritional analysis stating calorie count; grams of protein, carbohydrates, and total fat; and milligrams of cholesterol and sodium. Generally, the nutritional information applies to a single serving, based on the largest number of servings given for each recipe.

The nutritional analysis does not include optional ingredients or those for which no specific amount is stated. If an ingredient is listed with an option, the information was calculated using the first choice. Likewise, if a range is given for the amount of an ingredient, values were figured based on the first, lower amount.

Many of the recipes in this book give you a choice of fish to use; nutritional content will vary somewhat depending on which species of fish you select. When recipes offer too many choices to be accurately analyzed or when no reliable data is available (as for many salted seafood products), no nutritional data is given.

A Buyer's Guide to Seafood

*An A-to-Z primer to
fish and shellfish—
with cooking and serving tips
for every species*

Red

Abalone

From the turn of the century until the 1960s, divers took millions of pounds of abalone from beds along California's central coast each year. But overfishing and a variety of natural causes have shrunk the supply—and pushed up the price—of this highly prized shellfish.

Abalone farming in California and Hawaii may increase the supply in the future. Meanwhile, Alaska and British Columbia have a small commercial harvest of 3- to 4-inch pinto abalone, and some abalone is imported, primarily from Mexico and Australia.

Actually a large marine snail, abalone has a single shell and a tough, muscular "foot" with which it clings tenaciously to rocks as it grazes on seaweed. Four of California's seven species comprise most of the commercial catch. Red abalone is the largest (legal market size is 7¾ inches); pink and green abalone are a bit smaller.

Black abalone (legal market size is 5¾ inches) is the most affordable wild species today; the meat is tougher and requires more pounding, but it has an excellent sweet flavor.

■ **Size and forms.** Abalone is sold in the shell both live and frozen and as ready-to-use fresh or frozen tenderized steaks. Legal sizes for wild California abalone range from 5¾ to 7¾ inches, depending on the species. Most pintos are 3 to 4 inches. Some farm-raised abalone is being harvested at about 2 inches and is used for appetizers; other farms harvest abalone at 4 to 5 inches.

If you buy abalone in the shell, tickle its foot; if it wiggles and the foot feels rock-hard, you'll know it's alive and in good condition. A pound of abalone steaks yields 3 or 4 servings.

■ **Availability.** Because of its scarcity and cost, very little abalone is sold in retail markets.

■ **Taste and texture.** When properly tenderized and cooked, abalone steaks are meltingly tender, with mild, sweet flavor.

■ **Preparation.** The easiest way to shuck a live abalone is to sever the connector muscle from the shell, using a linoleum knife or heavy spoon, and then pry out the flesh. Trim and discard the viscera and scrub the meat to remove the black coating around the edges (or trim the dark edge meat). Remove the dark skin across the lower foot.

Using a thin, sharp knife, cut steaks across the grain, parallel to the bottom of the foot, into slices about ⅜ inch thick. Lightly pound each slice with a wooden mallet until the flesh is limp and velvety.

■ **Cooking methods.** Quick cooking is the key to delicious abalone—a moment too long and you'll have tough, not tender, meat.

Frying. To pan-fry, rinse 1 pound **abalone steaks** and pat dry. Dredge in **all-purpose flour,** shaking off excess. Heat a wide frying pan over high heat until a few drops of water sizzle and dance in pan. Add 2 tablespoons **salad oil** and heat until oil ripples when pan is tilted. Add abalone and cook for about 30 seconds on each side. Transfer to a warm platter and season to taste with **salt** and **pepper.** Makes 3 or 4 servings.

You can use abalone in Stir-fried Fish or Shellfish with Peas (page 95); cut abalone steaks into ½-inch strips and cook for 30 seconds, as for squid.

■ **Suggested recipes.** Use pounded abalone meat, cut into strips, in Seviche with Kiwi Fruit (page 100); use diced abalone in Seviche Salad (page 108).

■ **Serving ideas.** Serve pan-fried abalone with Almond or Filbert Browned Butter (page 92).

Glistening, freshly caught bonito and live oysters and clams are ready to go to market. Modern transportation methods provide shoppers with a great variety of seafood from around the world.

Albacore *see Tuna, page 74*

Amberjack *see Jack, page 35*

Angler *see Monkfish, page 42*

Arctic Char *see Trout, page 72*

California

Barracuda

Barracuda has a difficult reputation to overcome. In addition to its notoriously fierce nature, the fish in certain areas is susceptible to a dangerous poison called ciguatera (page 13). Even so, barracuda is an important food fish in many parts of the world, and local people generally know where fishing for it is safe. Some species, including California barracuda, are never toxic.

California barracuda (also called Pacific barracuda) ranges as far north as Alaska but is only abundant in Southern California waters, migrating there from Mexico in the spring and summer. This fish is not only completely safe to eat but also quite delicious. A close relative, sometimes called sea pike, is harvested in Hawaii.

The common Atlantic species is the *great barracuda*, found from Florida to Brazil and in certain areas of the Pacific. It can be contaminated with toxin. In general, the smallest fish of the species are considered safest to eat, but it's important to buy only from very reliable dealers. The fish the Hawaiians call kaku is also a great barracuda.

■ **Size and forms.** California barracuda ranges from 3 to 6 pounds and is usually sold either whole, with head on and cleaned, or as steaks. Great barracuda can grow up to 6 feet long, but market fish average 8 to 20 pounds; it's usually sold cleaned without the head,

sometimes as fillets. Almost all barracuda is sold fresh. Smoked barracuda is sometimes available.

■ **Availability.** The California species isn't plentiful, but it's in markets sporadically from June through August, mostly on the West Coast. Great barracuda is in season all year but is seldom sold outside Hawaii and Florida.

■ **Taste and texture.** The flesh of California barracuda is moderately firm, tender, and flaky. About 3 percent fat, it's mild to moderately pronounced in flavor and rich tasting. Like other fast-swimming fish, barracuda has streaks of dark red flesh, which have a more pronounced flavor.

The flesh of great barracuda is light gray in color and mild in flavor; larger fish tend to have coarse-textured flesh and taste drier than smaller ones.

■ **Preparation.** Barracuda skin, thin and tender, is difficult to remove. Cook steaks or fillets with the skin on. To cut a whole fish into steaks or fillets, see page 80.

■ **Cooking methods.** These fish are at their best barbecued or smoked (page 84). The flesh is tender and falls apart easily.

Baking. Bake cleaned whole fish or steaks in Piquant Vegetable Sauce. Oven-brown steaks or fillets. (See pages 82–85.)

Barbecuing and broiling. Barbecue larger whole California barracuda using indirect heat. Use direct heat to grill skin-on fillets or steaks, supporting them on perforated foil or in a hinged broiler. Use any baste or marinade. Broil steaks or fillets with dry heat or with a crumb coating. (See pages 86–89.)

Frying. Steaks and fillets are good pan-fried; a crumb coating adds nice texture. (See pages 90–92.)

Poaching and steaming. Barracuda steaks and fillets can be pan-poached or steamed Chinese-style. Poach cleaned whole fish the classic way. (See pages 92–95.)

■ **Suggested recipes.** Use barracuda steaks in Mackerel with Tart Onion Sauce (page 112), Grilled Salmon on

Wilted Chicory Salad (page 113), and Grilled Tuna with Teriyaki Fruit Sauce (page 117).

■ **Serving ideas.** Offer Aïoli (page 123) or Tomato-Caper Sauce (page 124) with distinctively flavored barracuda. To complement barbecued steaks or fillets flavored with Italian-style Marinade (page 87), serve a tangy red cabbage coleslaw or a fresh spinach and mushroom salad.

Hybrid striped

Bass

"Bass" and "sea bass" have become catchall terms used in fish markets to describe a variety of freshwater and saltwater fish. Conversely, "grouper" is an alternative name for some basses. It's important to know which species you're buying because the various basses can be very different when cooked.

Here we describe two related species: striped bass, a saltwater fish that spawns in freshwater rivers, and freshwater white bass. For fish called sea bass or grouper, see page 57.

Striped bass. Once one of the premium fish of the Atlantic coast, striped bass (also called striper or rockfish) has become a rarity because of overfishing and pollution, especially in Chesapeake Bay, its principal spawning grounds.

Pollution has taken its toll on the West Coast, too, where striped bass had thrived after being transplanted there in the last century. Commercial fishing for stripers is banned now in most Eastern states as well as in California. Sportfishing is still allowed, however. The biggest runs are in spring and fall.

The commercial future of this fish depends on aquaculture. Striped bass has been crossed successfully with white bass, and the hybrids are being farmed in geothermal-heated tanks in the California desert and in ponds in California and other states. Farmed fish are harvested year-round.

White bass. This small freshwater fish is a popular sports catch throughout the Middle West and much of the South and Southwest. Lake Erie provides most of the commercial fish, which are available in markets most of the year.

■ **Size and forms.** Striped bass can weigh more than 50 pounds, but 1 to 10 pounds is typical. Farmed fish are usually harvested at 1 to 5 pounds, pond-raised fish at about 1½ pounds. Almost all are sold fresh and whole, with the head on.

White bass usually run ½ pound to 2 pounds in size, but some 3- to 4-pound fish are caught. They're sold whole, cleaned, and sometimes filleted.

■ **Availability.** See individual species descriptions above.

■ **Taste and texture.** Striped bass is lean (about 2.3 percent fat), with flaky white flesh that's moderately firm and tender. The flavor is mild and slightly sweet; some farmed fish have a faintly earthy taste. White bass has a flavor and texture much like striped bass. Both species are subject to parasites, so they should not be eaten raw.

■ **Preparation.** Whole fish need to be scaled and cleaned. To fillet, follow directions for filleting a round fish; remove skin from fillets, if desired. Large fish can also be cut into steaks. For techniques, see pages 79–81.

■ **Cooking methods.** Striped bass and white bass can be cooked in the same ways.

Baking. Cleaned whole bass is an ideal fish to bake. Use Piquant Vegetable Sauce. Or bake larger bass stuffed; try Almond-Rice, Almond–Wild Rice, or Toasted Bread Cube Stuffing. You can also oven-brown fillets. (See pages 82–85.)

Barbecuing and broiling. Use the indirect-heat method to barbecue cleaned whole fish; brush with Lemon-Butter or Sesame-Soy Baste, or soak in Italian-style Marinade. To broil fillets, use the moist-heat technique or broil with a crumb coating. (See pages 86–89.)

Frying. Pan-fry fillets using a flour or light crumb coating, or coat with Golden Egg Wash. For small scaled and cleaned white bass, pan-fry with a cornmeal or crumb coating. (See pages 90–92.)

Poaching and steaming. Cleaned whole fish can be poached the classic way or foil-steamed. Pan-poach fillets or cleaned small fish, steep them, or steam them Chinese-style. (See pages 92–95.)

■ **Suggested recipes.** Fish Fillets with Dill and Tangerine (page 91), Rockfish Florentine (page 96), Bourride (page 102), Fish Pot-au-Feu (page 103), Fish Pil-Pil in Red Sauce (page 104), Veracruz Fish Salad (page 107), Fish Fillets with Sherry-Mushroom Sauce (page 111), Mr. Zhu's Steamed Fish (page 114), Pine Cone Fish (page 115).

■ **Serving ideas.** Browned Butter or Almond or Filbert Browned Butter (page 92) is good with pan-fried, foil-steamed, or poached striped bass. Also good with bass is Tomato-Caper Sauce (page 124).

Poached or barbecued bass is delicious served cold with a creamy dressing, such as Radish Tartar Sauce (page 123), or as a salad on a bed of mixed greens with Dijon Vinaigrette Dressing (page 124).

Black cod *see Sablefish, page 52*

Blackfish *see Tautog, page 70*

Bluefish

Named for the bluish green color along its back, the bluefish is a schooling fish notorious for its ferocious attacks on other fish. Because of its fighting nature, it's prized as a sport fish. Much of the commercial supply is taken by trawlers as an incidental catch. Bluefish is plentiful and inexpensive in areas near its migratory route from New England to the Gulf of Mexico.

The quality of bluefish is very dependent on freshness and handling. This fish needs to be bled, cleaned, and have its gills removed immediately after being caught, and it must be kept well iced or refrigerated, for the meat spoils quickly and can cause scombroid poisoning if not handled properly (page 13). When you buy bluefish, the skin should be smooth and tight and the eyes bright and clear; make sure it smells fresh, not fishy.

■ **Size and forms.** Average size is 3 to 6 pounds; any fish over 10 pounds is considered large. A bluefish under 1 pound is called a snapper, not to be confused with true snapper (page 65). Most bluefish are sold whole, head-on, and cleaned, or as fillets. They're almost always sold fresh. Bluefish does not freeze well.

■ **Availability.** Bluefish is usually sold near where it's caught. The season is from December to April in the Gulf of Mexico, from September to January in Florida, and from May through October in Chesapeake Bay, the top producing area.

■ **Taste and texture.** The flesh is soft textured, with loose, moist flakes. Bluefish is moderately oily (about 4.2 percent fat) and has relatively dark flesh that cooks to a light off-white.

The small snappers, which feed mainly on crustaceans, have a delicate, sweet flavor. The flavor is richer and more pronounced in larger bluefish, which often feeds on oily, strong-flavored fish. Fillets cooked without the skin are milder in flavor.

■ **Preparation.** Since bluefish has thin skin with small scales, whole fish only need scaling and cleaning. For mildest flavor, fillet the fish and skin the fillets; you can also cut out the dark, oily streaks of meat along the sides. For techniques, see pages 79–81.

■ **Cooking methods.** In addition to the cooking techniques that follow, smoking (page 84) is a delicious way to prepare bluefish.

Baking. A 3- to 6-pound cleaned whole fish is ideal for baking, either in Piquant Vegetable Sauce or stuffed (try Almond-Rice, Almond–Wild Rice, or Spinach-Mushroom Stuffing). Skinless fillets are good baked in Piquant Vegetable Sauce or oven-browned. (See pages 82–85.)

Barbecuing and broiling. Bluefish is delicious cooked over a smoky barbecue fire; adding wood chips, such as hickory or alder, enhances the flavor. Use direct heat for cleaned whole fish (under 1 lb.) and skinned fillets, placing a whole fish directly on the grill, fillets on perforated foil. Barbecue larger fish (2 to 8 lbs.) using indirect heat. Broil fillets using the dry-heat method or broil with a crumb coating.

For barbecuing or dry-heat broiling, brush with Lemon-Butter or Sesame-Soy Baste, or soak in Italian-style or Basil-Parmesan Marinade. (See pages 86–89.)

Frying. Scaled small bluefish (under 1 lb.) and skinless fillets are good pan-fried, dusted with flour or a crumb coating. (See pages 90–92.)

■ **Suggested recipes.** Fish Fillets with Dill and Tangerine (page 91), Veracruz Fish Salad (page 107), Five-Spice Fish (page 111), Orange Roughy Maître d'Hôtel (page 112), Mackerel with Tart Onion Sauce (page 112), Braised Sablefish (page 112), Grilled Tuna with Teriyaki Fruit Sauce (page 117).

■ **Serving ideas.** Baked or barbecued bluefish is delicious served cold, by itself or in fish salads. Its rich flavor is good paired with acidic ingredients or crisp bacon (replace the salad oil with bacon drippings for frying).

Serve pan-fried fish with Caper Butter (page 92). Offer baked or pan-fried fish with Tomato-Caper Sauce (page 124). Drizzle Dijon Vinaigrette Dressing (page 124) over poached cold bluefish arranged on a bed of lettuce.

Bonito see Tuna, page 74

Buffalo

This freshwater fish, a member of the sucker family, inhabits interior rivers and lakes from Canada to the Gulf of Mexico. There are three main species—big-mouth, small-mouth, and black buffalo. The small-mouth, which is caught in swift, clean rivers, is considered the best eating of the three. Buffalo is a bony fish but has fewer troublesome bones than carp, which it resembles.

Like other freshwater fish, buffalo varies in flavor according to its diet and the quality of the water in which it swims. This plentiful fish can be a real bargain if it's top quality, but freshness and quality are inconsistent, so buy it only from a reliable market. Purchase it scaled, if possible, since the scales are tough and heavy. Be leery of frozen fish, which is seldom handled carefully.

■ **Size and forms.** Most of the commercial catch runs from 3 to 12 pounds, but 20- to 30-pound buffalos are quite common, as are fish of 2 pounds or less. Most are sold whole or with head off, scaled, and cleaned. Because of their bone structure, they're difficult to fillet, but some markets dress them out into steaks or boneless strips for frying.

■ **Availability.** Buffalo is most popular in the Middle West but can be found throughout the country, primarily in ethnic markets. It's sold year-round, but supply and quality are best in spring and fall.

■ **Taste and texture.** At its best, the tender white flesh is moist and mild tasting, with only slight earthiness. Buffalo is quite fat but doesn't taste oily. The roe, available in spring, is considered a delicacy; it's served fried.

■ **Preparation.** Scale whole fish, if necessary; the skin is thin and tender and should be left on boneless strips, as it

keeps them from falling apart. Cook fish whole or cut into steaks; filleting is best left to experts. For techniques, see pages 79–81.

■ **Cooking methods.** In addition to preparing buffalo in the following ways, you can also smoke it (page 84).

Baking. Bake a cleaned whole fish in Piquant Vegetable Sauce or with a stuffing, such as Almond-Rice, Almond–Wild Rice, or Toasted Bread Cube. Steaks can be oven-browned. (See pages 82–85.)

Barbecuing and broiling. A smoky barbecue fire enhances the flavor of buffalo. Barbecue cleaned whole or headed fish over 2 pounds using the indirect-heat technique. For steaks or boneless strips, use direct heat (support them on perforated foil) or broil using the dry-heat method. Try Sesame-Soy Baste or Italian-style or Ginger-Soy Marinade. (See pages 86–88.)

Frying. Boneless strips are good deep-fried with British Beer or Lemon Batter. Use either a light or heavy crumb coating when you pan-fry steaks or boneless strips. (See pages 89–92.) Fry the roe as for shad roe (page 60).

Poaching and steaming. Pan-poach steaks or strips, or steam them Chinese-style. Steam cleaned whole fish in foil or poach the classic way. (See pages 92–95.)

■ **Suggested recipes.** Fish Pil-Pil in Red Sauce (page 104), Pan-fried Catfish with Jicama Salad (page 111; use steaks or boneless strips), Five-Spice Fish (page 111; use boneless strips), Orange Roughy Maître d'Hôtel (page 112), Mackerel with Tart Onion Sauce (page 112; use steaks or strips), Braised Sablefish (page 112), Grilled Salmon on Wilted Chicory Salad (page 113).

■ **Serving ideas.** Serve cooked buffalo with Caper Butter (page 92) or with Tartar Sauce or Aïoli (page 123).

Caviar—A Choice of Luxuries

Many consider caviar to be the ultimate luxury food. The finest is among the world's most expensive foods, but there are caviars offering good taste at all price levels.

True caviar is the roe, or eggs, of various species of sturgeon, preserved in salt. The eggs are gently separated from the connective membranes, rinsed, and bathed in a light brine.

The finest caviar is malossol, meaning little salt. It's stored at very cold temperatures and eaten fresh. The most sought-after roe comes from three species of sturgeon—beluga, osetra, and sevruga—from the Caspian Sea bordering Iran and the Soviet Union.

The good news is that eggs from other fish are prepared like true caviar, and all of them are less expensive. The most common of these is lumpfish caviar from Iceland, dyed black to resemble sturgeon eggs and sold pasteurized in jars. Its taste is reliable, though less complex than true caviar.

Golden whitefish caviar from the Great Lakes, sold fresh or pasteurized in jars, has a delicate, crunchy texture and good flavor. Salmon caviar has large, brilliant orange or red eggs and assertive flavor. An interesting newcomer is sturgeon caviar from China, labeled "Mandarin beluga" or "Mandarin osetra."

Storage and use. All fresh caviar must be refrigerated. The ideal storage temperature is 28° to 32°F, so choose the coldest spot in your refrigerator or pack the caviar on ice.

Fresh caviar sold in airtight jars keeps in the refrigerator for 2 to 3 weeks, but, once opened, it should be consumed within 2 or 3 days. Unopened pasteurized caviars can be stored in the refrigerator for up to 3 months.

If you're using a dyed caviar, such as lumpfish, put the caviar in a fine wire strainer just before serving and rinse well under cool running water to reduce excess salt, dyes, and off-flavors.

Remember that a little caviar goes a long way; one ounce is a generous serving. And while purists favor it served on toast points with just a bit of unsalted butter, you can easily extend caviar by

Fresh sturgeon caviar

Fresh whitefish caviar

offering such classic accompaniments as sour cream, grated onion, and mashed hard-cooked eggs.

Potato Salad with Caviar

About 4 large red thin-skinned
potatoes (2½ lbs. *total*)
Oil and Vinegar Dressing
(recipe follows)
½ teaspoon dill weed
½ cup chopped green onions
(including tops)
1 jar (about 4 oz.) black caviar
Parsley sprigs

Place potatoes in a 5- to 6-quart pan; add enough water to cover potatoes by 1 inch. Bring to a boil over high heat; cover and boil gently until tender when pierced (about 30 minutes). Drain and let cool completely. Cut into ¼-inch-thick slices and place in a shallow rimmed dish.

Prepare Oil and Vinegar Dressing; stir in dill weed and ¼ cup of the onions. Pour over potato slices. Cover and chill for at least 4 hours or for up to a day.

Rinse caviar as described at left and let drain. Meanwhile, lift out potato slices and arrange in slightly overlapping rows along sides of a large platter;

moisten with some of the dressing and sprinkle with remaining ¼ cup onions. Place caviar in a small container in center. Garnish with parsley.

Top individual servings of potatoes with a dollop of caviar. Makes 8 servings.

■ **Oil and Vinegar Dressing.** Combine ⅔ cup **salad oil**, ⅓ cup **white wine vinegar**, ½ teaspoon *each* **dry mustard** and **sugar**, 1 teaspoon **salt**, and ¼ teaspoon **pepper**. Mix until blended. Makes about 1 cup.

Per serving: 316 calories, 6 g protein, 27 g carbohydrates, 21 g total fat, 83 mg cholesterol, 499 mg sodium

Caviar Pie

Mustard Eggs (recipe follows)
1 cup chopped green onions
(including tops)
1 jar (2 oz.) sliced pimentos, drained
2 small packages (3 oz. *each*) cream
cheese, at room temperature
½ cup sour cream
1 jar (about 4 oz.) black lumpfish,
whitefish, or salmon caviar
Unsalted crackers

Prepare Mustard Eggs and spread smoothly in a 10-inch pie dish or plate. Top with onions and pimentos. Cover and chill for about 1 hour.

Blend cream cheese and sour cream until smooth. Spoon over onions. Cover loosely and chill for about 1 hour or for up to a day.

Just before serving, rinse caviar as described at left and let drain. Mound in center of pie. Cut pie into thin wedges and offer with crackers. Makes 12 to 16 servings.

■ **Mustard Eggs.** In a blender or food processor, combine 6 **hard-cooked eggs**; ⅓ cup **butter** or margarine, at room temperature; and 2 teaspoons *each* **Dijon mustard** and **white wine vinegar**. Whirl until smooth. Season to taste with **salt**.

Per serving: 129 calories, 6 g protein, 2 g carbohydrates, 11 g total fat, 167 mg cholesterol, 217 mg sodium

Atlantic butterfish

Butterfish

Sometimes called: Dollarfish, Silver dollar, Pumpkin-seed

A little coin-shaped fish with a silvery sheen, Atlantic butterfish is found from Maine to North Carolina. Two close relatives are the harvestfish, mainly caught in the South Atlantic, and a Pacific butterfish called California pompano (not related to Atlantic pompano), caught in small numbers off the Southern California coast.

An unrelated species, sablefish (page 52), is sometimes incorrectly called butterfish.

■ **Size and forms.** Because of its small size (3 to 12 oz.), butterfish is only sold whole or without the head and cleaned. You may also find it frozen or smoked. Plan on 1 to 3 fish per serving, depending on size.

■ **Availability.** Atlantic butterfish is most plentiful in the waters off the mid-Atlantic states, where some fish are caught year-round; peak seasons are late spring and late fall. The best seasons for the Pacific butterfish are spring and summer.

■ **Taste and texture.** True to its name, butterfish has a high fat content (about 8 percent). The off-white flesh is delicate, with fine, moist flakes. The flavor is mild to moderately pronounced and sweet.

■ **Preparation.** Butterfish has thin skin with small scales that are easily rubbed off; it doesn't need scaling. Simply remove the head and tail, if desired, and clean (pages 79–80).

■ **Cooking methods.** Butterfish can be smoked (page 84) as well as prepared in the following ways.

Baking. Bake cleaned whole butterfish in Piquant Vegetable Sauce, or oven-brown it. (See pages 82–85.)

Barbecuing and broiling. Use direct heat to barbecue butterfish, placing it on perforated foil or in a hinged broiler. You can broil whole fish using the dry-heat method. Brush barbecued or broiled fish with Lemon-Butter or Sesame-Soy Baste. (See pages 86–88.)

Frying. Pan-fry, dusting fish with flour; or use a crumb coating with cornmeal. (See pages 90–92.)

Poaching and steaming. Pan-poach, steep, or steam these little fish Chinese-style. (See pages 92–95.)

■ **Suggested recipes.** Mackerel with Tart Onion Sauce (page 112), Trout with Leeks & Vinegar (page 114).

■ **Serving ideas.** Serve cooked butterfish with Caper Butter or Almond or Filbert Browned Butter (page 92), or with Tomato-Caper Sauce (page 124) or Citrus Beurre Blanc (page 125).

Carp

A fast-growing freshwater fish that has been crossbred and farmed since the beginning of civilization, carp is traditional fare for many holidays and ceremonies in the Orient and in Eastern Europe. It was introduced into the United States in the 19th century, but when it strayed from farmers' ponds into nearby rivers and lakes and began squeezing out native game fish, interest shifted to finding ways to curb its numbers.

The recent introduction of two Oriental species of carp—the grass and bighead— found an eager market in Asian communities in the United States. As a result, many catfish farmers

are now farming these as well. Of the two, bighead has the fewest troublesome bones. Quality depends on how carp is raised and handled, so it's best to buy only from reliable markets. Carp roe is considered a delicacy; cook it as you would shad roe (page 60).

■ **Size and forms.** Carp grows to 30 or more pounds, but 7 to 10 pounds is average; 3- to 5-pound sizes have the best flavor. Carp is sold live or as fresh or frozen cleaned whole or lengthwise-split fish (splitting carp makes it easier to remove the bones). It's sometimes cut into fillets or steaks. Smoked carp is popular in the Middle West.

■ **Availability.** Though harvested year-round, carp is considered best in winter; it's fatter then and its diet consists of less algae, which tends to give fish an off-flavor. Carp is sold throughout the United States; look for it in markets that cater to Oriental or Jewish customers.

■ **Taste and texture.** Carp's flaky white flesh, soft and moist, has a high fat content—about 8.6 percent. Carp raised in clean, clear water has a mild and only slightly earthy flavor, resembling catfish. Taken from muddy waters, carp tastes muddy.

■ **Preparation.** If you have trouble removing carp's large, tough scales, boil the fish for 25 seconds; rub the skin off the hot fish and cool in cold running water. You can also skin carp like catfish (see facing page). If you cook the fish whole, the skin (with scales) can be removed before serving.

Cut steaks or fillets as directed for a round fish (page 80); remove the skin from fillets. For best flavor, also remove the tough, dark fat line.

■ **Cooking methods.** Carp is suitable for any of the following techniques.

Baking. Bake cleaned whole fish in Piquant Vegetable Sauce or with a stuffing. You can oven-brown steaks or skinless fillets. (See pages 82–85.)

Barbecuing and broiling. Place steaks and skinless fillets on perforated foil on the barbecue grill and use direct heat. Grill cleaned whole fish using indirect heat. Broil steaks and skinless fillets using the dry-heat method or with crumb coating. Before barbecuing or dry-heat broiling, marinate with Italian-style, Ginger-Soy, or Basil-Parmesan Marinade. (See pages 86–89.)

Frying. Deep-fry skinless fillets, using British Beer or Lemon Batter. To pan-fry steaks or skinless fillets, use flour or a crumb coating; one with cornmeal is good. (See pages 89–92.)

Poaching and steaming. Pan-poach steaks or skinless fillets, or steam them Chinese-style. Whole fish are good poached the classic way. (See pages 92–95.)

■ **Suggested recipes.** Puget Sound Salmon Gefillte Fish Soup (page 103; use in place of lingcod), Five-Spice Fish (page 111), Mackerel with Tart Onion Sauce (page 112), Pine Cone Fish (page 115).

■ **Serving ideas.** Serve poached or pan-fried carp with Caper Butter (page 92) or Tomato-Caper Sauce (page 124). Cold poached carp is good with Homemade Mayonnaise or Remoulade Sauce (page 123).

Catfish

Thanks to highly successful farming of channel catfish in the United States, this traditional Southern favorite has become popular all over the country. There's an abundant supply, so catfish is one of the most reasonably priced fish.

Mississippi produces about 85 percent of the supply, followed by Alabama, Arkansas, Louisiana, Texas, California, and Idaho. Though some other species are farmed or fished in U.S. waters, the

To skin a whole catfish, first slice through tough skin behind head and pectoral fins.

Grasp head firmly, using a towel or glove to protect your hand. Pull skin off with pliers.

channel "cats" are considered the most reliably good eating of the lot. A few wild catfish are imported from Brazil's Amazon River.

When farmed catfish is ready to be harvested, it's taken live in a tank truck to the processing plant, where it's processed immediately. Quality is carefully controlled and fish are tested for taste. Wild and imported fish usually sell for a lower price; they can be high quality, but they're not subject to the same quality controls as farmed fish. Catfish is a bottom-feeder; when caught in muddy water, it can taste muddy.

For ocean catfish, see Wolffish, page 77.

■ **Size and forms.** Catfish, harvested from about 1½ to 5 pounds, is sold both fresh and frozen as whole fish (usually with head off, skinned, and cleaned), skinless fillets, steaks, strips, or "nuggets" (cut from belly flaps). Frozen catfish is usually individually quick-frozen.

■ **Availability.** Catfish is available year-round in most markets.

■ **Taste and texture.** The flesh of catfish is white, moist, flaky, fairly soft, and moderately lean (about 4.3 percent fat). Its flavor is mild, rather sweet, and sometimes slightly earthy.

■ **Preparation.** Most catfish is now sold skinless, but if the skin is on, remove it before cooking. To skin, cut through the skin just behind the head and pectoral fins. Wearing a glove or using a towel to protect your hand, hold the head in one hand; grasp the skin with pliers and pull towards the tail, as shown above. Cut off the head and tail.

Catfish can be cut into steaks or fillets (page 80). To minimize the earthy taste of catfish, marinate pieces in buttermilk or lemon juice for 15 to 30 minutes before cooking.

■ **Cooking methods.** Deep-fried catfish is traditional, but this versatile fish can be cooked in other ways as well.

Baking. Bake cleaned, skinned whole fish or steaks or fillets in Piquant Vegetable Sauce. Or oven-brown catfish fillets. (See pages 82–85.)

Barbecuing and broiling. Barbecue catfish over direct heat, using a hinged broiler to enclose cleaned, skinned whole fish (up to 16 oz.) or placing small whole fish, steaks, or fillets on perforated foil. Use the dry-heat technique for broiling catfish fillets or steaks, or broil them with a crumb coating. When you barbecue or broil with dry heat, use Sesame-Soy Baste or Italian-style Marinade. (See pages 86–89.)

Frying. When deep-frying, coat strips or small fillets with British Beer or Lemon Batter. Use a light or heavy crumb coating when you pan-fry cleaned, skinned small catfish (up to 16 oz.), fillets, or steaks. (See pages 89–92.)

Poaching and steaming. Use the pan-poaching technique for catfish fillets, steaks, or cleaned, skinned small fish. Foil-steam skinned whole fish of any size or poach them the classic way. (See pages 92–94.)

■ **Suggested recipes.** Fish Fillets with Dill and Tangerine (page 91), Fish & Chard Pie (page 99), Quenelles with Creamy Shallot Sauce (page 100), Quick Colorful Chowder (page 102), Veracruz Fish Salad (page 107), Pan-fried Catfish with Jicama Salad (page 111), Five-Spice Fish (page 111), Orange Roughy Maître d'Hôtel (page 112), Baked Fish & Ratatouille (page 112).

■ **Serving ideas.** The soft flesh of catfish is enhanced by a crisp coating. In the classic Southern presentation, pieces of catfish are dredged in cornmeal, deep-fried, and served with hush puppies (a fried cornbread batter) and potatoes. Or you can serve pan-fried catfish with crisp bacon, using the bacon drippings to fry the fish.

When you pan-fry or foil-steam catfish, serve it with Tartar or Creamy Horseradish Sauce (page 123) or Tomato-Caper Sauce (page 124); or offer plenty of lemon or lime wedges to squeeze over.

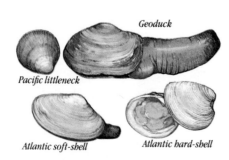

Geoduck

Pacific littleneck

Atlantic soft-shell   Atlantic hard-shell

Clams

Clams live in intertidal zones and in deeper offshore waters of both the Atlantic and Pacific coasts and throughout much of the world. These double-hinged mollusks fall into two broad categories: those with hard shells that close tightly and those with thin ("soft") shells and long necks that can't be retracted into the shell. The latter, with their breakable shells, are the more perishable.

Atlantic hard-shell clams. Dug off the coast from Newfoundland to Florida, these clams (also called quahogs) range from about 1½ to 3½ inches across. *Little necks,* the smallest and most tender, and medium-size *cherrystones* are sold live. Both are suitable for eating raw on the half-shell or for steaming, but cherrystones quickly become tough if overcooked. Little necks usually cost about three times as much as cherrystones.

The largest size, *chowders,* as well as several kinds of deep-sea clams including *surf clams* and *ocean quahogs,* are shucked and chopped for canned and frozen products. The meat is tough but makes flavorful chowder.

Pacific hard-shell clams. The two main species of these clams now come mostly from cultivated beds, though a few are still harvested wild in Puget Sound, the center of the West's clam industry. *Littlenecks,* properly spelled as one word in contrast to Atlantic little necks, are native Pacific clams; they're sometimes called rock clams. *Manilas* were accidental imports, probably hitchhiking here years ago with Japanese oyster seed; they can now be found from California to British Columbia, often growing with littlenecks.

Both range from 1 to 2 inches across and are typically sold either live or frozen. Littlenecks have white shells and

pink meat; they're chewier and tend to not open all at the same time when cooked. Manilas, with their darker shells and light orange meat, are a little sweeter and more tender, and they open at the same time when cooked; small ones are delicious raw. Both species are usually steamed. The two species are often sold mixed, making it difficult to cook them properly.

Butter clams grow almost to the size of geoducks. Because of their perishability, they're usually minced and canned. Very small ones can be eaten raw or steamed.

Cockles. A number of hard-shell clam species around the world are sold as cockles; their eating quality varies. Small New Zealand cockles are sold in the United States from time to time. Their meat is sweet and tender enough to eat raw, but they're usually steamed.

Atlantic soft-shell clams. Found from the Arctic to Cape Hatteras, North Carolina, Atlantic soft-shells (also called longnecks, belly clams, steamers, and Ipswitch) are also harvested in Puget Sound in a small colony transplanted from the Atlantic. They grow up to 2 inches in size and are sold both live and as fresh shucked meat. The long neck is chewy, but the rest of the meat is tender. They're good fried, steamed, or raw.

Razor clams. Soft-shelled razor clams, so called because of their sharp, brittle shells, are found on both coasts, but the two kinds are quite different. Few Eastern razors are harvested, and Western razors are largely a recreational catch; a few from the Pacific Northwest and Alaska are sold commercially. The Eastern variety are good steamed or minced and made into fritters. The Western ones are usually sold shucked; they're good fried whole or minced for chowder.

Geoducks. Though 3 pounds is average, the giant geoducks (pronounced "gooey-ducks") can exceed 5 pounds in weight, and their necks can extend 3 feet or more. Divers harvest them in Puget Sound. About 3 steaks can be cut from each clam; when fried, they have a sweet, distinctive flavor similar to abalone. The neck is quite tough, but it can be skinned and minced for chowder or cut in thin slices and tenderized. Geoducks are sold live, as steaks, or minced.

■ **Size and forms.** The many species of clams range from tiny cockles to large geoducks. See individual species descriptions on the facing page for details.

When you buy live clams, always make sure they're actually alive. The shell of a hard clam should be tightly closed or, if gaping, should close when tapped. The neck of a soft clam should contract when touched. Discard dead clams and those with broken shells. Shucked clams should be plump, with clear liquid, and free of shell particles.

■ **Availability.** Most species are sold year-round, depending on weather and tidal conditions. When clams spawn in summer, their shelf life is shorter, but they're still good to eat.

As with all filter-feeders, clams sometimes ingest toxic levels of planktonic micro-organisms during a condition called red tide and can also become contaminated from pollution. For these reasons, the commercial harvest is closely monitored. If you dig your own clams, check with your local fish and game department regarding regulations on season, size, daily bag limit, and approved method of digging.

■ **Taste and texture.** All clams share a sweet taste and chewy texture; the most tender are the smaller Atlantic and Pacific hard-shells and the Atlantic soft-shell (except for the neck).

■ **Preparation.** Keep live clams covered with damp paper towels in the refrigerator; they should stay alive for up to a week after harvest or for several days after purchase. Never store them in water, on ice, or in an airtight container; they'll die.

Before sending live clams to market, most producers hold them in sea water to purge them of sand; just scrub them under cool running water. If you dig your own, let them stand for several hours in sea water (or use ⅓ cup salt to 1 gallon fresh water); change the water at least once. Adding about 1 cup cornmeal to the bucket helps clean the clams' stomachs. Don't use fresh water; it will kill the clams.

Shucking live clams. If you put clams in the freezer for 5 to 10 minutes before shucking them, they'll be easier to open. Working over a bowl, grasp the

clam firmly with the hinge toward your palm. Insert the blade of a clam or paring knife between the shell halves (see below) and work the blade around to sever the muscle at the hinge so you can open the shell. Sever the muscles attaching the clam to each shell half and separate the shells. To serve raw, arrange the clam on one of the half-shells; spoon on any reserved juice.

Soft-shell clams are easily shucked because their shells don't close tightly; just slide a thin knife between the body and shell, and cut the meat away from the shell. To eat Atlantic soft-shells raw, discard the neck and thin, dark "veil"; eat the tender meat. To eat them steamed, use the neck as a handle to pull the clam from the shell; discard after eating the rest.

For Pacific razors, remove from the shell, as described above, and snip off the tip of the neck with scissors or a knife. Cut the clam open lengthwise from the base of the foot to the tip of the neck; also split the digger muscle

(opposite the neck) so it will lie flat. Remove the gills and digestive tract (dark parts of clam) and discard. The clam is now ready to fry.

For geoducks, bring water almost to a boil and dip the geoduck in water for 20 seconds. Rinse under cool running water. Pull off and discard the shell, neck skin, membrane covering the stomach, and stomach. Cut off and discard a 1-inch piece from the end of the neck. Slice across where the neck joins the body and flush water through the neck holes.

Butterfly the neck by cutting lengthwise almost through to the other side; then cut crosswise into thin slices. Cut the body meat crosswise into 2 or 3 pieces, or "steaks."

One at a time, place the neck and body pieces in a plastic bag and, using a smooth-surfaced mallet, pound until soft and about ⅛ inch thick. The meat can also be ground, using the medium blade of a food chopper or a food processor, and used for chowder or fritters.

(Continued on next page)

To shuck, hold live clam over a bowl with hinge toward palm; work a knife blade between shell halves and cut muscle at hinge.

Open shell and sever muscles connecting clam to each half of shell; catch juices in bowl.

■ **Cooking methods.** Hard-shell clams are most often steamed—or eaten raw (see descriptions of individual species, page 22). Soft-shell clams are often fried.

Barbecuing. See page 87 for directions on barbecuing hard-shell clams.

Frying. For either deep-frying or pan-frying, rinse 1 to 1½ pounds cleaned **Pacific razor or Atlantic soft-shell clams or geoduck steaks;** dry well. (For deep-frying, cut geoduck steaks into 1-inch strips.) Have ready ½ cup **all-purpose flour** on a sheet of wax paper, 2 **eggs** lightly beaten with 2 tablespoons **milk** in a shallow bowl, and 1½ cups **fine dry bread crumbs** or seasoned crumbs in another shallow bowl. Dredge each piece in flour to coat, shaking off excess, and dip in egg mixture; drain briefly. Dredge in crumbs to coat. Let dry on a rack for about 30 minutes.

To deep-fry, heat 1½ to 2 inches **salad oil** in a deep pan to 375°F on a deep-frying thermometer. Lower clams, 4 or 5 pieces at a time, into hot oil and cook until lightly browned (about 30 seconds). Lift out clams and drain on a paper towel–lined plate; keep warm until all are cooked.

To pan-fry, place a wide frying pan over medium-high heat. Add 1 tablespoon **salad oil** and heat until oil ripples when pan is tilted. Add 1 tablespoon **butter** or margarine and heat until melted. Place clams, without crowding, in pan and cook, turning once, until browned (about 1 to 1½ minutes total); add more oil and butter as needed. Lift out clams and place on a paper towel–lined plate; keep warm. Makes 4 to 6 servings.

Steaming. For up to 5 pounds **live hard-shell clams,** pour ¼ cup **water** into a 5- to 7-quart pan. Add clams, cover, and boil over medium-high heat just until shells open (5 to 10 minutes); remove clams as they open. Serve warm in wide bowls. Strain cooking liquid and serve in small bowls as a dip. Offer **melted butter** and **lemon wedges,** if desired. Or remove steamed clams from shells and use in other recipes.

■ **Suggested recipes.** Garlic Clams on the Half Shell (page 101), Fish Pil-Pil in Red Sauce (page 104), Thai Seafood Firepot (page 105), San Francisco-style Cioppino (page 105), Steamed Clams with Linguisa & Pasta (page 106), Hearty Clam Chowder (page 106), Seafood Linguine (page 119). For smoked clams: Smoked Mussels with Lemon-Garlic Mayonnaise (page 116).

■ **Serving ideas.** Serve raw clams on the half shell with lemon wedges and pepper, liquid hot pepper seasoning, or chopped parsley. With fried clams, offer Tartar Sauce (page 123) or Warm Garlic Butter (page 125).

Cobia

Sometimes called: Ling, Lemonfish, Crabeater, Sergeant fish

A solitary wanderer found in tropical and subtropical waters worldwide, cobia has no close relatives. It's a large, handsome brown fish with distinctive dark, lateral streaks (hence, the name sergeant fish). Sometimes cobia is mistaken for shark. In the United States, most cobia is taken as an incidental catch along the Gulf Coast of Florida and other Gulf states, but it's caught as far north as Chesapeake Bay. Mexico is a leading producer.

■ **Size and forms.** Cobia up to 6 feet long and 100 pounds in weight has been taken, but 20 to 50 pounds is more common. Almost all is sold fresh, either as steaks or fillets.

■ **Availability.** Cobia can be found all year on a limited basis, with much of the catch sold near where it's landed. A small amount of imported frozen cobia is also sold.

■ **Taste and texture.** The meat is firm (similar to swordfish) and moderately oily (about 5 percent fat); rosy pink when raw, it turns light tan when cooked. The flavor is moderately pronounced but not strong.

■ **Preparation.** If you buy cobia whole, cut it into steaks or fillets as for round fish. Skin the fillets unless you plan to barbecue them. For techniques, see pages 80–81.

■ **Cooking methods.** Cobia is especially delicious smoked (page 84) or grilled over a smoky fire.

Baking. Bake steaks and skinned fillets in Piquant Vegetable Sauce or oven-brown them. (See pages 82–85.)

Barbecuing and broiling. Grill steaks and skin-on fillets over direct heat, placing them right on the grill. Use indirect heat for large whole fillets and thick chunks. Chunks can also be cubed and skewered for kebabs. To broil cobia, use dry or moist heat. Soak fish in Ginger-Soy, Italian-style, or Basil-Parmesan Marinade before barbecuing or dry-heat broiling. (See pages 86–89.)

Frying. Pan-fried cobia steaks and skinned fillets brown well without a coating; or simply dust with flour. Cut into cubes for stir-frying. (See pages 90–92, 95.)

Poaching and steaming. Cobia is suitable for pan-poaching or poaching the classic way. (See pages 92–94.)

■ **Suggested recipes.** Burmese Fish with Sweet Onions (page 96), Fish Pot-au-Feu (page 103), Thai Fish & Watercress Salad (page 108), Grilled Tuna with Teriyaki Fruit Sauce (page 117), Swordfish Steaks with Mushrooms (page 117), Skewered Fish, Northwest Style (page 118).

■ **Serving ideas.** Flour-dusted, pan-fried cobia steaks or fillets are enhanced by a drizzling of Warm Garlic Butter, Provençale Butter, or Garlic-Lemon Butter (page 125). Accompany with baked small red thin-skinned potatoes.

Rediscovering
Salt
Cod

Salting foods to preserve them has given us some of our favorite tastes: ham, bacon, aged cheeses, and corned beef, to name a few. Though refrigeration has eliminated the need for curing, we still enjoy these foods because of their special flavor. Often overlooked, however, is salted fish. It's worth rediscovering for the added taste dimension it gives to many dishes.

The most common dry-cured fish is salt cod, long popular in Scandinavian, Canadian, and Mediterranean cuisine. You'll find salt cod fillets in wooden crates in the refrigerated section of many markets specializing in Scandinavian or Mediterranean foods.

If salt cod is still flexible when you buy it, wrap it in a damp towel and refrigerate for up to 3 weeks. If it's fully dehydrated and stiff, wrap it in plastic wrap or aluminum foil and store it in the refrigerator for up to 3 months.

Before you can use salt cod, it must be reconstituted. Rinse the cod well and then immerse it in a container of cold water (cut it into chunks, if necessary, to fit). Refrigerate, changing the soaking water 2 or 3 times, until softened (12 to 24 hours, depending on how stiff it was when purchased).

Drain the cod and place it in a large pan; pour in cold water to cover. Bring to a boil; reduce heat, cover, and simmer until fish is opaque and plumped and falls into heavy flakes when prodded (about 20 minutes). Drain and pat dry. Remove bones and skin, if necessary. Use in recipes or, if made ahead, cover and refrigerate for up to 2 days.

The robust flavors of Mediterranean cuisine are a perfect match for salt cod.

This hearty stew from Italy, known there as *baccalà,* is a favorite winter dish served atop polenta.

Braised Salt Cod

About 2 pounds salt cod
2 **bunches Swiss chard**
¾ **cup olive oil**
2 **large onions, chopped**
2 **large leeks (including tender green tops), thinly sliced (about 4 cups *total*)**
4 **cloves garlic, minced or pressed**
½ **head green cabbage, coarsely chopped**
1½ **cups dry white wine**
1 **can (about 1 lb.) pear-shaped tomatoes**
3 **cans (8 oz. *each*) tomato sauce**
2 **tablespoons chopped fresh rosemary or 1 tablespoon dry rosemary**
1 **can (14½ oz.) regular-strength chicken broth**
Hot Cooked Polenta (recipe follows)

Soak and cook cod as directed at left. Refrigerate until ready to use.

Tear chard leaves from stems. Chop leaves and stems separately; reserve 2 cups of the leaves.

Heat oil in a 5- to 6-quart pan over medium-high heat. Add remaining chard, onions, leeks, garlic, and cabbage. Cook, stirring, until vegetables are soft (about 15 minutes).

Stir in wine, tomatoes (break up with a spoon) and their liquid, tomato sauce, rosemary, and broth. Bring to a boil; reduce heat, cover, and simmer, stirring occasionally, for 1½ hours. (At this point, you may cool, cover, and refrigerate until next day; reheat to use.)

Add cod to sauce and continue to cook for 1 more hour, stirring in reserved chard leaves in last 15 minutes of cooking time. Meanwhile, prepare Hot Cooked Polenta.

Evenly spoon polenta into wide bowls. Ladle stew over. Makes 8 to 10 servings.

■ **Hot Cooked Polenta.** In a 4-quart pan, bring 6 cups **water** and 1 teaspoon **salt** to a boil over high heat. Add 2 cups **polenta** in a steady stream, stirring constantly. Reduce heat and simmer, stirring often with a long-handled wooden spoon, until mixture is very thick and pulls away from sides of pan (about 30 minutes). Stir in ¼ cup **butter** or margarine, if desired.

Salt cod, an old-world favorite, combines with robust vegetables and seasonings in Braised Salt Cod (recipe at left), a Mediterranean-style stew. Serve with golden polenta.

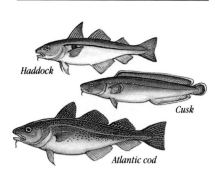

Haddock

Cusk

Atlantic cod

Cod

European sailors were fishing for cod in the North Atlantic hundreds of years before the first settlements in North America. Cod's firm white flesh was easily preserved by salting, and salt cod (page 25) became a staple in both the diet and trade of the New England colonists. Cod's commercial importance continues to this day.

Haddock, pollock, hake, whiting, and New Zealand's hoki are all members of the cod family. With the exception of the small Atlantic whiting (silver hake), all are medium-size fish, usually sold as fresh or frozen fillets; they have similiar cooking and eating qualities. "Scrod" is simply a term used to describe small (1½ to 2½ lbs.) cod, haddock, or pollock. Cusk is another member of the cod family, though its unusual, firm texture requires special preparation (see at right).

Several other fish are sometimes called cod, though they don't belong to the same family. For black cod, see Sablefish, page 52; for rock cod, see Rockfish, page 51; for Lingcod, see page 37.

Atlantic cod. This is the cod on which New England's fishing industry has been based since colonial times. Today, most New England–caught cod is sold fresh as skinless fillets; cleaned whole fish and steaks are occasionally available. Fresh cod is caught year-round, with most landings in late winter and early spring. Canada, Norway, and Iceland produce frozen Atlantic cod fillets.

Pacific cod. This cod (also called true cod), almost identical to the Atlantic species, is found from California to the Gulf of Alaska, its major source. The harvesting of Alaska's cod for salting was pioneered by New Englanders in the last century and continued until the advent of refrigerated transport for fresh fish in the 1940s. Today, freezer trawlers catch, fillet, and freeze Alaska's cod at sea; the skinless fillets make an excellent frozen product.

Haddock. Smaller than cod (generally 2 to 5 lbs.), with softer flesh that doesn't make good salted fish, haddock is found only in the North Atlantic. Fresh fish is sold in steaks or fillets; the fillets are usually sold with the skin on to distinguish them from cod. Very little fresh fish is available between March and June, the haddock spawning season. Frozen haddock fillets, usually sold skinless, are available year-round.

Atlantic pollock. The meat of this fish is more strongly flavored and less white than cod, but it turns white when cooked. Pollock is considerably less expensive than cod. Pollock is landed in New England waters throughout the year, but heaviest landings are usually in the fall. The skinless fillets are sold fresh and occasionally frozen.

Alaska pollock. Sometimes called walleye pollock, this fish, abundant in the Gulf of Alaska and the Bering Sea, is harvested primarily by factory ships and frozen at sea; it's the main species used for surimi (page 69). With its snow-white flesh and fairly firm texture, it's quite different from Atlantic pollock and tastes almost identical to cod. The fresh fish doesn't keep well, but skinless frozen-at-sea fillets are a good value.

Cusk. A solitary fish that's often taken incidentally along the New England coast, cusk has chewy flesh, similar to monkfish though not quite as firm. Cusk is sold as skinless fillets; once the dense muscle has been tenderized, it can be cooked like cod. Chunks of cusk hold their shape well in soups and stews.

Whiting and hake. Some 15 species of fish around the world are sold by these names, often used interchangeably. In North America, the *Atlantic whiting* (also called silver hake) is the most important. These small fish (usually about 1 lb.) are sold fresh or frozen, usually headed and cleaned; they're most popular in the Northeast and Middle West.

Small amounts of the East Coast's *white hake* and *red hake* are sold in markets; they're much softer than cod and must be processed or frozen very quickly after they're caught. Some of the West Coast's *Pacific whiting* is available fresh and sometimes smoked; it can be a good fish if properly handled.

Antarctic whiting, caught off the southern coast of Chile, is a good-tasting fish that yields large, snow-white fillets. Some is sold in the United States under the name of *Antarctic queen.* Hoki, or blue hake, is landed off the New Zealand and Chilean coasts. Skinless fillets of hoki are sold frozen; much also goes into surimi (page 69).

■ **Size and forms.** The various cod family members can range in size from 1 to 25 pounds or more, but most market fish are under 10 pounds and are sold as fillets. See individual species descriptions above for details.

■ **Availability.** See individual species descriptions above. Cod and haddock are also available lightly smoked as finnan haddie.

■ **Taste and texture.** With the exception of cusk, cod and its cousins all have tender, flaky flesh that's light in color, mild in flavor, and very lean (about 1 percent fat). The different species vary in firmness, with cod having the firmest flakes, whiting and hake the softest, but they can be used interchangeably in most recipes. Cusk's flesh is also white, lean, and mild, but it has a slightly chewy texture.

■ **Preparation.** Whole fish, where available, are usually headed and cleaned; they may need to be scaled. Fillet as for round fish. For techniques, see pages 79–80.

To tenderize cusk's dense muscle before cooking, place it on a board and cut it on the bias into 1-inch-thick slanting slices.

■ **Cooking methods.** Cod and most of its cousins can be used interchangeably in cooking.

Baking. Steaks, fillets, and cleaned whole Atlantic whiting can be baked in Piquant Vegetable Sauce. Oven-brown fillets and steaks or bake them with a creamy topping. (See pages 82–86.)

Barbecuing and broiling. Support steaks or fillets on perforated foil on the barbecue; use direct heat. Use Lemon-Butter Baste or Italian-style or Basil-Parmesan Marinade to grill. Broil fillets or steaks using moist heat or broil with a crumb coating. (See pages 86–89.)

Frying. Deep-frying is one of the most popular ways to cook fish in the cod family; try British Beer or Lemon Batter. Pan-fried steaks and fillets brown best if coated; try a light or heavy crumb coating or Golden Egg Wash. Pan-fry whole Atlantic whiting with a cornmeal or crumb coating. (See pages 89–92.)

Poaching and steaming. Steaks, fillets, and whole Atlantic whiting can be pan-poached, foil-steamed, or steamed Chinese-style. If you poach pieces of fish the classic way, support them with cheesecloth. (See pages 92–95.)

■ **Suggested recipes.** Fish Fillets with Dill and Tangerine (page 91), Rockfish Florentine (page 96), Fish & Chard Pie (page 99), Quenelles with Creamy Shallot Sauce (page 100), Faux Salmon Terrine (page 101), Quick Colorful Chowder (page 102), Puget Sound Salmon Gefillte Fish Soup (page 103), Fish Pot-au-Feu (page 103), Fish Pil-Pil in Red Sauce (page 104), Veracruz Fish Salad (page 107), Fish Fillets with Sherry-Mushroom Sauce (page 111), Orange Roughy Maître d'Hôtel (page 112), Baked Fish & Ratatouille (page 112).

■ **Serving ideas.** These mild-flavored fish accept a wide range of flavorings. After poaching or steaming, arrange fish in a shallow casserole, cover with Mornay Sauce (page 124), and broil briefly until the sauce is dappled with golden brown flecks. Serve cold cooked fish with Homemade Mayonnaise or any of its variations (page 123).

Corbina & Corvina *see Seatrout/ Weakfish, page 59*

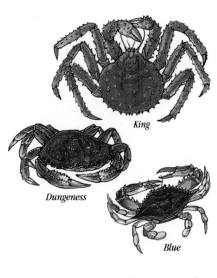

King

Dungeness

Blue

Crab

Of the dozens of kinds of crabs found in Atlantic and Pacific waters, four species—blue, Dungeness, king, and snow—account for the bulk of the catch in the United States. Some others are becoming more common, so you may see other species as well. The different crabs vary widely in size and shape, which often determine how they're sold and used.

To eat cooked crab once it's been cleaned and cracked, you pluck the meat from the body and legs with a metal pick, a small fork, or the tip of a crab leg. Soft-shell crabs are the exception—you can eat almost the entire crab, shell and all.

Blue crab. The largest crab fishery in the United States is centered on the blue crab. This small crab, weighing from 4 to 16 ounces and averaging 5 to 7 inches across the back, is found along the Atlantic coast from Massachusetts to Florida and in the Gulf of Mexico. Most of the meat is in the body and two pincer claws; it takes about 3 to make a serving.

Some blue crabs are caught year-round, but summer is the peak season. They're sold live, cooked, and as picked crabmeat.

Soft-shell blue crabs are a special delicacy. As they mature, crabs periodically grow a slightly larger shell. When harvested immediately after shedding their old shell and before the new shell has hardened, these crabs are almost completely edible. Crabs molt between April and September, but live soft-shell crabs are most available June through August. They're sold frozen the rest of the year.

Dungeness crab. This, the most important West Coast crab, was named for a small community on the Strait of Juan de Fuca in Washington State. It grows to 4 pounds, though most market crabs weigh between 1¼ and 2½ pounds; larger crabs (2½ to 3½ lbs.) are still fairly common in Alaska. Only males measuring at least 6¼ inches across the back are taken. Dungeness have a higher proportion of meat to body weight than most other crabs, and it's relatively easy to remove the meat.

The commercial fishing area for Dungeness is from central California to Kodiak, Alaska. Supply fluctuates widely from year to year and region to region. The main harvest season runs from early December through August in California, Oregon, and Washington. In Alaska, the season is from May through August. Usually, these crabs are most abundant early in the season. They're sold live or as fresh or frozen cooked whole crab, frozen crab sections, or fresh or frozen crabmeat.

King crab. Three species of kings, the largest of all crabs, are caught in the North Pacific and Bering Sea: red (the most important), blue, and brown (or golden). Red and blue kings, which are similar, can reach 6 feet across and weigh 20 pounds, but most are under 10 pounds. Brown kings, found in deeper waters along the continental shelf, are a little smaller.

Most king crab is landed between September and February, but virtually all is sold cooked and frozen as sections, legs or claws, or crabmeat and is available all year.

Another species of crab is taken in the Antarctic by Chilean fishermen and sold as king crab; it's usually marketed as frozen cooked crabmeat.

Snow crab. Two principal species of this crab (also called tanner and, in Canada, queen crab) are harvested commercially. Bairdi, the larger, grows to about 2½ pounds and is found only in the

To kill live crab, place a heavy knife over center of belly and rap sharply with a mallet to cut through crab and kill instantly.

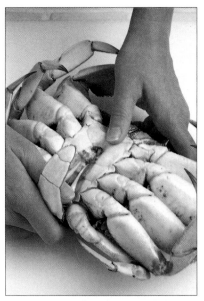

To clean raw or cooked crab, first break off triangular belly flap on underside of crab; discard.

Turn crab over and, starting from rear of crab, pull firmly to lift off back of shell; discard.

Pull off and discard spongy gills from body and tiny paddles from front. Scoop out golden crab butter (reserve, if desired). Rinse body well.

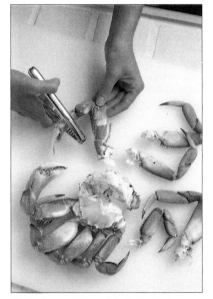

Twist claws and legs off body. Crack claws and legs along edges of shells, using a heavy cracker or hitting softly with a small hammer.

Cut body into halves or quarters; extract crabmeat from body, claws, and legs, using a metal pick, small fork, or tip of a crab leg. If raw, cook crabmeat.

North Pacific. Opilio is taken in both the North Pacific and Atlantic by Canadian fishermen. Snow crab is sold as cooked frozen clusters or as crabmeat.

Stone crab. Florida fishermen harvest only the claws of stone crab; they twist off one claw and return the crab to the sea to regenerate another one. The cooked claws are sold fresh or frozen. A few stone crabs are also taken in Texas. The season for the fresh claws runs from October through March in Florida and until June in Texas. Stone crab has especially rich-tasting meat.

Rock and Jonah crabs. These small crabs, found throughout the Northeast, rarely weigh more than a pound. Both live and cooked Jonah crabs are available in most East Coast cities during the summer. The rock crab is more important in Maine; it's sold as cooked whole crab or as crabmeat. The meat yield from both crabs is low—it takes about a dozen crabs to yield a pound of picked meat.

Before cooking, quickly kill live soft-shell crab by snipping off face directly behind eyes.

Gently lift one side of top shell; pull off spongy gills and discard. Repeat on other side.

Turn crab over and pull off "apron," or flap; soft-shell crab is now ready for cooking.

California has a limited fishery for rock crab and red rock crab. Red rock and box crab are sometimes sold in Northwest markets. Almost all the fine-tasting meat of these crabs is in the two large claws.

Red crab. Found along the edge of the continental shelf from Nova Scotia to Cuba, these deep-sea dwellers have developed commercial importance only in recent years. They're fairly small (males grow to 2¼ pounds and females to 1¼ pounds), but their meat yield is high. The meat's flavor and appearance compare with king crab, but the pieces are much smaller. Most red crab is sold as frozen leg or salad meat. Because of their fragile nature, these crabs are rarely sold live or whole.

■ **Size and forms.** Crab is sold live, as cooked whole crab or picked crabmeat, or frozen (see individual species descriptions above). Crabs that are alive until shortly before cooking and eating have the freshest flavor. For cooked dishes (to avoid cooking the crab twice), it's always best to start with live crab, if possible; you may need to order it a few days ahead. If only cooked crab is available, add it to hot dishes during the last minutes of cooking and cook just until hot.

Figure on about 3 ounces of picked crabmeat per serving in salads and casseroles. For a cracked-crab dinner, allow 1 to 1¼ pounds Dungeness or about 3 blue crabs per serving.

■ **Availability.** See individual species descriptions preceding.

■ **Taste and texture.** The tender, flaky meat of all crabs has similar delicate, sweet flavor.

■ **Preparation.** To clean and crack live or cooked Dungeness crab, see the facing page.

To crack cooked hard-shell blue crab, twist off the claws and legs. With the crab on its back, lift up the "apron," or flap, and, in one motion, remove the top shell with your fingers; discard. Remove and discard the spongy white gills. Snap the body in half.

To prepare soft-shell blue crab for cooking, see the photos above.

■ **Cooking methods.** Cooking technique depends on the type of crab you have.

Simmering live crab. For up to 5 pounds **live crabs,** bring about 5 quarts **water** to a rapid boil in a 10- to 12-quart pan. Pick up each crab, holding from rear, and plunge it headfirst into water. Reduce heat, cover, and simmer, allowing 15 to 20 minutes for 1½- to 2-pound Dungeness, 5 to 10 minutes for smaller crabs. Remove with tongs and immerse briefly in cold water.

To clean and crack, see facing page. For a cracked-crab feast (see "Serving ideas," page 30), refrigerate crabs for at least 2 hours.

Pan-frying soft-shell blue crab. Prepare live crabs for cooking as shown above. Rinse prepared crab or thawed frozen crab under cool running water; let drain and pat dry. For 6 **crabs** (about 2 oz. *each*), combine 6 tablespoons **all-purpose flour** or 3 tablespoons *each* flour and yellow cornmeal with ¼ teaspoon *each* **salt** and **pepper.** Dust the crabs, 1 at a time, with the flour mixture, shaking off excess.

Heat 2 tablespoons **salad oil** in a wide frying pan over medium heat; add 2 tablespoons **butter** or margarine and heat until melted. Lay crabs, backs down, in pan without crowding. Cook, turning once, until browned on both sides (8 to 10 minutes total). Lift out and keep warm until all are browned. If desired, offer with **Ginger or Cayenne Sauce** (page 120). Allow 1 crab as an appetizer serving, 2 or 3 for a main dish.

Broiling king crab legs. Thaw frozen crab legs completely. Break at the joints, if necessary. Using scissors, cut down both sides of each shell; lift off and discard the upper half, leaving the meat on the lower half.

For about 1½ pounds **crab legs,** melt ¼ cup **butter** or margarine and stir in 2 teaspoons **lemon juice** and ½ teaspoon **dry tarragon.** Arrange crab legs, shell sides down, in a shallow baking pan and brush generously with butter mixture. Broil 5 to 6 inches from heat just until hot (4 to 5 minutes). Makes about 4 servings.

■ **Suggested recipes.** Maki or Temaki Sushi (pages 54–55), Crabby Jack Quesadillas (page 101), Thai Seafood Firepot (page 105), San Francisco-style Cioppino (page 105), Red Chile Louis (page 109), Pan-fried Soft-shell Crab with Ginger or Cayenne Sauce (page 120), Laurita-style Crab & Pasta (page 121), Crab Lace Patties on Lettuce (page 121).

■ **Serving ideas.** Good sauces with crab are Lemon Mayonnaise and other variations of Homemade Mayonnaise (page 123). Or try Ginger or Cayenne Sauce (page 120).

For a cracked-crab feast, pile chilled cooked crab legs and body pieces onto a platter. Accompany with melted butter (about ½ cup for 4 servings) and lemon wedges. Or serve with small dishes of one of the sauces suggested above.

Crayfish

Sometimes called: Crawfish

Crayfish are small, lobsterlike crustaceans found in freshwater lakes, rivers, and streams. The commercial harvest comes primarily from Louisiana, California, Oregon, and Washington. Crayfish are also farmed on a large scale in Louisiana. After harvest, crayfish are usually held overnight in a cleaning tank. Hearty creatures, they can be shipped live just about anywhere.

To remove sand vein, grasp live crayfish behind pincers and turn belly side up. Twist off center section of tail, gently pulling out sand vein with it.

Eating crayfish is something of an art. The tail, which readily breaks away, contains most of the meat; those who take time to crack the claws of West Coast crayfish are rewarded with the sweetest, most succulent segments. Sip juices that linger in the shells and, if you like, eat the green-to-gold "butter" in the body. In females, you may find clusters of delicious bright red eggs.

■ **Size and forms.** Market size ranges from 3½ to 7 inches long. Most crayfish is sold live, but fresh or frozen cooked whole crayfish and peeled and deveined tail meat are also available. About 7 pounds of whole crayfish yields a pound of meat (allow about a pound of live crayfish per person).

■ **Availability.** The harvest season in Louisiana is from November to June, with heaviest production from March through May. In the West, crayfish is most available from May to October. Though some markets carry crayfish in season, you may need to order in advance.

■ **Taste and texture.** Crayfish meat has a sweet, lobsterlike flavor but is not quite as rich or firm as lobster.

■ **Preparation.** Spray crayfish with cool water just before cooking to rinse away any silt; inspect and remove any

dead crayfish. To remove the sand vein, if desired, grasp the crayfish behind the pincers and turn it stomach side up; twist the center tail section, snapping the shell, and gently pull out the vein (shown at left).

■ **Cooking methods.** The classic way to cook crayfish is to boil them in a spicy mixture.

To boil, rinse about 4 pounds **live crayfish** in cool water and, if desired, remove sand vein (see above). Prepare either **Spicy or Dill Boil** (recipes follow). Drop in crayfish, a few at a time (to maintain boil), and boil rapidly for 30 seconds; reduce heat and simmer until tail meat is opaque throughout when tail is pulled off and cracked open (6 to 7 minutes). Remove with a slotted spoon and mound on a serving platter. Makes about 4 servings.

Spicy Boil. In an 8-quart or larger pan, combine 4 quarts **water;** ½ cup **lemon juice** or cider vinegar; 1 medium-size **onion,** sliced; 2 or 3 **carrots,** sliced; 6 to 8 **parsley sprigs;** 2 tablespoons **salt;** 8 to 10 **whole black peppercorns;** 2 **bay leaves;** 8 **whole cloves;** 6 **whole allspice;** and 1 to 1½ teaspoons **ground red pepper** (cayenne). Cover and simmer for 15 minutes. Increase heat to high and bring to a rolling boil.

Dill Boil. In an 8-quart or larger pan, combine 4 quarts **water,** ½ pound **fresh mature dill** (including flower heads), and 2 tablespoons **salt.** Cover and bring to a rolling boil over high heat.

■ **Suggested recipes.** Tahoe Crayfish Bisque (page 106).

■ **Serving ideas.** Offer small bowls of melted butter or margarine, Aïoli, or Homemade Mayonnaise (page 123) for dipping. It's a Louisiana custom to serve small new potatoes and shucked ears of corn with crayfish that's been cooked in Spicy Boil. Cook the potatoes in the same liquid until almost tender; add the corn with the crayfish.

Atlantic

Croaker

Different species of croaker, named for the croaking sounds they make by vibrating muscles against their air bladders, are sold around the world, but Atlantic croaker and spot are the most important in North America. Both are closely related to the drum (below right).

Atlantic croaker (also called hardhead and golden croaker) is a schooling, bottom-dwelling fish caught in inshore waters from Chesapeake Bay to Argentina and in the Gulf of Mexico.

Spot (also called spot croaker) takes its name from the dark spot it wears on its shoulder. It's caught along the mid-Atlantic and Gulf coasts.

■ **Size and forms.** Typical Atlantic croaker size is 1 to 1½ pounds. This fish is usually sold whole or cleaned, with head and tail off; larger fish are sometimes filleted. Most spots weigh less than a pound and are sold whole or cleaned.

■ **Availability.** Both Atlantic croaker and spot are subject to wide swings in supply. Some are landed year-round, but they're most plentiful from March to October. Most of the fish caught domestically are sold near where they're landed. Some frozen Atlantic croaker is imported from South America.

■ **Taste and texture.** The flesh of croaker is light in color, with moist, tender flakes. It has mild to moderately pronounced flavor and is moderately lean (about 3.2 percent fat). These fish are subject to parasites, so don't eat them raw.

■ **Preparation.** Whole croaker or spot may need scaling and cleaning; remove the head and tail, if desired. For techniques, see pages 79–80.

■ **Cooking methods.** These pan-size fish can be cooked in a number of ways.

Baking. Bake whole croaker or spot in Piquant Vegetable Sauce or with a stuffing. Oven-brown spot and small croakers. (See pages 82–85.)

Barbecuing and broiling. Barbecue with direct heat, using perforated foil or a hinged broiler. You can also broil a whole fish using the dry-heat method. Use a baste or marinade for barbecuing or broiling. (See pages 86–88.)

Frying. Pan-fry small fish, using a light or heavy coating with cornmeal or crumbs, or simply flour these fish. (See pages 90–92.)

Poaching and steaming. Pan-poaching, classic poaching, foil-steaming, and Chinese-style steaming are all good ways to cook these fish. (See pages 92–95.)

■ **Suggested recipes.** Bourride (page 102), Orange Roughy Maître d'Hôtel (page 112), Trout with Leeks & Vinegar (page 114), Calico Stuffed Trout (page 114).

■ **Serving ideas.** Serve pan-fried croaker or spot with Almond or Filbert Browned Butter or Caper Butter (page 92). With fried or poached croaker or spot, try Homemade Mayonnaise or any of its variations (page 123), or offer with Tomato-Caper Sauce (page 124).

Cusk see Cod, page 26

Dolphin see Mahi Mahi, page 41

Red

Drum

Drums represent a large and diverse family of fish that get their name from the noise they make when a drumming muscle hits their air bladder. Some drums are known as croakers (above left), others as seatrout or weakfish (page 59); white sea bass (page 57) and California corbina (page 59) are also family members.

All drums are prone to parasites, which are harmless when the fish is cooked. But drum should not be eaten raw.

The recent popularity of Cajun cuisine, especially a dish called blackened redfish, created a tremendous demand for *red drum* (also called redfish, channel bass, or red sea bass). Once plentiful along the South Atlantic coast and in the Gulf of Mexico, these fish are now in short supply and are reserved for recreational anglers in most Atlantic and some Gulf states. (Red drum should not be confused with the Atlantic ocean perch, a rockfish also sometimes called redfish.)

As supplies of red drum have decreased and prices increased, the demand for the less-expensive and more plentiful *black drum* has escalated. In markets and restaurants, black drum is often sold as redfish.

The two are easy to tell apart if you see them whole: black drum has a thicker body with a humped back and distinctive barbels on its lower jaw; red drum has coppery scales and several black spots near the tail. Black drum is found from Cape Cod to Argentina but is most abundant in the Gulf of Mexico.

The smaller *freshwater drum* (also called gaspergau or sheepshead) is found in rivers and lakes from the Hudson Bay to the Gulf of Mexico.

■ **Size and forms.** Though red drum grows to more than 25 pounds and black drum to 100 pounds, the best are under 10 pounds. Larger fish are more prone to parasites. Both are usually sold as fresh skinless fillets and taste almost identical. Some cleaned whole red drums (with heads) are also available.

Freshwater drum typically runs from 1½ to 5 pounds; it's usually sold whole.

■ **Availability.** A few red drums are available all year, but these fish are most plentiful in the fall when they feed close to shore. Black drum supplies are best in the cooler months; there's a fairly steady supply all year.

■ **Taste and texture.** The cooked meat of both red and black drum has tender-firm, moist flakes. Black drum is slightly coarser, red drum more flaky. The meat is lean and light in color, with mild to moderately pronounced flavor. Fresh-water drum is more coarsely textured and earthy tasting, and is only fair in quality.

■ **Preparation.** To scale, clean, and fillet a whole fish, see pages 79–80.

■ **Cooking methods.** The different drums can be cooked in the same ways.

Baking. Bake whole fish or fillets in Piquant Vegetable Sauce; or bake whole fish stuffed with Almond-Rice or Spinach-Mushroom Stuffing. Fillets are good oven-browned or baked with a creamy topping. (See pages 82–86.)

Barbecuing and broiling. Drum is especially good barbecued—the smoke enhances its flavor. Fillets are firm enough to place directly on the grill, using direct heat; a baste or marinade is optional. Use indirect heat to grill whole fish. For broiling fillets, use the moist-heat method or broil with a crumb coating. (See pages 86–89.)

Frying. Pan-fried fillets brown well without a coating. Also use drum for Stir-fried Fish or Shellfish with Peas. (See pages 90–92, 95.)

Poaching and steaming. Pan-poach, foil-steam, steep, or steam fillets Chinese-style. Poach fillets or whole fish the classic way. (See pages 92–95.)

■ **Suggested recipes.** Fish Fillets with Dill and Tangerine (page 91), Burmese Fish with Sweet Onions (page 96), Faux Salmon Terrine (page 101), Bourride (page 102), Quick Colorful Chowder (page 102), Fish Pot-au-Feu (page 103), Fish Pil-Pil in Red Sauce (page 104), Veracruz Fish Salad (page 107), Thai Fish & Watercress Salad (page 108), Fish Fillets with Sherry-Mushroom Sauce (page 111), Mr. Zhu's Steamed Fish (page 114).

■ **Serving ideas.** Serve poached or pan-fried drum fillets with Browned Butter (page 92), Béarnaise Sauce (page 124), or Provençale or Diable Butter (page 125). Serve cold cooked fish with Homemade Mayonnaise or Remoulade Sauce (page 123) or with Dijon Vinaigrette Dressing (page 124).

Eel

Despite its serpentine appearance, eel is indeed a finfish. Known variously as American, common, silver, or fresh-water eel, the best-known species is caught along the Atlantic coast, both in brackish tidewaters and in inland rivers, lakes, and ponds. It's most plentiful from Chesapeake Bay north to Long Island.

Eel is catadromous, living most of its life in fresh water but returning to the ocean to spawn and die (just the reverse of salmon). It starts and ends its life in the Sargasso Sea near Bermuda.

■ **Size and forms.** Eel can grow to several feet in length and weigh 10 pounds or more, but it's generally sold at 1 to 2 pounds. Baby eel (less than 3 inches in length) is known as elver.

Most eel is sold live from freshwater tanks. Some cleaned whole eels and eel fillets are available fresh or frozen, but they're hard to find. Eel is also available smoked, canned, pickled, and jellied.

■ **Availability.** Eel is sold on a limited basis all year but is easiest to find in November and December. Look in European ethnic markets.

■ **Taste and texture.** Eel is oily (as much as 16 percent fat) but mild in flavor. The flesh is quite dense.

■ **Preparation.** Live eel can be killed with a blow to the head and then cleaned and skinned; most vendors will do this for you. Another way to kill eel is to smother it in a container of coarse salt.

To skin an eel, follow the directions for catfish (page 21); trim the fins with scissors. Cut the body into 2- to 3-inch lengths or carefully cut the meat away from the backbone into 2 long fillets.

Eel meat freezes well.

■ **Cooking methods.** Though used mainly in soups and stews, eel can be smoked (page 84) or cooked in the following ways. It requires more time to cook than most fish.

Baking. Bake sections in Piquant Vegetable Sauce or oven-brown them. (See pages 82–85.)

Barbecuing and broiling. Place meaty chunks of eel on skewers to barbecue; to broil, use dry heat. Use Italian-style or Basil-Parmesan Marinade. (See pages 86–88.)

Frying. Pan-fry sections or fillets, dusting pieces with flour. (See pages 90–92).

Poaching and steaming. Pan-poach sections or poach the classic way. (See pages 92–94.)

■ **Suggested recipes.** Matelote of Eel (page 104).

■ **Serving ideas.** Accompany pan-fried or poached eel with Tomato-Caper Sauce (page 124).

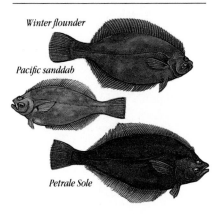

Winter flounder

Pacific sanddab

Petrale Sole

Flounder/Sole

Fish called flounder, sole, plaice, dab, turbot, and halibut all belong to a unique family of flatfish. These fish have platter-shaped bodies, dark on top and light on the bottom, and eyes curiously placed on the same side of the head. They swim with an undulating motion near the bottom of the sea.

With the exception of halibut (described on page 34) and some large flounders and turbots, flatfish are small. Sole and flounder in U.S. markets come from the East, West, and Gulf of Mexico coasts; some are imported. The different species vary in quality.

East Coast varieties. Gray sole (also called witch flounder), the premium variety, makes a thick fillet, the most expensive produced in the United States. *Winter flounder,* better known as blackback flounder when under 3½ pounds and as lemon sole when larger, produces both a white and a gray fillet from each fish, but both turn pure white when cooked.

American plaice (often sold as dab or sanddab on the East Coast) makes a thick, firm fillet. *Yellowtail flounder* (also called dab or rusty flounder) makes a delicate, thin fillet, less sweet tasting than other Eastern species.

Summer flounder, or fluke, can grow to 20 pounds but usually weighs from 3 to 5 pounds; in quantity, it's the most abundant flatfish on the East Coast. *Southern flounder* ranges from the Carolinas to Texas, but most is harvested in the Gulf of Mexico.

West Coast varieties. Petrale sole, the finest flounder on the West Coast, makes large, firm fillets. The smaller *sand sole* is a close second for flavor. *English sole* has firm texture and good flavor but sometimes tastes slightly like iodine. *Rex sole* and *Pacific sanddab* are usually too small to fillet and are sold whole or trimmed; they're the favorites of many sole connoisseurs.

Dover sole, the most plentiful of the West Coast flatfish, has soft flesh. Most frozen sole is Dover. *Arrowtooth flounder* (sometimes incorrectly called turbot) and *starry flounder* are two large fish that often show up in markets as incidental catches; the flesh, especially of arrowtooth flounder, is soft and rather low in quality.

California halibut is a large flounder that can weigh as much as 20 pounds, big enough to cut into steaks that resemble Pacific halibut (page 34), a fish with finer texture and firmer meat. Most of the California catch is sold fresh within the state, where it's often labeled simply "halibut" and easily confused with true Pacific halibut. Though not as high in quality as true halibut, this flounder is a tasty, mild-flavored fish.

To bone a cooked, trimmed sole easily, first cut through center crease down to backbone.

Lift top fillets off backbone; using a dull knife, ease out embedded bones.

Imported varieties. The only true soles come from Europe; in general, they have thicker bodies and more oval shapes than any of the North American flatfish. *Dover sole,* not to be confused with the Pacific fish with the same name, is the common sole of Europe and is the choicest of all soles. Another fine-tasting species is the *sand sole* (sometimes called French or lemon sole), also different from its West Coast namesake.

■ **Size and forms.** Most of the small flatfish are sold as fresh or frozen fillets; usually, they're less than ½ inch thick and weigh under 8 ounces, though some are as heavy as a pound. Very small sole are sold whole, often with head and tail off and trimmed deeply on both sides to remove the fin bones.

Some summer flounder, arrowtooth flounder, starry flounder, and California halibut are large enough to be cut into steaks.

■ **Availability.** Fresh flatfish are in U.S. markets year-round. In the East, prices rise a lot in winter, when supplies are limited. In the West, sole is most plentiful in spring and summer, most limited in fall.

■ **Taste and texture.** The premium species are noted for their fine, tender-

firm texture with delicate taste, often sweet and nutlike. Less choice species have coarser, softer flesh and less delicate flavor. All are lean (usually under 1 percent fat).

■ **Preparation.** Flatfish are easy to fillet (page 81). And cooked whole sole is easily boned before serving. Before cooking, trim whole sole deeply on both edges, if necessary, to remove the fin bones.

To bone a cooked, trimmed sole, run a knife along the center crease to the backbone (shown above left); slide fillets off. Grasp the bone at the tail end and lift off, easing the bone from the meat (shown above right). Set fillets back in place.

Thin fillets are easily rolled before cooking; fasten with picks or twine.

■ **Cooking methods.** Fillets less than ½ inch thick usually require different treatment than thicker pieces.

Baking. You can bake flounder fillets over ¾ inch thick in Piquant Vegetable Sauce; or oven-brown them. (See pages 82–85.)

Broiling. Only thicker flounder fillets should be broiled; use moist heat. (See pages 88–89.) These fish are not suitable for barbecuing.

Frying. You can deep-fry boneless strips from large flounders. Use flour coating when pan-frying thin fillets or small whole fish; thicker flounder pieces may be coated with a crumb coating or Golden Egg Wash. (See pages 89–92.)

Poaching and steaming. Pan-poach thin fillets or steam Chinese-style; roll fillets to poach the classic way or steep. Thicker flounder fillets or small whole fish can be cooked flat by any of these methods, but handle them gently. (See pages 92–95.)

■ **Suggested recipes.** For small flounder/sole: Sole Fillets with Peas and Sesame Oil (page 91), Sole-wrapped Belgian Endive Rolls (page 110), Sole with Mushroom Velvet (page 110).

For large flounder: Fish Fillets with Dill and Tangerine (page 91), Rockfish Florentine (page 96), Fish & Chard Pie (page 99), Quenelles with Creamy Shallot Sauce (page 100), Faux Salmon Terrine (page 101), Quick Colorful Chowder (page 102), Puget Sound Salmon Gefillte Fish Soup (page 103), Fish Pot-au-Feu (page 103), Fish Pil-Pil in Red Sauce (page 104), Veracruz Fish Salad (page 107), Fish Fillets with Sherry-Mushroom Sauce (page 111), Orange Roughy Maître d'Hôtel (page 112), Baked Fish & Ratatouille (page 112).

■ **Serving ideas.** Complement the delicate flavor of these flatfish with an elegant sauce, such as Almond or Filbert Browned Butter (page 92); for a variation, substitute coarsely chopped macadamia nuts or pistachios. Citrus Beurre Blanc (page 125) is also a perfect finish for pan-fried fillets. Offer Hollandaise or Béarnaise Sauce (page 124) with cold cooked fish.

Fluke see Flounder/Sole, page 32

Greenland turbot see Halibut, at right

Grouper see Sea bass, page 57

Grunion see Smelt, page 65

Haddock see Cod, page 26

Hake see Cod, page 26

Pacific

Halibut

Not all fish that go by the name are really halibut. The true halibuts are Pacific (or northern) and Atlantic halibut, both very large flatfish with a firm texture. California halibut (page 33), most of which is sold within California, is a large flounder with softer and coarser flesh than true halibut. Greenland turbot is in the halibut family, but its flesh is softer and oilier than that of true Pacific or Atlantic halibut.

Pacific halibut. This fish (also called northern or Alaska halibut) ranges from Northern California to the Bering Sea, but most is taken in the Gulf of Alaska. For years, Pacific halibut was overfished, but fishing is now carefully regulated and supplies are increasing. Fresh Pacific halibut is available sporadically during spring and summer. Much of the catch is frozen and available year-round.

Atlantic halibut. Though this giant flatfish ranges across the North Atlantic, it's not very abundant. Most is landed as an incidental catch in Canada, Iceland, Norway, and the United States. It's available sporadically all year; almost all is sold fresh.

Greenland turbot. Greenland turbot is the legal name in the United States for this fish, neither a turbot nor a true halibut. Found in the northern Atlantic and Pacific, it's landed mostly from late summer to early fall; some is taken in winter in Greenland, where it's fished through the ice.

■ **Size and forms.** Pacific halibuts weighing 100 to 300 pounds are fairly common, but most are 100 pounds or less. Atlantic halibut can grow even larger. Greenland turbot is usually 10 to 15 pounds. Most true halibut is sold as thick steaks or fillets, fresh or frozen; halibut chunks, or roasts, and halibut cheeks are sometimes available.

Greenland turbot is usually available only as frozen fillets.

■ **Availability.** During much of the year, only frozen true halibut is available (most markets thaw it before displaying it). Frozen fish cooked from the frozen state usually tastes fresher than thawed fish, but you may need to ask for unthawed fish where you shop. See individual species descriptions at left for seasons for fresh fish.

■ **Taste and texture.** The fine-grained, snow-white flesh of true halibut has dense, firm flakes and very mild, sweet flavor. Its lean meat (about 2.3 percent fat) dries out easily if overcooked. Greenland turbot has about 10 percent fat; its flesh is dense and darker in color than true halibut.

■ **Preparation.** No preparation necessary.

■ **Cooking methods.** Because of their different textures and fat content, true halibut and Greenland turbot sometimes require different cooking techniques. Greenland turbot is also good smoked (page 84).

Baking. Bake steaks, fillets, or roasts of true halibut with Piquant Vegetable Sauce or a creamy topping. Oven-brown Greenland turbot fillets. (See pages 82–86.)

Barbecuing and broiling. True halibut is firm enough to skewer for kebabs; or place steaks directly on a well-greased grill and use direct heat. Barbecue roasts with indirect heat. Use Italian-style or Basil-Parmesan Marinade and baste frequently; avoid overcooking. Use moist heat for broiling. (See pages 86–89.)

Barbecuing is a favorite way to cook Greenland turbot; support fillets on perforated foil and use direct heat. Use dry heat when broiling. Try Sesame-Soy or Lemon-Butter Baste when barbecuing or broiling. (See pages 86–88.)

Frying. Pan-fry true halibut plain or use a flour coating. It can also be stir-fried or deep-fried. To pan-fry Greenland turbot, use a light or heavy crumb coating; this species is not suitable for stir-frying or deep-frying. (See pages 90–92, 95.)

Poaching and steaming. True halibut is excellent pan-poached, poached the classic way, steeped, foil-steamed, or steamed Chinese-style. You can pan-poach Greenland turbot. (See pages 92–95.)

■ **Suggested recipes.** For true halibut: Gravlax Plus (page 47), Maki Sushi (page 54), Burmese Fish with Sweet Onions (page 96), Faux Salmon Terrine (page 101), Fish Pot-au-Feu (page 103), Salmon Salad with Tarragon Vinaigrette (page 107), Thai Fish & Watercress Salad (page 108), Skewered Fish, Northwest Style (page 118).

For Greenland turbot: Fish Fillets with Dill and Tangerine (page 91), Veracruz Fish Salad (page 107), Five-Spice Fish (page 111), Baked Fish & Ratatouille (page 112), Braised Sablefish (page 112).

■ **Serving ideas.** Serve hot cooked true halibut with a buttery sauce, such as Hollandaise, Mousseline, or Béarnaise (page 124), or with slices of Basil Garlic Butter (page 125). Cold cooked halibut is good in salads with Tarragon Vinaigrette Dressing (page 107).

Atlantic herring

Herring/Sardine

The term "sardine" is used to describe a number of small sea herrings that are brined and canned. (The method originated on the island of Sardinia, hence the name.) In Maine, the sardine industry cans juvenile *Atlantic herring,* a species abundant in the North Atlantic. The other major commercial species, the *Pacific herring,* ranges from California north to the Bering Straits and across to Japan.

Another species, the *Pacific sardine,* was once a major fishery centered in Monterey, California (responsible for the town's Cannery Row). This fish disappeared mysteriously in the 1940s but is now beginning to reappear; its excellent flavor is similar to that of Spanish and Portuguese sardines.

A close relative of the sea herring is the *freshwater alewife,* also called river or spring herring.

Most of the herring consumed in the United States is in the form of canned

sardines and various other marinated, salted, and smoked herring products. Though not too easy to find, there are also some fresh and frozen herring and Pacific sardines available in markets from time to time.

The fresh fish are very fragile and need to be handled carefully; buy them only from reliable markets and cook them as soon as possible. High-quality frozen herring is often a good buy; use it within a day of thawing.

■ **Size and forms.** The average size of fresh or frozen sea herring is about a pound, a little smaller for Pacific sardines. Freshwater herring is usually 4 to 8 ounces. Herring is sold whole and occasionally as butterflied fillets.

■ **Availability.** Fresh herring is easiest to find from late fall through spring.

■ **Taste and texture.** Herring is oily (about 11 percent fat) and pronounced in flavor, resembling mackerel. The meat is soft and tender.

■ **Preparation.** Whole fish need to be scaled and cleaned (pages 79–80) to cook whole. Herring can also be filleted to remove most of the bones. Cut the head, tail, and fins from the scaled and cleaned fish; then split it the length of the belly and spread it out, skin side up. Rub firmly up and down the backbone and turn the fish over. Grasp one end of the backbone (with small bones attached) and lift up gently. Leave fillets attached (butterflied) or cut them apart.

■ **Cooking methods.** Aside from the methods below, herring is also good smoked (page 84).

Baking. Bake whole herring in Piquant Vegetable Sauce. (See pages 82–83.)

Barbecuing and broiling. Whole fish and butterflied fillets cook well over direct heat, supported on perforated foil. Broil using the dry-heat method or with a crumb coating. Try Ginger-Soy or Basil-Parmesan Marinade when broiling with dry heat or barbecuing. (See pages 86–89.)

Frying. Pan-fry whole fish or fillets after coating with flour or a light crumb coating. (See pages 90–92.)

■ **Suggested recipes.** Mackerel with Tart Onion Sauce (page 112).

■ **Serving ideas.** To complement the rich taste of herring, offer with Tomato-Caper Sauce (page 124). Along the Mediterranean coast of France, grilled sardines are paired with lemon wedges and spicy Diable Butter (page 125).

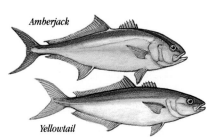

Amberjack

Yellowtail

Jack

The many members of the jack family are widespread throughout the world's tropical and subtropical waters. In addition to fish called jack, the family includes the amberjack and yellowtail, as well as the pompano (page 50).

Except for pompano, the important jacks in U.S. markets are large fish with firm flesh. Smaller jacks with flakier flesh and less commercial importance include the blue runner in the western Atlantic, rainbow runner in the western Atlantic and Hawaii (where it's often called Hawaiian salmon), and jack mackerel (page 40), caught along the Pacific Coast.

Amberjack. One species, the greater amberjack, is well known in the Southeast, where it's taken off the Carolina coast in summer and in the Gulf of Mexico in winter. An amberjack caught in Hawaii is called kahala. Amberjacks grow to more than 100 pounds, but average market size ranges from 7 to 40 pounds; those under 15 pounds are considered best.

The larger fish sometimes have parasites in their belly cavity, but they're easy to spot and remove and are harmless when the fish is cooked. Amberjack is available year-round; in spring and fall it has fewer parasites.

A species closely related to the greater amberjack is often called Japanese yellowtail. Sashimi aficionados know it as *hamachi.*

Yellowtail. This sought-after game fish is often available in markets, especially in late summer and early fall when it migrates into Southern California waters. It's most abundant off the Pacific coast of Mexico. Catches fluctuate from year to year, so its appearance in markets is unpredictable. These fish can weigh more than 100 pounds, but 4 to 20 pounds is more typical. It's popular for sashimi (page 54).

Other species. *Jack crevalle* is found worldwide by various names, including cavally, cavalla, toro (in Mexico), common jack (in Florida), trevally (in Australia), and jackfish (in New Zealand). Most weigh between 2 and 7 pounds, though some reach more than 40 pounds. They're available year-round.

Hawaii has about 10 species of fish in this family, among them the *ulua,* or giant trevally, which reaches 100 pounds, and the smaller *papio,* or trevally. In general, fish under 10 pounds of any of these species are called papio. Peak season for both is fall.

■ **Size and forms.** Jacks vary widely in size (see individual species descriptions above). Amberjack, crevalle, yellowtail, and ulua are usually sold as fresh fillets, steaks, or chunks. Papio and other small jacks are sold whole, fresh or frozen.

■ **Availability.** See individual species descriptions above.

■ **Taste and texture.** The flesh of most jacks is firm to very firm and meaty; papio has softer, flakier flesh. Amberjack and cravelle have tan-colored flesh, yellowtail's is deep rose, and ulua's is pinky white. Properly bled and handled, the meat is rich but mild tasting. Amberjack is about 9 percent fat, yellowtail about 5 percent fat.

■ **Preparation.** For best flavor, skin fillets and remove as much of the red muscle underneath as possible. Papio, however, is often just scaled and cleaned before being cooked whole. For techniques, see pages 79–81.

■ **Cooking methods.** Jack is best smoked (page 84) or barbecued; the smoke enhances its rich flavor.

Baking. Steaks and fillets are good with Piquant Vegetable Sauce or baked with a creamy topping. (See pages 82–86.)

Barbecuing and broiling. Use direct heat to barbecue steaks or fillets, placing them directly on a greased grill. Use indirect heat for whole fish. Jacks make fine fish kebabs. Use either dry or moist heat for broiling. Any of the suggested bastes or marinades works well. (See pages 86–89.)

Frying. Pan-fried steaks and fillets brown well without a coating. Cut into chunks, the meat holds its shape for stir-frying. (See pages 90–92, 95.)

Poaching and steaming. Pan-poaching works well for steaks and fillets, as does poaching the classic way and steaming Chinese-style. (See pages 92–95.)

■ **Suggested recipes.** Burmese Fish with Sweet Onions (page 96), Seviche with Kiwi Fruit (page 100), Fish Pot-au-Feu (page 103), Thai Fish & Watercress Salad (page 108), Five-Spice Fish (page 111), Grilled Tuna with Teriyaki Fruit Sauce (page 117), Swordfish Steaks with Mushrooms (page 117), Skewered Fish, Northwest Style (page 118).

■ **Serving ideas.** Present barbecued steaks or fillets atop a crisp salad of chopped tomatoes, slivered bell peppers, thinly sliced celery, and shredded romaine lettuce, mixed lightly with Basil Vinaigrette Dressing (page 109). Or season hot fish with Citrus Beurre Blanc, Basil Garlic Butter, or Diable Butter (page 125).

John Dory

Sometimes called: St. Pierre

Though seldom seen in fish markets, John Dory is popular in restaurants featuring continental cuisine. It's an odd-looking fish with a thin, vertically compressed body and a thumbprint-shaped spot on each side.

Most of the fish sold in the United States is imported from Europe, Morocco, or New Zealand. However, the New Zealand fish is often confused with several species of oreo dories, incorrectly sold as St. Pierre. The oreos are good tasting and less expensive, but are not as choice as the John Dory.

John Dory can weigh up to 12 pounds. Most is sold fresh and whole—the best way to be sure it's the real John Dory. It yields only about a third of its weight when filleted. The flesh is fine grained, flaky, moist, and very lean; the flavor is mild and sweet. Fillets are thin and can be cooked similarly to sole (page 32).

Kingklip

Sometimes called: Cusk eel, Ling

Widely distributed in southern oceans, kingklip imported from South America, New Zealand, or South Africa is now available in some U.S. markets. Though it looks a little like eel, the two are not related. Of the four species sold, golden kingklip is the most abundant and rivals the rarer red species in quality; both have whiter and more tender flesh than South African kingklip or black king-klip, the poorest in quality.

■ Size and forms. Kingklip can grow to 6 feet in length and weigh 50 pounds, but most is smaller. Almost all is sold as fresh or frozen skinless fillets.

■ Availability. Year-round.

■ Preparation. No preparation necessary.

■ Taste and texture. Kingklip has an unusual dense and chewy texture some-what like monkfish, but softer and with large, loose flakes. Very lean (under 1 percent fat), the flesh tastes quite bland, with just a hint of sweetness.

■ Cooking methods. Kingklip's lean, white flesh accepts a wide variety of added flavors.

Baking. Bake fillets in Piquant Vegetable Sauce, oven-brown, or bake with a creamy topping. (See pages 82–86.)

Barbecuing and broiling. To grill, place fillets on perforated foil and use direct heat. A baste or marinade, such as Sesame-Soy, Italian-style, or Basil-Parmesan, adds needed flavor. Broil with a crumb coating or with moist heat. (See pages 86–89.)

Frying. Pan-fry with a light or heavy crumb coating to add texture contrast. Use kingklip for Stir-fried Fish or Shell-fish with Peas, or deep-fry it. (See pages 89–92, 95.)

Poaching and steaming. Use any of the moist-heat cooking methods on pages 92–95.

■ Suggested recipes. Fish Fillets with Dill and Tangerine (page 91), Rockfish Florentine (page 96), Fish & Chard Pie (page 99), Faux Salmon Terrine (page 101), Quick Colorful Chowder (page 102), Fish Pot-au-Feu (page 103), Vera-cruz Fish Salad (page 107), Fish Fillets with Sherry-Mushroom Sauce (page 111), Orange Roughy Maître d'Hôtel (page 112).

■ Serving ideas. Sprinkle deep-fried kingklip fillets with a splash of malt vinegar to taste. Or, for a more formal dish, pour Sweet & Sour Sauce (page 115) over hot cooked fish just before serving, or top with a browned butter sauce (page 92) or one of the butters on page 125.

Lingcod

Its confusing name works against this fine-tasting, usually modestly priced Pacific Coast fish. Unrelated to cod and not ling (a common name given to a variety of different fish), lingcod is actually a greenling. It ranges from Cali-fornia to Alaska but is harvested mostly in Washington and British Columbia.

Fish caught by longline or hook and line that are individually bled, cleaned, and iced are superior to trawl-caught fish, often not handled as carefully. A limited amount of high-quality, frozen-at-sea lingcod comes from Alaska.

■ Size and forms. Lingcod grows to 50 pounds, though average is about 10 pounds. Most is sold fresh, whether whole, cleaned, and without the head; filleted, with skin off; or cut into steaks. Whole fillets usually weigh 2 pounds or more.

■ Availability. Lingcod is fished the year around, peaking from mid-April through November. It's sold primarily on the West Coast.

■ Taste and texture. The flesh is tender-firm and a little chewy, with soft, moist flakes. It often has a green or blue tint when raw but turns white when cooked. Lingcod is very lean (about 1 percent fat) and mild in flavor.

■ Preparation. If you buy a whole fish, cut it into steaks or fillet as for round fish; skin fillets, if desired. For techniques, see pages 80–81.

■ Cooking methods. Cuts of lingcod are fairly dense and take a little longer to cook than other fish of the same thickness.

Baking. Bake small fish, steaks, or fillets in Piquant Vegetable Sauce. Or stuff small fish with Almond-Rice, Spinach-Mushroom, or Toasted Bread Cube Stuffing. Oven-brown steaks or fillets, or bake them with a creamy topping. (See pages 82–86.)

Barbecuing and broiling. The smoke of the barbecue doesn't particularly enhance the flavor of this fish, but steaks and fillets do grill well; place them on perforated foil over direct heat. Try Ginger-Soy or Italian-style Marinade. Broil with moist heat or with a crumb coating. (See pages 86–89.)

Frying. Lingcod is good deep-fried; use British Beer or Lemon Batter. Pan-fry thinner cuts with a light or heavy crumb coating to add flavor and texture. (See pages 89–92.)

Poaching and steaming. Steaks and fillets can be pan-poached, poached the classic way, or steamed in foil. Steam whole fish in foil or poach the classic way. (See pages 92–95.)

■ Suggested recipes. Gravlax Plus (page 47), Fish Fillets with Dill and Tan-gerine (page 91), Rockfish Florentine (page 96), Fish & Chard Pie (page 99), Quenelles with Creamy Shallot Sauce (page 100), Seviche with Kiwi Fruit (page 100), Faux Salmon Terrine (page 101), Quick Colorful Chowder (page 102), Puget Sound Salmon Gefillte Fish Soup (page 103), Fish Pot-au-Feu (page 103), Fish Pil-Pil in Red Sauce (page 104), Veracruz Fish Salad (page 107), Seviche Salad (page 108), Fish Fillets with Sherry-Mushroom Sauce (page 111), Orange Roughy Maître d'Hôtel (page 112), Mr. Zhu's Steamed Fish (page 114).

■ Serving ideas. Poached lingcod is good hot or cold, paired with almost any sauce (pages 123–125).

This versatile fish is often used com-mercially for fish and chips. For your own version, pass malt vinegar to sprin-kle on deep-fried lingcod and french fried potatoes.

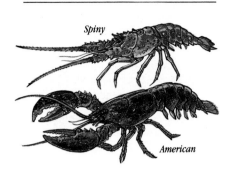

Spiny

American

Lobster

This king among crustaceans can be divided into two groups: large, clawed lobsters and spiny lobsters. Of the first group, the species eaten in the United States is the American lobster. Spiny lobster usually appears in U.S. markets as frozen lobster tails. Both are coveted for their sweet, succulent meat.

Several varieties of smaller lobsters are also available, with tail meat that can be delicious eating.

A small relative of the lobster is the freshwater crayfish (page 30).

American lobster. Often called Maine lobster, this is the species many consider "true lobster"—the large variety with meaty claws found in the Atlantic from Newfoundland to South Carolina. Most of the catch comes from Maine and Massachusetts. Lobsters are not as abundant now as in the past, but continuing efforts to regulate the industry should help keep supplies steady.

Though this lobster can weigh as much as 45 pounds, anything over 3 pounds is rare now; most are 1 to 2 pounds. The bulk of the U.S. catch is taken from July to November; Canadian imports are heaviest in spring.

Spiny lobsters. This clawless variety is also called rock lobster and, in some parts of the world, crawfish, langouste, or langosta. It's caught in warm and cold waters worldwide; the U.S. catch comes from Florida, Southern California, and Hawaii. Normally, only the frozen uncooked tails are sold in U.S. markets,

though some live and cooked fresh whole spiny lobsters can be found in California from October to March and in Florida from August to March.

Of the imported varieties, cold-water tails are generally preferred to warm-water ones, with Australian and New Zealand products consistently of highest quality.

Small lobsters. Small lobsters abound in seas worldwide; you can often find their frozen cooked tails in restaurants (retail sales are limited). Most common are *scampi* (not the garlicky shrimp dish of the same name), also known as Norway lobster or Dublin Bay prawn, and *langostino* from Chile.

The tails of both scampi and langostino are roughly the size of shrimp. Their flavor and texture are a cross between lobster and shrimp.

Slipper lobsters shipped from Thailand and Australia as frozen tails average 2 to 3 ounces and are usually less expensive than other lobster tails. Eating quality can be good.

■ Size and forms.
Most American lobster is sold live in tanks and can be found year-round; some cooked whole lobster and lobster meat, fresh or frozen, is also sold. Other lobsters are usually sold as frozen raw or cooked tails.

When selecting live lobsters, look for active ones; their tails should curl under when they're lifted. Listlessness is a sign that the lobster has been in the tank too long. If you buy cooked lobster in the shell, the tail should be pulled in tightly under the body.

Usually, a 1- to 1½-pound lobster serves one; a 1½- to 2½-pound one can be split to serve two. Figure on about ¼ pound cooked lobster meat or 6 to 8 ounces tails per serving.

■ Availability.
See individual species descriptions above.

■ Taste and texture.
All lobster meat is sweet and mild, and the flesh tender.

■ Preparation.
No preparation is required if live lobster is to be boiled. To broil, the lobster needs to be killed, split, and cleaned (not for the squeamish); or it can be boiled until almost done and then broiled until hot.

To prepare live American lobster for broiling, hold it, stomach down, on a board and kill instantly by inserting

the tip of a sharp knife between the tail section and body shell, severing the spinal cord.

For one serving, split the lobster lengthwise through the undershell and flesh; to serve two, cut through the back shell. Remove and discard the stomach sac (behind the head) and pull out the dark intestinal vein, which runs to the end of the tail. Save the lobster "tomalley" (yellow-colored liver) and roe (when present), if desired. Rinse well.

To prepare lobster tails for broiling, thaw, if frozen. With kitchen scissors, cut along the inner edges of the soft undershell of each tail. Clip off the fins. Peel back the undershell and discard. Bend the tail back, cracking some of the joints so it won't curl when cooked. If the tails are large, cut them lengthwise through the shell. Rinse.

■ Cooking methods.
For cooked dishes, it's best to start with either live lobster or raw lobster tails—cooking the meat twice tends to toughen it. To use cooked lobster meat in hot dishes, add it only during the last few minutes of cooking.

All lobster shells turn bright red when cooked, regardless of their color when raw.

Boiling. For up to 5 pounds **live lobsters** or thawed frozen raw lobster tails, pour enough **water** into a large pan to generously cover. Add 2 teaspoons **salt,** if desired, for each quart water; bring to a boil over high heat. Add lobster tails or plunge live lobsters head first into water, tucking tails under to prevent splashing. Cover pan.

When water resumes boiling, reduce heat and simmer until meat is opaque when cut. For American lobster, allow 10 to 15 minutes if small (¾ to 1¼ pounds), 15 to 20 minutes if large (1½ to 2½ pounds); for whole spiny lobster, allow 12 to 15 minutes if small (1 to 1¼ pounds), 15 to 18 minutes if large (1½ to 2 pounds). For lobster tails, allow 3 to 5 minutes for 2- to 4-ounce size, 5 to 7 minutes for 4- to 6-ounce size, 7 to 9 minutes for 6- to 8-ounce size. Simmer scampi and langostino for 1 to 1¼ minutes if frozen, ¾ to 1 minute if thawed.

To crack and eat, see the photos on the facing page.

Broiling. Prepare raw or partially cooked **whole lobster** as directed under "Preparation." Place, meat side up, on

To boil live lobster, grasp firmly behind claws and lower headfirst into boiling water. Cook as directed on facing page.

When lobster is cooked and cool enough to handle, twist off large whole claws where they join body.

Grasp lobster by body and tail and separate at joint. Twist off 8 small legs and lift off top body shell.

Scoop out lobster tomalley (yellow-colored liver) and any coral-colored roe from body cavity; if desired, mix with melted butter to make a dipping sauce for lobster meat.

To extract tail meat, slide a fork between soft underside of tail and meat, and firmly pull out meat.

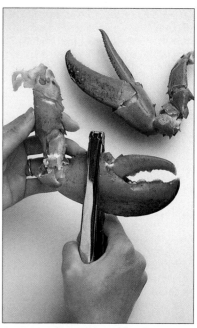

Crack open claws and legs using a heavy cracker; or strike softly with a hammer. Pluck out meat with a small fork or metal pick.

a broiler pan. Brush generously with melted **butter,** margarine, or Lemon-Butter Baste (page 87); if desired, stir any reserved **tomalley** (liver) and **roe** into butter. Broil 4 inches from heat until opaque when cut or until heated through (10 to 12 minutes for raw lobster, 4 to 5 minutes for cooked lobster).

To broil raw lobster tails, prepare as directed on page 38. Place lobster tails, shell sides up, on a broiler pan and broil 4 inches from heat for 4 minutes. Turn and brush generously with melted **butter,** margarine, or Lemon-Butter Baste (page 87); broil until meat is opaque when cut (about 5 more minutes).

■ **Suggested recipes.** Lobster Soup with Leeks (page 105).

■ **Serving ideas.** Serve warm boiled lobsters with melted butter or margarine (about ¼ cup per serving); add lemon juice to taste and, if desired, any reserved tomalley and roe. Or offer Homemade Mayonnaise or Lemon Mayonnaise (page 123).

Mix diced cooked lobster meat with Mornay Sauce (page 124) in individual ramekins; top with buttered bread crumbs and place under the broiler until sauce bubbles.

Atlantic

Mackerel

Mackerel is in the same fish family as tuna (page 74). What the two have in common are bands of oilier outer red muscle with lighter interior meat. The various mackerel species differ in the proportion of red and lighter meat.

Though mackerel is considered an oily fish, this varies with the species and season. In general, mackerel is very perishable—its quality depends on the care taken in getting it to market.

Also included here is the Pacific jack mackerel, actually in the jack family (page 35) but a lot like mackerel in size and uses.

Atlantic mackerel. Found in the North Atlantic, this mackerel (sometimes erroneously called Boston mackerel) is the most important market species. With a considerable amount of red meat (12 to 28 percent), it's also one of the more assertively flavored species. The flesh, good raw, is often used in sashimi (page 54). This fish, which weighs between 1¼ and 2½ pounds, is almost always sold whole, fresh or frozen. It's available year-round.

Spanish mackerel. One of the leanest and most mildly flavored of the mackerels, with a minimum of red meat, this fish ranges from Cape Cod to Brazil. Most of the catch in the United States is taken in the South Atlantic and Gulf of Mexico. Market size is 2 to 4 pounds. Caught primarily from December to March, these fish are sold whole, cleaned, or filleted.

King mackerel. One of the largest mackerels, king (also called kingfish or cavalla) runs from 5 to 20 pounds. It's found from North Carolina to Brazil, but most is taken off Florida. It's oilier, firmer in texture, and has more red meat and a more assertive flavor than the Spanish and cero species. Peak season is January through early March. King is usually sold as steaks but is sometimes available whole or filleted.

Cero mackerel. The cero (also called cerro or painted) looks like a small king mackerel but has less red meat and a milder flavor. Most is caught off Florida from December to March.

Pacific mackerel. Also called American, blue, or chub, Pacific mackerel has staged a remarkable comeback since the 1970s, when it practically disappeared from California waters. Now, most is taken off the Southern California coast.

Pacific mackerel grows to about 4 pounds, but most market fish weigh less than a pound. This is one of the oilier and more strongly flavored species. Fish over about 12 ounces can be filleted, but most are sold whole. Though much of the catch is canned, some fresh fish are available most of the year.

Pacific jack mackerel. This jack (also called horse mackerel) resembles the Pacific mackerel in size and shape; like the Pacific, much of the catch is canned. The two fish are often caught together,

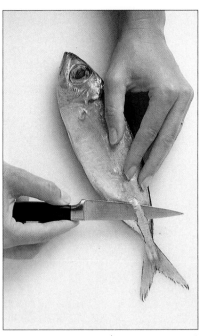

To remove surface bones from jack mackerel, insert knife point under bones at tail end. Keeping knife flat, slice under bones toward head; sever each end and remove row of bones. Repeat on other side.

and markets in the West sell them interchangeably as "mackerel." You can recognize the jack by a row of tiny, shallow surface bones along the lateral strip on each side; it's leaner and milder in flavor than Pacific mackerel.

Wahoo. The Hawaiian name of this fish, ono, means sweet and delicate, a fitting name for this choice mackerel found in tropical and subtropical seas worldwide. Wahoo has been caught in Florida waters, but most is taken in the Pacific. The light-colored flesh has a firm, flaky texture and a fairly high oil content (about 8 percent fat); it's popular for sashimi (page 54).

Whole fish average 35 pounds and are usually sold as skin-on fillets. There's also a good frozen-at-sea product. Fresh fish are available all year but are most abundant from May through July.

■ **Size and forms.** Mackerel ranges in size from less than a pound to 35 pounds or more; see individual species descriptions above.

■ **Availability.** Some mackerel is available year-round; see individual species descriptions above.

■ Taste and texture. In general, mackerels have moist, tender flesh; the exceptions are king and wahoo, which are firm and meaty. Fat content varies, as does flavor. See individual species descriptions on the facing page.

■ Preparation. To prepare whole mackerel for cooking, remove the scales and clean. Fish over 12 ounces can be filleted as for round fish. For techniques, see pages 79–81.

Before cooking jack mackerel, remove the shallow layer of surface bones, as shown on the facing page. All mackerels will taste milder if skinned and trimmed of red meat.

■ Cooking methods. Smoking (page 84) or barbecuing over a smoky fire are ideal treatments for these robustly flavored fish, but mackerel can be cooked in other ways as well.

Baking. Whole fish and thicker fillets or steaks are good baked in Piquant Vegetable Sauce. Or oven-brown fillets or steaks. (See pages 82–85.)

Barbecuing and broiling. Place steaks and fillets on perforated foil to barbecue; small whole fish can be placed directly on the grill. Use direct heat. Fillets and steaks are good broiled with dry heat or with a crumb coating. Soak in Italian-style, Ginger-Soy, or Basil-Parmesan Marinade before barbecuing or broiling with dry heat. (See pages 86–89.)

Frying. Pan-fry small whole fish, steaks, or fillets after coating with flour or a light crumb coating. (See pages 90–92.)

Poaching and steaming. Pan-poaching, classic poaching, and steaming Chinese-style are all suitable, especially for the milder flavored species. (See pages 92–95.)

■ Suggested recipes. For all species: Burmese Fish with Sweet Onions (page 96), Five-Spice Fish (page 111), Mackerel with Tart Onion Sauce (page 112), Braised Sablefish (page 112), Grilled Salmon on Wilted Chicory Salad (page 113), Trout with Leeks & Vinegar (page 114), Grilled Tuna with Teriyaki Fruit Sauce (page 117).

For king and wahoo only: Swordfish Steaks with Mushrooms (page 117), Skewered Fish, Northwest Style (page 118).

■ Serving ideas. Include morsels of mackerel steaks or fillets in boldly seasoned seafood stews. Or coat small fish or fillets with a light crumb coating (page 92), using a mixture of half flour and half quick-cooking oatmeal; pan-fry and serve with Creamy Horseradish Sauce (page 123).

Complement hot mackerel with Tomato-Caper Sauce (page 124). Aïoli (page 123) is good with either hot or cold cooked fish.

Mahi Mahi

Sometimes called: Dolphin, Dorado

Most people equate mahi mahi with Hawaii, but this fish is found in warm waters all over the world. Some is caught in Hawaii and Florida, but most mahi consumed in the United States is imported. The tuna-fishing industry is the source of most of the frozen product in markets—mahi is often caught on tuna longlines.

Properly called dolphin, this fish is not related to the mammal called dolphin. A sportfishing prize, mahi puts on a dazzling display of acrobatics when hooked. Its skin is a brilliant silver blue streaked with yellow, fading as it dies.

Quality of frozen mahi varies; the best is now frozen at sea. Check for any signs of mishandling, such as yellowing around the belly flap. Poorly handled fish can result in scombroid poisoning (page 13).

■ Size and forms. Mahi ranges in size from 10 to 40 pounds. Most of the fresh fish is sold as fillets or as loins, or sides, with the skin on; some is cut into steaks. Most frozen mahi is sold as fillets, with the skin on.

■ Availability. Mahi is available year-round, with heaviest landings in spring and summer. Demand often exceeds supply.

■ Taste and texture. The meat, tender-firm with large, moist flakes, has a sweet, mildly pronounced flavor. Trim away the darker portions of meat for a milder flavor. It's a lean fish (under 1 percent fat) with thin skin.

■ Preparation. For most cooking methods, leave the skin on—it helps keep the fish intact.

■ Cooking methods. Fresh-caught or well frozen mahi is ideal as sashimi (page 54). In cooked preparations, it's best when slightly underdone.

Baking. Bake steaks or fillets with Piquant Vegetable Sauce or a creamy topping; or oven-brown them. (See pages 82–86.)

Barbecuing and broiling. Place steaks or fillets, skin sides down, on a greased grill; use direct heat. For a large whole fillet or loin, line the skin side with foil and grill using indirect heat. Use Lemon-Butter or Sesame-Soy Baste. Broil either with a crumb coating or by the moist-heat method. (See pages 86–89.)

Frying. A light coating of flour or crumbs is optional when pan-frying. (See pages 90–92.)

Poaching and steaming. Mahi is excellent pan-poached, poached the classic way, foil-steamed, or steamed Chinese-style. (See pages 92–95.)

■ Suggested recipes. Maki Sushi (page 54), Fish Fillets with Dill and Tangerine (page 91), Burmese Fish with Sweet Onions (page 96), Seviche with Kiwi Fruit (page 100), Faux Salmon Terrine (page 101), Quick Colorful Chowder (page 102), Fish Pot-au-Feu (page 103), Fish Pil-Pil in Red Sauce (page 104), Veracruz Fish Salad (page 107), Thai Fish & Watercress Salad (page 108), Fish Fillets with Sherry-Mushroom Sauce (page 111), Grilled Tuna with Teriyaki Fruit Sauce (page 117).

■ Serving ideas. To make a quick topping for hot cooked mahi, brown sliced mushrooms in butter or margarine, pour in a little dry white wine, vermouth, or lime or lemon juice, and stir until the liquid is reduced by half. Or try a browned butter sauce (page 92) or another butter, such as Citrus Beurre Blanc, Basil Garlic Butter, or Diable Butter (page 125).

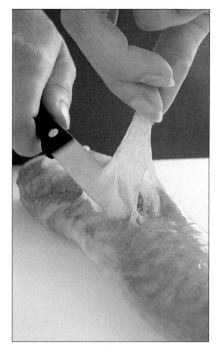

Pull off silvery membrane from monkfish fillets before cooking. Slide a knife underneath to loosen.

To prepare monkfish scaloppine-style, thinly slice fillet at a 45° angle, starting at narrow end.

Place monkfish scaloppine slices between plastic wrap and pound gently with a heavy mallet until ⅛ inch thick.

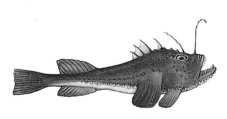

Monkfish

Sometimes called: Angler, Goosefish, Lotte (in France)

It would be hard to find an uglier, more bizarre-looking creature than monkfish. Its huge head supports an antenna it uses to entice prey into its toothy mouth. Only the tail—a thick, tapering section—is eaten; the rest is discarded at sea. In the western Atlantic, monkfish is found from Newfoundland to North Carolina. Most is taken as an incidental catch. Monkfish is a prized fish in Europe, where it's a classic ingredient of many soups and stews.

■ Size and forms. Monkfish grows to 50 pounds, but the usable tail section ranges from 2 to 10 pounds. One tail yields two tapering, boneless fillets, usually sold fresh and skinless. Some frozen fillets are also available.

■ Availability. Though available all year, monkfish is most plentiful in spring and summer.

■ Taste and texture. The firm, sweet meat is very lean, chewy, and nonflaky; it's surprisingly similar to lobster in texture and taste.

■ Preparation. Most fillets are covered with a tough membrane; pull it off before cooking, as shown above left. Because of its tapering shape, monkfish is difficult to pan-fry unless it's sliced. Cut it lengthwise, or cut crosswise into ⅜- to ¾-inch slanting slices.

To slice for monkfish scaloppine, start 3 or 4 inches from the narrow end and, using a sharp knife, cut toward that end at a 45° angle into ¼- to ⅜-inch slices (shown above center). Continue until you reach the thick end and pieces become too short for large slices. Cut the remaining chunk almost through the thickest part, open, and flatten,

butterfly-style. Place the slices between plastic wrap. Gently pound with a smooth mallet until the slices are ⅛ inch thick (shown above right).

■ Cooking methods. Especially versatile because of its unique texture, monkfish holds its shape for stir-frying or in soups, won't fall off skewers, and can even be pounded thin. It does take a little longer to cook than most other fish.

Baking. Bake whole fillets in Piquant Vegetable Sauce. Or oven-brown slices of equal thickness. (See pages 82–85.)

Barbecuing and broiling. Monkfish is easiest to grill or broil if cut into cubes for kebabs. Barbecue with direct heat; broil with dry heat. Use Italian-style or Basil-Parmesan Marinade. (See pages 86–88.)

Frying. To deep-fry, use strips, dipping them in Japanese Tempura Batter. Pan-fry equally thick slices of monkfish, using a flour coating. Cut into chunks to stir-fry. (See pages 89–92, 95.)

Poaching and steaming. Pieces of equal thickness can be pan-poached or steamed Chinese-style. A whole fillet can be poached the classic way. (See pages 92–95.)

■ **Suggested recipes.** Fish Pot-au-Feu (page 103), Fish Pil-Pil in Red Sauce (page 104), San Francisco-style Cioppino (page 105; use in place of shrimp), Thai Fish & Watercress Salad (page 108), Stir-fried Scallops & Asparagus on Cool Pasta (page 109; use in place of scallops), Monkfish Scaloppine with Shallots (page 115), Skewered Fish, Northwest Style (page 118), Seafood Brochettes with Champagne Sauce (page 119; use in place of scallops).

■ **Serving ideas.** Use monkfish in soups, stews, and casseroles. Poached, it's good served cold. Such buttery, creamy sauces as Creamy Shallot Sauce (page 100) and Béarnaise Sauce (page 124) enhance its sweet flavor. For a colorful complement to baked or pan-fried monkfish, offer ratatouille (hot or at room temperature).

Moonfish see Opah, page 45

Mullet

Many different species of mullet are found throughout the world, but only one—the striped mullet—is harvested commercially in the United States. Sometimes called black mullet or jumping mullet, it's caught in shallow bays along the Gulf of Mexico and North Carolina coasts and in Hawaii, where it's called ama'ama.

A number of fish called mullet actually aren't. One is a freshwater sucker called mullet by Canadians. Another is the kingfish, caught from Virginia to Florida and often called sea mullet or Virginia mullet. The famous red mullet of French cuisine is actually a goatfish.

Mullet is prized for its delicious roe. Most of the catch, in fact, is fished for the roe. Mullet is one of the few fish with a gizzard that can be prepared and eaten much as chicken gizzard.

■ **Size and forms.** Striped mullet usually weighs under 2 pounds. It's sold whole or cleaned; fresh fish actually keep longer if not cleaned (once cleaned, use within 2 days). Mullet is rarely filleted because the yield is low. Frozen mullet should be used within 90 days. The roe is available fresh and frozen. Mullet is sometimes available smoked.

■ **Availability.** Mullet is available year-round, but peak season is from October to December. The fish are also in the best condition then, prior to spawning. Mullet is most popular in the Southeast.

■ **Taste and texture.** The moderately firm, tender meat is light in color, with a darker streak along the midline. About 3.7 percent fat, mullet has a rich, moderately pronounced, often sweet and nutlike flavor. But mullet can also taste earthy or muddy, depending on where it was feeding.

■ **Preparation.** Mullet's coarse scales should be removed before cooking. For mildest flavor, fillet as for round fish and remove the skin and dark streak of meat. For techniques, see pages 79–81.

Whole fish can be boned and butterflied as you would trout (page 73).

■ **Cooking methods.** Mullet is at its best when smoked (page 84) or grilled over a smoky fire. Pan-fry the roe as directed for shad roe (page 60).

Baking. Bake whole fish in Piquant Vegetable Sauce or with a stuffing, such as Almond-Rice, Spinach-Mushroom, or Toasted Bread Cube Stuffing. Oven-brown fillets. (See pages 82–85.)

Barbecuing and broiling. Grill small whole fish over direct heat. Broil boned and butterflied fish using dry heat. Brush with Lemon-Butter Baste or soak in Italian-style, Ginger-Soy, or Basil-Parmesan Marinade when barbecuing or broiling. (See pages 86–88.)

Frying. Pan-fry whole fish or fillets, covering with a crumb or cornmeal coating or dusting with flour. (See pages 90–92.)

Poaching and steaming. Small whole fish can be pan-poached, poached the classic way, or foil-steamed. Fillets can be steeped or steamed Chinese-style. (See pages 92–95.)

■ **Suggested recipes.** Bourride (page 102), Mackerel with Tart Onion Sauce (page 112), Baby Salmon with Sautéed Leeks (page 113; use boned and butterflied fish), Mr. Zhu's Steamed Fish (page 114).

■ **Serving ideas.** With cornmeal-coated pan-fried mullet, offer a creamy coleslaw or tart-sweet Jicama Salad (page 111). The flavors of anise and fennel contrast nicely with this fish; use the seasoning mixture for Five-Spice Fish (page 111) as a marinade before foil-steaming or barbecuing. Or serve pan-fried mullet with butter-steamed sliced fresh fennel.

Green

Blue

Mussels

Blue mussels, the most common species in the United States, are abundant in the colder waters along the New England and Pacific Northwest coasts. These bivalve mollusks grow in large colonies on any firm surface; each is bound to its bed by a tuft of anchor threads called the byssus, or beard.

Though blue mussels are now farmed on both coasts, wild mussels from New England still account for some of the U.S. supply. As a general rule, cultivated mussels have clean, black shells; wild mussels have rougher, silver-colored shells.

Blue mussels are farmed in two different ways. Those grown on ropes or in mesh bags suspended from rafts grow fast and have a high proportion of meat to shell; but their thin shells make them more perishable than other mussels. Today, more mussels are being produced by a bottom-culture technique; though not as high in quality as rope-cultured ones, they can be harvested with dredges, and growing them is far more profitable.

Some New Zealand green (or green-lipped) mussels are also available in U.S. markets. They're larger, meatier, and have a slightly more pronounced flavor than blue mussels. The indigenous California mussel can be gathered at low tides (except in summer when quarantined), but it's not harvested commercially; only those under 3 inches are tender.

Of all shellfish, mussels are the most susceptible to pollution and paralytic shellfish poisoning (page 13). Strict monitoring is required to detect both natural and man-made pollutants. In some areas, mussels are routinely run through purification plants.

■ Size and forms.
Blue mussels in the shell average 12 per pound, green mussels 4 to 6 per pound. Most are cleaned and shipped live to markets (allow about a pound of live blue mussels per main-dish serving). Some are also sold frozen in the shell or as frozen and canned meat.

■ Availability.
Blue mussels are best and most plentiful from October to May. When spawning in late spring, they're more watery and have a short shelf life but are still edible. In some areas, they're sold all year.

■ Taste and texture.
Mussels are sweeter and more tender than clams, and richer in taste than oysters.

■ Preparation.
Inspect mussels carefully and make sure they are alive—the shells should be tightly closed or should close when lightly tapped. Clean mussels just before cooking; they don't live long afterwards. To clean, pull off the beard with a quick tug (shown above right), scrub with a stiff brush if needed, and rinse well.

To remove the meat, either steam them (see at right) or pry the shells open as directed for clams (page 23).

■ Cooking methods.
Mussels are usually steamed in water or a flavorful liquid and then served on the half shell

Pull beard off mussel with a firm tug. Live mussels have tightly closed shells; beard anchors mollusk to bed.

or in a bowl with the cooking liquid; or use the meat in other preparations. The meat can also be fried.

Frying. Remove the meat from the shells (see "Preparation," at left); pat dry. For 1 to 1½ cups **shucked mussels,** place a 10- to 12-inch frying pan over medium-high heat until a drop of water sizzles and dances in pan. Add 1 tablespoon **butter** or margarine, tipping pan to coat bottom. Add mussels and ¼ teaspoon **dry thyme leaves.** Cook until lightly browned on both sides (2 to 3 minutes). Makes 2 to 4 servings.

Steaming. For up to 5 pounds **mussels,** pour **water** to a depth of ¼ inch into a 5- to 7-quart pan. Add mussels, cover, and bring to a boil over high heat; reduce heat to low and boil until shells open (about 5 minutes); discard any that don't open.

For mussels in wine broth, use 1¼ cups **dry white wine** (or 1 cup water and ¼ cup lemon juice) instead of water; add 6 **green onions** (including some tops), chopped, and ¼ teaspoon **dry thyme leaves.** Steam as directed above; transfer to serving bowls. Boil liquid until reduced to 1½ cups.

Blend 6 tablespoons **butter** or margarine, at room temperature, with 1½ teaspoons **cornstarch;** add to liquid and cook, stirring, until it boils and thickens slightly. Pour over mussels.

■ Suggested recipes.
Garlic Mussels on the Half Shell (page 101), Thai Seafood Firepot (page 105; use in place of clams), Mussel & Potato Salad (page 109), Smoked Mussels with Lemon-Garlic Mayonnaise (page 116), Sesame-Ginger Steamed Mussels (page 119), Seafood Linguine (page 119).

■ Serving ideas.
After steaming mussels, discard the top shells and serve the mussels warm in the bottom shells to dip in melted butter or in Warm Garlic Butter (page 125). Offer lemon wedges to squeeze over.

Combine cold steamed mussels, removed from the shell, with chopped tomato and Basil Vinaigrette Dressing (page 109) and serve over cold cooked green beans or crisp leaves of assorted baby lettuces for a dramatic first-course salad. For a satisfying pasta, heat steamed mussels in Tomato-Caper Sauce (page 124) and spoon over steaming hot linguine or green fettuccine.

Ocean Perch see *Rockfish, page 51*

Ocean Pout

An odd-looking long and narrow fish without a tail, ocean pout is an Atlantic member of the eelpout family. Largely ignored until recently, ocean pout is now being harvested along the New England coast. Its flesh is unusually dense and needs to be pounded or tenderized before cooking.

■ Size and forms.
Ocean pout ranges in size from 1½ to 5 pounds. It's sold as long, thin skinless fillets.

■ Availability.
This fish is sold fresh, mainly in New England, from December to May. Frozen ocean pout is also available.

■ Taste and texture.
The dense, chewy white flesh is very mild and sweet tasting—and almost free of bones.

Preparation. Cut fillets into serving-size pieces. To tenderize, use a meat tenderizer to pound each piece gently and evenly. (Or use a sharp knife to score pieces from one end to the other at about ½-inch intervals; then turn and repeat at a different angle.)

Cooking methods. Because of its unusually chewy texture, ocean pout is especially good in soups and chowders and for stir-frying. When tenderized and pan-fried, it's a little like veal or chicken scaloppine.

Baking. Bake tenderized fillets in Piquant Vegetable Sauce or oven-brown them. (See pages 82–85.)

Frying. For deep-frying, cut tenderized fillets into 3- by 5-inch pieces; coat and deep-fry as for squid. To pan-fry, coat tenderized fillets with a flour or crumb coating or with Golden Egg Wash. To stir-fry, cut tenderized fillets into 1-inch strips. (See pages 89–92, 95.)

Poaching and steaming. Pan-poach tenderized fillets. (See pages 92–93.)

Suggested recipes. Quick Colorful Chowder (page 102), Fish Pot-au-Feu (page 103), Fish Pil-Pil in Red Sauce (page 104), Veracruz Fish Salad (page 107), Thai Fish & Watercress Salad (page 108), Scaloppine with Monkfish Shallots (page 115).

Serving ideas. Ocean pout's mild flavor calls for buttery or creamy sauces. Try Browned Butter (page 92), Home-made Mayonnaise or any of its variations (page 123), Aïoli (page 123), or Basil Garlic Butter (page 125).

Octopus

Octopus, a shy member of the mollusk family, is considered a delicacy in many countries. More than 140 species of this shell-less shellfish inhabit tropical and temperate waters worldwide. All octopus available on the market can be handled in the same way.

Size and forms. Though different species vary tremendously in size, most market octopus weigh between 1 and 5 pounds. The larger specimens command a higher price.

Octopus is usually sold frozen whole (cleaned and debeaked), but it's sometimes available fresh. Octopus legs, sold separately, can be found in limited quantity. Buy octopus that is free of off-odors; it's hard to judge freshness any other way. Canned and smoked octopus are sold in some specialty food shops.

Availability. Octopus is plentiful year-round; look for it in large fish markets or in Italian or Oriental markets.

Taste and texture. Because octopus feeds on shellfish exclusively, the white flesh is mild and sweet. The texture is firm, however, and requires a fairly long cooking time to ensure tenderness.

Preparation. It's best to use rubber gloves when handling octopus, as it could cause a temporary skin rash. If frozen, thaw octopus completely in the refrigerator.

If the octopus hasn't been cleaned, cut open the head cavity with a sharp knife and discard the interior. Cut away and discard the tough beak (near where the tentacles attach). Separate the tentacles from the head.

Octopus needs to be precooked before it can be used in most preparations. To precook, drop the cleaned head and tentacles into a pan of boiling salted water; simmer gently until the skin can be peeled off (30 to 60 minutes). Remove from heat and let stand in cooking water until cool enough to handle. Remove the skin, if desired.

Cooking methods. Use precooked octopus (see above) for the following cooking methods.

Baking. Oven-brown, using 3- to 4-inch lengths of precooked octopus. (See page 85.)

Broiling. Broil with a crumb coating as for fish or oysters, using 3- to 4-inch lengths of precooked octopus. (See page 89.)

Frying. For up to 2 pounds **octopus**, beat 2 **eggs** with 2 tablespoons **milk** in a shallow bowl; have ready 1 cup **fine dry bread crumbs** or cracker crumbs. Dip pieces of precooked octopus (3- or 4-inch lengths) in egg mixture. Drain briefly; then dredge in crumbs to coat. Place on a wire rack and refrigerate for about 20 minutes.

In a deep pan, pour **salad oil** to a depth of 1½ inches and heat to 375°F on a deep-frying thermometer. Cook octopus, a few pieces at a time, until golden brown. Drain on paper towels.

Suggested recipes. Use precooked octopus in place of cooked squid in Mexican-style Squid Salad (page 110).

Serving ideas. Dress cooked octopus with a vinaigrette sauce or bottled Italian dressing and refrigerate for 3 to 4 hours. Serve as an appetizer or add to salads. Accompany pan-fried or broiled octopus with Tomato-Caper Sauce (page 124).

Opab

Sometimes called: Moonfish

The exotic opah was a curiosity, rarely eaten until recently. Large (30 to 140 pounds) and colorful, it resembles a garbage can lid in size and shape; it has no near relatives. Like swordfish and tuna, opah is a worldwide wanderer found in both tropical and temperate waters. Though it ventures as far north as Alaska, most opah is taken in Southern California waters as an incidental catch. Some is also caught in Hawaii.

■ Size and forms. Average size is 80 pounds. Almost all opah is sold fresh as thick fillets.

■ Availability. In California, most is taken from May to November, coinciding with swordfish season. In Hawaii, it's caught year-round, though winter is peak season. Opah is never plentiful.

■ Taste and texture. Opah's firm, coarse meat is oilier than that of most fish. It has four types of flesh, each a different color—amber red behind the head and along the backbone, pale pink and slightly stringy toward the belly, red in the cheeks, and bright ruby red inside the breastplate. The chunk of meat inside the breastplate cooks up brown and tastes something like beef; the other areas all cook up white.

Opah is rich tasting, sweet, and mild to moderately pronounced in flavor. Some compare it to chicken.

■ Preparation. Opah has thick, heavy scales and a fatty layer of meat under the skin. If you buy skin-on fillets, remove the scales (page 79) before cooking. Or cut away the skin and fatty layer before or after cooking.

■ Cooking methods. Smoking (page 84), barbecuing, and broiling are the best ways to cook opah, but you can also pan-fry, poach, or bake it. It's also suitable for sashimi.

Baking. Bake fillets in Piquant Vegetable Sauce or oven-brown them. (See pages 82–85.)

Barbecuing and broiling. Place skin-on fillets on a greased grill over direct heat or use the skinned meat for kebabs. Broil using dry heat. Brush with Lemon-Butter or Sesame-Soy Baste or soak in one of the suggested marinades before grilling or broiling. (See pages 86–89.)

Frying. Coat skinless fillets with a crumb coating before pan-frying. (See pages 90–92.)

Poaching and steaming. Pan-poach skinless fillets or steam them Chinese-style. (See pages 92–95.)

■ Suggested recipes. Fish Pot-au-Feu (page 103), Five-Spice Fish (page 111), Mackerel with Tart Onion Sauce (page 112), Braised Sablefish (page 112), Grilled Tuna with Teriyaki Fruit Sauce (page 117), Swordfish Steaks with Mushrooms (page 117), Skewered Fish, Northwest Style (page 118).

■ Serving ideas. Serve hot-cooked opah with Tomato-Caper Sauce (page 124) or Hot Ginger Sauce (page 94).

Orange Roughy

This popular fish wasn't even discovered until 1975, when a research vessel exploring deep-water plateaus off New Zealand brought up a netful. Orange roughy is now a well-established catch, though a rather unusual one. Large factory boats haul in the fish from depths of more than 2,000 feet, well offshore. The freezer-equipped boats stay at sea for up to 2 months.

As the fish are caught, they're headed, cleaned, and frozen in blocks. On shore in New Zealand, they're then thawed to the point when they can be filleted and skinned. Most orange roughy is refrozen but some is air-freighted directly to U.S. markets, where it's sold as "fresh." This fish stands up to handling remarkably well; even after being frozen twice, it tastes good. The least expensive and best way to buy it is frozen unthawed.

■ Size and forms. Orange roughy averages 3 pounds, yielding 2 fillets weighing 4 to 10 ounces each, sold skinless and boneless.

■ Availability. Year-round.

■ Taste and texture. The pearly white flesh, with moist flakes and tender-firm texture, has a mild, sweet, crablike flavor much like petrale sole. Though it's

about 8 percent fat, it has a unique type of fat that doesn't taste oily.

■ Preparation. No preparation necessary.

■ Cooking methods. This very versatile fish is delicious cooked by almost any method, and you can often use the individually frozen fillets without defrosting them first.

Baking. Bake in Piquant Vegetable Sauce or oven-brown. (See pages 82–85.)

Barbecuing and broiling. Place fillets directly on a greased grill over direct heat. To broil, use dry heat. When grilling or broiling, use any of the suggested bastes or marinades. Or broil with a crumb coating. (See pages 86–89.)

Frying. To deep-fry, use Japanese Tempura or Lemon Batter. Pan-fry, using a flour or light crumb coating, or dip in Golden Egg Wash. (See pages 89–92.)

Poaching and steaming. Choose any poaching or steaming method. (See pages 92–95.)

■ Suggested recipes. Fish Fillets with Dill and Tangerine (page 91), Rockfish Florentine (page 96), Seviche with Kiwi Fruit (page 100), Quick Colorful Chowder (page 102), Fish Pot-au-Feu (page 103), Veracruz Fish Salad (page 107), Five-Spice Fish (page 111), Orange Roughy Maître d'Hôtel (page 112), Baked Fish & Ratatouille (page 112).

■ Serving ideas. Orange roughy holds its shape well enough to use in soups, stews, and casseroles. Cold poached orange roughy is good in salads; dress it with Dijon Vinaigrette Dressing (page 124). Or offer Radish Tartar Sauce (page 123) with cold fish. Serve pan-fried or hot poached orange roughy with Browned Butter (page 92) or Citrus Beurre Blanc (page 125).

Gravlax: More Than Just Salmon

The Swedes have special ways with salmon. One favorite is gravlax, salmon cured with salt, sugar, and dill. The process draws moisture out of the fish, firms its texture, and introduces pleasing flavor changes.

This classic Swedish process also produces excellent results with other kinds of fish, such as lingcod, halibut, tuna, and trout. These may be more economical than salmon.

It takes about 24 hours in the refrigerator to produce this cured fish. Once cured, gravlax keeps for several days, ready to serve as an elegant appetizer or first course. Or, for a main dish, offer as open-faced sandwiches with potato salad or scrambled eggs.

Because the fish is not cooked, it should be frozen (either commercially or in a home freezer below 0°F for at least 3 days) before you prepare the gravlax. This ensures that the fish is free of parasites.

Rub fish with oil. Mix sugar, salt, and pepper. Lightly rub mixture all over fish. Lay fish, skin side down, in a glass baking dish that fish almost fills. Pat remaining mixture on fish; spoon cognac over.

Place onion and 1 to 2 cups of the dill on fish. Cover dish tightly with plastic wrap. Refrigerate for 12 hours, basting 3 or 4 times with accumulated juices. Turn fish over, placing dill and onions underneath. Cover and refrigerate for 12 more hours, basting 3 or 4 times with juices.

Meanwhile, prepare Mustard Sauce.

After 24 hours, fish is ready to serve. If made ahead, leave fish in brine for 24 more hours. To keep for 2 more days, remove from brine, pat dry, enclose in a plastic bag, and refrigerate.

To serve whole, place fish, skin side down, on a serving board; discard dill and onion. Garnish with remaining fresh dill. With a sharp knife, cut fish into paper-thin slanting slices. Offer with lemon wedges, sour cream, and sauce.

To make open-faced sandwiches, spread bread with sour cream and Mustard Sauce and top with fish; eat with a knife and fork. Makes 10 to 12 first-course servings.

Mustard Sauce. Combine ⅔ cup **Dijon mustard,** ½ cup **salad oil,** 1½ tablespoons **white wine vinegar,** and 1 tablespoon **sugar.** Mix until smooth. Just before using, stir in ¼ cup chopped **fresh dill;** season to taste with **pepper.** Makes about 1¼ cups.

Gravlax Plus

- 1 **boned frozen salmon, lingcod, or Pacific (northern) halibut fillet (about 2 lbs.), thawed; 2 pounds skinned frozen tuna loin (1 to 1½ inches thick), thawed; or 2 pounds boned, unskinned frozen trout fillets, thawed**
- ¼ **cup salad oil**
- ⅓ **cup *each* sugar and salt**
- 1½ **tablespoons whole white pepper, coarsely crushed**
- ¼ **cup cognac (optional)**
- 1 **small red onion, thinly sliced**
- 2 **to 3 cups lightly packed fresh dill sprigs**
  Mustard Sauce (recipe follows)
  Lemon wedges and sour cream
  Crisp flat bread or dense pumpernickel bread

Cut Swedish gravlax—salmon cured with salt, sugar, and dill—into paper-thin slices for an elegant appetizer. Accompany with lemon, sour cream, and a tart-sweet sauce.

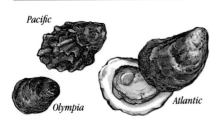

Pacific

Olympia

Atlantic

Oysters

Though oysters are called by many different names and may look and taste different, only two main types—Atlantic and Pacific—are harvested on a large scale in the United States. The other names—Blue Point, Chincoteague, Malpeque, and Apalachicola, for example—simply refer to where they're grown. The various marine plants they feed on account for differences in flavor and appearance.

Atlantic oysters. The traditional half-shell oyster, the Atlantic (also called Eastern or American) was once abundant from the Gulf of St. Lawrence to Mexico. But due to pollution and loss of habitat, the supply has diminished. Commercial oystering—primarily a wild harvest—is now centered on the Atlantic coasts of Nova Scotia, Maryland, Virginia, and on the Gulf coasts of Florida and Louisiana.

This species is smaller and milder in flavor than the Pacific; most develop naturally as single oysters. Though somewhat softer and poorer in quality during the summer, they're harvested all year and shipped live all over the United States.

Pacific oysters. This species, found from Northern California to British Columbia, was planted from Japanese seed in the early 1920s.

In the United States, most Pacific oysters are raised in the Pacific Northwest in cultivated beds. They develop heavy protective shells and often grow attached to each other in clumps. Most are sold shucked; since they're shucked by hand, smaller ones are more expensive.

There's a growing trend to raise more single (unattached) Pacific oysters to sell live in the shell. Usually grown continuously immersed in water or exposed only occasionally, these oysters grow faster, have thinner shells, and produce more meat in proportion to shell. Harvested small, they're tender and succulent eaten raw or cooked. You may find these oysters sold as Wescott Bays, Shoalwaters, Quilcenes, and Willapa Bays, for example.

Normally, Pacific oysters aren't harvested during the summer spawning season, when they become watery and soft, but that may be changing with the recent introduction of genetically engineered oysters. Called triploid, these don't spawn and can be harvested all year.

Kumamoto, a fairly new variety of Pacific oyster, is increasing in production. Relatively small in size, with a deep shell, it's ideal for the half-shell trade.

Other oysters. Olympia, the West Coast's native oyster, once grew from Los Angeles to Alaska. It was farmed in Puget Sound until the 1930s, when pollution and overharvesting almost destroyed the species. Now the tiny oyster is being cultivated again in Puget Sound, but it's still rare and expensive. Olympias have a distinctive, slightly metallic taste.

A few *European flat oysters,* often incorrectly called Belons after a region in France where they're grown, are farmed on both U.S. coasts. A little smaller than Atlantic or Pacific oysters, they're used almost entirely for the half-shell market.

■ **Size and forms.** Oysters are sold either as shucked meat in various sizes (indicating the number per gallon) or live in the shell, usually by count. Atlantic and Pacific oysters are also available frozen as meat or raw on the half shell (properly handled, frozen oysters are a good product, hard to distinguish from fresh). Thawed oysters should be used the same day and not refrozen.

Allow 6 to 9 small to medium-size oysters per serving.

■ **Availability.** Though available year-round, oysters are at their best in late fall and winter. During the summer, markets often carry imported Pacific oysters, primarily from New Zealand, and Atlantic oysters from the cold waters of eastern Canada.

■ **Taste and texture.** Depending on the season and where they're grown, these tender mollusks vary in flavor and firmness from bland and tender to salty and firm.

To shuck, firmly hold oyster, cup side down, in a towel and work tip of an oyster knife between shells near hinge; twist to sever.

After severing top muscle, run knife under oyster to loosen from bottom shell, working over a bowl to catch juices.

■ Preparation. Live oysters need to be cleaned shortly before shucking (opening). To clean, scrub with a stiff brush under cold running water; rinse.

To shuck a live oysters safely, you'll need an oyster knife (available in cookware stores); never use a sharp knife. Using several layers of towel or a heavy glove to protect your hand, hold the oyster firmly, cup side down (to retain the flavorful juices). Slide the tip of the oyster knife between the shells near the hinge (look for a small crevice), twisting and pushing the knife firmly into the opening to sever the hinge (shown on facing page).

Then slide the knife in along the top shell and sever the adductor muscle (about two-thirds of the way from the hinge). Remove the top shell; sliding the knife under the meat, cut the muscle away from the bottom shell. Remove any shell particles and serve from the bottom shell within 5 or 10 minutes.

■ Cooking methods. The simplest way to open live oysters is to steam or barbecue them until the shells open. When cooking oysters, remember that they cook very quickly and become tough if overcooked.

Barbecuing and broiling. To barbecue live oysters, follow the directions for barbecuing oysters over direct heat. Use a crumb coating when broiling shucked oysters. (See pages 86–89.)

Frying. Drain 1 jar (8 to 10 oz.) **shucked oysters;** pat dry. Heat a 10- to 12-inch frying pan over medium-high heat until a drop of water sizzles and dances in pan. Add 1 tablespoon **butter** or margarine and tilt pan to coat bottom. Add oysters and sprinkle with ⅛ teaspoon **dry thyme leaves.** Cook, turning once, until lightly browned on both sides (2 to 3 minutes total). Makes 2 servings.

Steaming. For up to 3 dozen small to medium-size **live oysters,** pour **water** or beer to a depth of ¼ inch into a 5- to 7-quart pan. If desired, add 1 clove **garlic,** crushed, and 1 **bay leaf.** Add oysters, cup sides down, cover, and boil over medium-high heat until shells open (8 to 20 minutes); remove oysters as shells open enough to insert knife inside. Serve as soon as cool enough to handle.

■ Suggested recipes. French Oyster Soup (page 106), Smoked Mussels with Lemon-Garlic Mayonnaise (page 116; use smoked oysters), Hangtown Fry (page 122), Garlic Oyster Sandwiches (page 122).

■ Serving ideas. Serve raw oysters on the half shell with lemon wedges, freshly ground black pepper, or liquid hot pepper seasoning. Barbecued oysters are good with lemon wedges and Warm Garlic Butter (page 125).

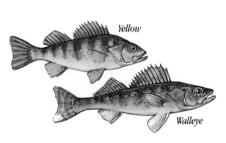

Yellow

Walleye

Perch

True perch are freshwater fish. Two species—the walleye and the yellow perch—are important market fish in the United States, especially in the Great Lakes region. They are among the best tasting of all freshwater fish.

Walleye, also called walleye pike, yellow pike, or pike-perch, is the largest member of the perch family; it's not related to pike, despite its common names. The smaller, slow-growing *yellow perch* is widely distributed in the eastern half of the northern United States and Canada.

A number of unrelated freshwater and saltwater fish are commonly called perch, but most are actually something else. The so-called white perch is a small bass (page 16). Both the Atlantic and Pacific ocean perches are rockfish (page 51). The various surfperch and seaperch on the Pacific coast belong to the surfperch family; few are sold commercially.

■ Size and forms. Walleye grows to 20 pounds or more, but 2 to 3 pounds is the most common market size. It's sold whole, cleaned, and as skin-on fillets weighing 6 to 10 ounces each.

Yellow perch normally does not exceed 1 pound; most is between ¼ and ¾ pound. Typically, the fish is boned through the belly cavity to make a 2- to 3-ounce butterflied skin-on fillet.

■ Availability. Heaviest landings of walleye are in spring and fall, but frozen fillets are available all year. Peak season for yellow perch is April through November; frozen fish are available year-round, mostly in the Great Lakes area.

■ Taste and texture. Both perch species have lean, tender-firm, flaky white flesh. The flavor of walleye is very mild; yellow perch is delicate and sweet tasting.

■ Preparation. If you buy a whole walleye, it may need to be scaled. Fillet as for round fish; walleye is relatively easy to fillet, and the fillets are almost boneless. For techniques, see pages 79–80.

The thin, tender skin of both walleye and yellow perch is usually eaten with the fish.

■ Cooking methods. Walleye is a very versatile fish that's good cooked by almost any method except barbecuing. Small yellow perch are usually pan-fried.

Baking. Walleye fillets and whole fish can be baked in Piquant Vegetable Sauce. You can also bake whole walleye with a stuffing; bake fillets with a creamy topping. Oven-brown fillets of walleye or whole yellow perch. (See pages 82–86.)

Broiling. Fillets can be broiled with moist heat or with a crumb coating. (See pages 88–89.)

Frying. Deep-fry fillets, using any of the suggested batters. Pan-fry fillets, using flour or a crumb coating. (See pages 89–92.)

Poaching and steaming. Fillets and small fish can be pan-poached, steeped, or steamed Chinese-style. Whole walleye can be poached the classic way or foil-steamed. (See pages 92–95.)

■ **Suggested recipes.** Fish Fillets with Dill and Tangerine (page 91), Rockfish Florentine (page 96), Quenelles with Creamy Shallot Sauce (page 100), Faux Salmon Terrine (page 101), Bourride (page 102), Quick Colorful Chowder (page 102), Puget Sound Salmon Gefillte Fish Soup (page 103), Fish Pot-au-Feu (page 103), Fish Pil-Pil in Red Sauce (page 104), Veracruz Fish Salad (page 107), Fish Fillets with Sherry-Mushroom Sauce (page 111), Orange Roughy Maître d'Hôtel (page 112), Baked Fish & Ratatouille (page 112), Mr. Zhu's Steamed Fish (page 114).

For small whole yellow perch: Steamed Trout with Lettuce & Peas (page 96), Baby Salmon with Sautéed Leeks (page 113), Trout with Leeks & Vinegar (page 114).

■ **Serving ideas.** When broiling perch fillets, reserve some of the crumb coating and sprinkle it over cut surfaces of tomato halves; dot with butter and then broil until lightly browned. Offer with fish. Or drizzle pan-fried perch fillets with a browned butter (page 92) or Garlic-Lemon Butter (page 125).

Pike

Sometimes called: Pickerel

Only one species of the pike family— the northern pike—is important as a market fish in the United States. Its larger, look-alike relative, the muskellunge, is a popular game fish. The fish called walleye pike or yellow pike is actually a perch (page 49).

Also called common pike or pickerel, northern pike is a fast-growing fish with a very long body and a large mouth

shaped like a duck's bill. It's common in the Great Lakes and other large lakes in the northern United States and Canada.

■ **Size and forms.** Market size is usually between 2 and 10 pounds, though pike grows much larger; those under 6 pounds are the most tender. Pike is sold whole, cleaned, or as fillets, both fresh and frozen.

■ **Availability.** Most of the commercial supply is imported from Canada and is available year-round in major cities.

■ **Taste and texture.** The very lean, flaky meat tends to break up easily; it's often used in quenelles, mousses, and stuffings. Pike's mild flavor varies somewhat, depending on the quality of the water where the fish is caught and its diet.

■ **Preparation.** Pike's complicated bone structure makes it difficult to fillet, and the dense slime on its body makes it difficult to scale the usual way. But a quick bath in scalding water coagulates the slime and loosens the scales. Simply place the fish in a bucket and pour boiling water over both sides; then scale.

Because of pike's long shape, you'll probably need to remove the head and tail to fit a whole fish inside your pan or oven. Or you can bake just a center section. Larger fish can be cut into steaks.

For techniques, see pages 79–80.

■ **Cooking methods.** Be careful not to overcook pike; its lean meat easily becomes dry. This fish can also be smoked (page 84).

Baking. Bake whole fish, whole sections, steaks, or fillets in Piquant Vegetable Sauce. Bake whole fish or sections with a stuffing. Oven-brown fillets or steaks or bake them with a creamy topping. (See pages 82–86.)

Barbecuing and broiling. Place fillets or steaks on perforated foil to barbecue and use direct heat. Barbecue whole fish or sections using indirect heat. Choose any of the suggested bastes or marinades. Broil fillets or steaks with moist heat or with a crumb coating. (See pages 86–89.)

Frying. To deep-fry fillets, use British Beer or Lemon Batter. Fillets and steaks are good pan-fried with a crumb or cornmeal coating. (See pages 89–92.)

Poaching and steaming. Fillets or steaks can be pan-poached, steeped, or steamed Chinese-style. Whole fish or sections can be poached the classic way or foil-steamed. (See pages 92–95.)

■ **Suggested recipes.** Fish Fillets with Dill and Tangerine (page 91), Rockfish Florentine (page 96), Fish & Chard Pie (page 99), Quenelles with Creamy Shallot Sauce (page 100), Faux Salmon Terrine (page 101), Bourride (page 102), Quick Colorful Chowder (page 102), Puget Sound Salmon Gefillte Fish Soup (page 103), Fish Pot-au-Feu (page 103), Fish Pil-Pil in Red Sauce (page 104), Veracruz Fish Salad (page 107), Fish Fillets with Sherry-Mushroom Sauce (page 111), Orange Roughy Maître d'Hôtel (page 112), Baked Fish & Ratatouille (page 112), Mr. Zhu's Steamed Fish (page 114).

■ **Serving ideas.** A classic in Sweden is poached pike, served with melted butter and horseradish and accompanied by boiled potatoes and chopped hard-cooked eggs. You could also offer hot cooked pike with a browned butter sauce (page 92) or with Basil Garlic or Diable Butter (page 125). Pike is good cold with Homemade Mayonnaise or any of its variations (page 123).

Plaice *see Flounder/Sole, page 32*

Pollock *see Cod, page 26*

Pompano

This aristocrat of fish, one of an extensive family that includes all the jacks, is both scarce and expensive. Some of its near relatives are commonly sold as pompano, but there is only one real pompano—the Florida pompano. This fish ranges from Massachusetts to Brazil, but most is caught and consumed in Florida.

Of the pompano pretenders, the paloma most closely resembles pompano in size, shape, and edibility; it's found from Peru to California, where only a few are caught and sold.

Permits are much larger fish than pompano, but small permits closely resemble pompano. The palometa and gafftopsail pompano are more strikingly colorful than the rather plain true pompano, but neither these fish nor the permits compare in eating quality.

For California pompano, see Butterfish (page 20).

■ **Size and forms.** True pompano averages 2 pounds and is sold whole fresh, occasionally whole frozen. If you find fillets, they aren't from real pompano. Imported pompano, often unidentified, is available both fresh and frozen. Pompano freezes well.

■ **Availability.** Pompano is taken year-round in Florida, with peaks in late fall and spring.

■ **Taste and texture.** Pompano's light-colored meat is tender-firm and moist; it's about 9.5 percent fat. The flavor is sweet, mild, rich, and distinctive.

■ **Preparation.** Whole fish may need cleaning, but they don't require scaling. Fillet as for round fish. For techniques, see page 80.

■ **Cooking methods.** The simplest preparations are best—you won't want to overpower pompano's flavor. Baking the fillets in parchment—called *en papillote*—is the classic presentation (page 91). Barbecuing and broiling are also favorite ways to cook pompano.

Baking. Bake whole fish with a stuffing, such as Almond-Rice or Toasted Bread Cube; oven-brown fillets. (See pages 83–86.)

Barbecuing and broiling. Barbecue fillets and whole fish over direct heat, using a well-greased hinged wire broiler or placing fish on perforated foil. Broil fillets by the dry-heat method. For barbecuing or broiling, use Lemon-Butter Baste. You can also broil fillets with a crumb coating. (See pages 86–89.)

Frying. Pan-fry fillets, using flour or a light crumb coating. (See pages 90–92.)

Poaching and steaming. Fillets can be pan-poached or steeped. Poach whole fish the classic way or foil-steam. (See pages 92–94.)

■ **Suggested recipes.** Fish Fillets with Dill and Tangerine (page 91), Salmon Salad with Tarragon Vinaigrette (page 107), Five-Spice Fish (page 111), Orange Roughy Maître d'Hôtel (page 112), Baked Fish & Ratatouille (page 112), Grilled Salmon on Wilted Chicory Salad (page 113), Mr. Zhu's Steamed Fish (page 114).

■ **Serving ideas.** Choose subtle sauces such as Browned Butter (page 92), Watercress Cream (page 94), or Mousseline Sauce (page 124) to enhance this distinctively flavored fish. You can dress up flour-dusted pan-fried pompano fillets with a simple sauce made by warming small cooked shrimp in melted butter with a little lemon juice and chopped parsley.

Porgy see Sea Bream, page 58

Rainbow Runner see Jack, page 35

Redfish see Drum, page 31; Rockfish, below

Red Snapper see Snapper, page 65

Canary rockfish

Rockfish

Sold often by other names, members of the rockfish family are a major source of moderately priced fish in the United States. More than 50 different species are found along the West Coast and one, the Atlantic ocean perch, on the East Coast.

Slow growing and easily caught with nets, the overfished rockfish takes a long time to replenish itself. Total catches are not as large as in earlier years, though for the most part, they're now regulated to sustain the population at the present level.

Atlantic ocean perch, also called redfish in New England, is found in cold, deep waters on both sides of the North Atlantic; most of the U.S. supply now comes from Iceland and Canada. This fish has bright red skin; both fresh and frozen fish are always sold as skin-on fillets. Atlantic ocean perch is a different "redfish" from the fish popularized by Cajun cooking (see Drum, page 31).

About eight species make up the bulk of the commercial catch of Pacific rockfish, often misnamed Pacific red snapper, rock cod, or a variety of local names. One rockfish with bright red skin is sold as *Pacific ocean perch;* the skin-on fillets are indistinguishable from those of Atlantic ocean perch. Both freeze well and often are sold that way.

Other important species are the *widow* (or brown), *canary, chilipepper, China, vermilion, yelloweye, quillback,* and *bocaccio rockfish;* any of these may be sold in California as Pacific red snapper or Pacific snapper, though they're entirely different from true red snapper (page 65). Those with red skin may be sold with skin on, but much of the "Pacific red snapper" landed off the Pacific Coast is brown-skinned widow rockfish, sold as skinless fillets.

One fine-tasting but very ugly small rockfish is the *scorpionfish,* or sculpin, caught and sold in Southern California. Its spines are very poisonous, but markets normally trim them off; if not, handle these fish carefully and cut off the spines with heavy scissors.

Quality of rockfish depends more on handling than color of skin. Though most rockfish is still caught with nets by trawlers, a growing fleet of boats on the West Coast is fishing rockfish with hook and line. Many of these top-quality fresh fish are sold whole; expect to pay higher prices for them. Some good frozen-at-sea headed and gutted rockfish from Alaska is also available, but most species of rockfish do not freeze well.

■ **Size and forms.** Though the largest species can reach 20 pounds, whole market rockfish ranges from 2 to 5 pounds. Most is sold as fresh or frozen fillets. Each fish makes 2 thick fillets.

■ **Availability.** Year-round.

■ **Taste and texture.** The flaky, tender-firm flesh is moist and lean (about 1.5 percent fat). The flavor is mild and slightly sweet.

The best rockfish—caught by hook and line and properly bled—has flesh that is clear and free of pink color; it cooks up pure white. Trawl-caught fish often have rose or pink flesh due to bruises.

(Continued on next page)

Rockfish (cont'd)

■ **Preparation.** Whole fish may need to be scaled and cleaned. Fillet as for round fish; because rockfish has a large head, the yield of filleted meat is fairly low (about 30 percent by weight). For techniques, see pages 79–80.

■ **Cooking methods.** Rockfish adapts well to most cooking methods. Its mild flavor is not particularly enhanced by barbecuing or smoking.

Baking. Bake whole fish or fillets in Piquant Vegetable Sauce or bake whole fish with a stuffing. Fillets can be oven-browned or baked with a creamy topping. (See pages 82–86.)

Barbecuing and broiling. Barbecue whole fish by the indirect method, using any of the suggested bastes or marinades. Broil fillets with moist heat or with a crumb coating. (See pages 86–89.)

Frying. Remove the skin from skin-on fillets (page 81). Deep-fry with British Beer or Lemon Batter. Pan-fry with flour or a crumb coating or with Golden Egg Wash. (See pages 89–92.)

Poaching and steaming. Fillets (skinned or skin-on) can be pan-poached, steeped, or steamed Chinese-style. Whole fish are good poached the classic way or foil-steamed. (See pages 92–95.)

■ **Suggested recipes.** Fish Fillets with Dill and Tangerine (page 91), Rockfish Florentine (page 96), Fish & Chard Pie (page 99), Quenelles with Creamy Shallot Sauce (page 100), Faux Salmon Terrine (page 101), Bourride (page 102), Quick Colorful Chowder (page 102), Puget Sound Salmon Gefillte Fish Soup (page 103), Fish Pot-au-Feu (page 103), Fish Pil-Pil in Red Sauce (page 104), Veracruz Fish Salad (page 107), Fish Fillets with Sherry-Mushroom Sauce (page 111), Orange Roughy Maître d'Hôtel (page 112), Baked Fish & Ratatouille (page 112), Mr. Zhu's Steamed Fish (page 114), Pine Cone Fish (page 115).

■ **Serving ideas.** To prepare rockfish fillets for stylish pan-frying, use half sesame seeds and half flour to make a light crumb coating (page 92). Serve with Ginger Sauce (page 120) or Garlic-Lemon Butter (page 125). Browned butter sauces (page 92) are also good with rockfish.

Sablefish

Sometimes called: Black cod, Butterfish

Sablefish has an identity problem: fishermen usually call it black cod, and when it's commercially smoked, as much is, it's sold in the West as smoked black cod. Understandably, sablefish is often confused with cod, a lean and very different fish.

To further confuse matters, fresh sablefish is sometimes incorrectly sold as butterfish, a name given to several other fish as well. But by any name, sablefish is unique in that it combines high fat content with very mild flavor.

Though sablefish is found from Southern California to the Bering Sea, most of the catch is now taken in Alaska. Sablefish is an especially fragile, perishable fish, and its quality varies, depending on how it was caught and how carefully it was handled. Quality also seems to be related to the depth of the water where these fish are found, with fish from shallower water being firmer, fatter, and tastier than fish from deeper water.

The best guarantee is to buy sablefish only from a reliable market and cook it as soon as possible after purchase. Some good-quality fish is processed and frozen at sea.

■ **Size and forms.** Most sablefish weighs between 3 and 10 pounds, but it can reach 40 pounds. In general, larger fish are better. Most sablefish is sold as fresh or frozen skinless fillets, but it's sometimes available whole, headed and cleaned, or cut into steaks. If you buy frozen fish, be sure it's well glazed.

■ **Availability.** The fresh fish is available from January through September, or until the yearly quota is met. Heaviest landings usually occur in spring. Frozen fillets are available all year.

Much of the catch is either exported to Japan or smoked, so this once plentiful and inexpensive fish is often in short supply.

■ **Taste and texture.** Its high oil content (over 14 percent) gives sablefish an unusual velvety soft texture. The flesh is tender and delicate to handle. It tastes rich, yet is very mild.

■ **Preparation.** The skinless fillets are ready to cook. Cut whole fish into thick steaks or fillets as for round fish; skin fillets unless directed otherwise for your cooking method. For techniques, see pages 80–81.

■ **Cooking methods.** Sablefish is one of the best candidates for smoking (page 84) or barbecuing.

Baking. Bake steaks or fillets in Piquant Vegetable Sauce, or oven-brown them. (See pages 82–85.)

Barbecuing and broiling. Wood chips, such as alder or hickory, enhance the flavor of sablefish; use direct heat to barbecue, supporting pieces on perforated foil. Broil using the dry heat method or coat fish with a crumb coating. Use Lemon-Butter or Sesame-Soy Baste or Ginger-Soy Marinade when you barbecue or broil with dry heat. (See pages 86–89.)

Frying. Pan-fry fillets and steaks (handling them carefully); coat with flour or crumbs. (See pages 90–92.)

Poaching and steaming. Pan-poach, foil-steam, or steam Chinese-style. (See pages 92–95.)

■ **Suggested recipes.** Five-Spice Fish (page 111), Mackerel with Tart Onion Sauce (page 112), Braised Sablefish (page 112), Grilled Tuna with Teriyaki Fruit Sauce (page 117). For smoked sablefish: Steamed Smoked Fish with Dill Butter (page 116).

■ **Serving ideas.** Hot cooked sablefish is delicious served with steamed new potatoes; drizzle with Garlic-Lemon Butter (page 125). Or offer Hot Ginger Sauce (page 94) or Tomato-Caper Sauce (page 124).

King

Salmon

Probably the most fascinating and popular of the world's fish, Pacific salmon lives most of its life at sea and then heads instinctively to the freshwater stream where it was born to spawn and die. Six species of Pacific salmon and one Atlantic salmon account for most of the world's salmon. Steelhead trout (page 72) closely resembles salmon in size and cooking qualities.

Farming of salmon, a skyrocketing business in many countries, has dramatically increased supplies and affected sizes, varieties, and seasonal availabilities. Some of the farmed fish are hatched and released as tiny fry to return years later; others are hatched and raised in pens in salt water or fresh water until they reach marketable size.

Salmon's quality and flavor depend on many factors. The different species vary in fat content and flavor. Quality of wild fish diminishes as they migrate from the open sea into bays and then up rivers and streams; and fish from different river systems have unique qualities. Fish caught by hook and line (trolling) are regarded as superior to net-caught fish, which bruise more easily; but of greater importance is the way fish are handled after being caught.

Atlantic salmon. The only salmon native to the Atlantic is sometimes labeled by its country of origin, for example, Norwegian salmon or Nova Scotian salmon. Most Atlantic salmon sold in the United States is farm-raised in Norway, but the species is also farmed in Scotland, Iceland, Australia, Canada, and in the states of Maine and Washington.

Unlike Pacific salmon (but similar to steelhead), the Atlantic species can spawn more than once. Wild fish can grow to 40 pounds, but most farmed fish are sold at 6 to 9 pounds. Because of its relatively high oil content (about 6 percent fat), Atlantic salmon is best smoked, barbecued, or broiled; it's also good poached or baked.

King (Chinook). The largest and most expensive Pacific salmon, king or Chinook (also called spring, tyee, or blackmouth) is sometimes marketed by its river of origin and season (such as the renowned Columbia River spring king), sometimes by flesh color (from deep red to white), and sometimes by the method of capture (such as troll-king). The natural range is from Northern California to the Yukon River in Alaska, and the main season is May through September. Some pen-raised kings from New Zealand and Chile are sold in the United States in winter.

Most of the commercial catch runs 7 to 30 pounds, though 100-pound fish have been taken. High in oil content (ranging from 7 to 15 percent fat), kings are best smoked, barbecued, broiled, baked, or poached.

Silver (Coho). Silver salmon, often called coho, ranges from Northern California to Bristol Bay in Alaska. Wild fish run from 2 to 12 pounds; very small silvers are sometimes called jacks. Season is from mid-June to October, but fish caught late in the season are best. This is the species most often pen-raised to 1 or 2 pounds to be sold as baby salmon.

The flesh of silvers is medium red; it's less oily and firmer than that of kings. Larger fish are ideal as steaks or fillets to broil, barbecue, or pan-fry.

Pink. Pink salmon, also known as humpback or humpie, is the smallest (3 to 4 pounds) and most abundant of the wild Pacific salmons. Pinks are still sold mainly as a canned product, but they're increasingly being recognized for their delicate eating qualities.

Pink salmon requires careful handling, but some troll-caught pinks are sold fresh, and many are being sold frozen. Largest catches are in Alaska from late June through September. The pink meat is softer and usually has a lower oil content than other salmon; pinks are best poached, baked, or pan-fried.

Sockeye. Ranging from the Columbia River to Bristol Bay, this salmon (also called red, blueback, or Quinault) runs 3 to 12 pounds. Like king, it's often named for its river of origin (for instance, Copper River red). Sockeye season extends from May through August, peaking around the Fourth of July.

Sockeye's culinary prestige approaches that of king salmon. Its deep red flesh, firm texture, and high oil content have made it the preferred choice for eating out of a can, but because demand for fresh and frozen sockeye is growing, fewer are now canned. The fresh fish is best smoked, barbecued, broiled, baked, or poached.

Chum. Just slightly larger than the silver, chum (other names include keta and dog) averages about 9 pounds. The terms "silverbrite" and "semibrite" are used to grade chum according to skin color. Ocean-caught silverbrites have the lightest skin and pinkest meat; as the fish move into fresh water, the skin darkens and the flesh loses color and quality.

This salmon is always net caught, and the largest fisheries are in Alaska. Most of the fresh chums are sold in the fall, when few other salmon are being landed, but the bulk of the production is either frozen or canned. The meat is pale pink, low in fat, and considered less flavorful than other types; however, chums can be fine eating if poached or pan-fried.

■ **Size and forms.** Salmon can run from 1 to 100 pounds; see individual species descriptions above.

Whole fish are usually sold cleaned, with the head on or headed. You can also buy fresh or frozen steaks, fillets, whole fillets (or sides), and chunks or sections of whole fish (sometimes called roasts). A variety of smoked and kippered products is also available.

■ **Availability.** The main season for wild fish begins in May with kings and extends into fall with the last of the silvers and chums. However, imported and farmed fish are sold in American markets when local salmon is out of season.

■ **Taste and texture.** Salmon's moist meat is flaky and tender; flavor varies by species from delicate and mild to rich and distinctive. See individual species descriptions above.

■ **Preparation.** If you buy whole fish, cut steaks or fillet as for round fish (page 80). One word of caution: Don't

Continued on page 56

Sushi Made Simple

Simplicity, freshness, and elegance are the fundamentals of Japanese raw fish presentations. The most straightforward is *sashimi*—decoratively sliced, flawlessly fresh fish arranged with simple garnishes, such as daikon radish or carrot shreds. When vinegared rice is added to the presentation, it becomes *sushi,* popular for centuries in Japan and gaining an enthusiastic following in the United States as well.

Among the easiest forms of sushi to make at home is *maki,* or rolled sushi, in which rice is spread on toasted sheets of *nori* (dried seaweed), topped with fish and other ingredients, and then rolled into a neat cylinder and cut. The same elements are rolled together by hand to form *temaki sushi.* An American sushi variation adopted with gusto by the Japanese is the California roll: crabmeat, avocado, and rice are rolled in nori with an extra layer of rice on the outside.

To make sushi at home, start with firm-fleshed, parasite-free fish or use cooked crabmeat, cooked shrimp, or smoked salmon. By far the most important step is careful selection of the fish, since there is no cooking to kill any parasites. For guidelines on using raw fish, see page 13.

Sushi is invariably accompanied with *shoga,* sliced pickled ginger, to cleanse the palate between bites. A dipping sauce of soy stirred with a bit of *wasabi,* pungent Japanese horseradish, is also common. The Japanese usually offer hot miso soup and thinly sliced cucumbers seasoned in rice vinegar.

You can purchase nori, wasabi, pickled ginger, and miso soup stock mix in Oriental markets. For maki sushi, you'll also need a bamboo rolling mat (*sudare*), available in Oriental shops and some cookware stores.

To serve sushi, set a small dish of soy sauce, a plate with a small mound of prepared wasabi and some thinly sliced pickled ginger, and a covered bowl of hot miso soup at each place. Offer premade rolled sushi or arrange platters of ingredients for hand-rolled sushi for each diner to prepare. Allow 6 to 8 pieces of sushi per person.

Tea, beer, and hot or chilled sake are compatible beverages. Follow up with fresh fruit, such as tangerines or sliced kiwi fruit.

Maki Sushi (Rolled Sushi)

5 sheets toasted or untoasted nori
Sushi Rice (recipe follows)
Prepared Vegetables (directions follow)
Wasabi Paste (recipe follows)

½ **pound sashimi-grade tuna or frozen tilefish, mahi mahi, Pacific or Atlantic halibut, or salmon, boned, skinned, and cut into ½- by ½- by 5-inch strips; or ½ pound shredded crabmeat or smoked salmon**
Soy sauce
Pickled red ginger (shoga)

Toast nori (if untoasted) until crisp by drawing it, a sheet at a time, back and forth over a low gas flame or an electric element set on low. (If done ahead, let cool; then package airtight.)

Prepare Sushi Rice, vegetables of your choice, and Wasabi Paste.

To assemble, place a sheet of nori on a sudare or bamboo placemat with slats running parallel to you. Place a fifth of the rice on nori (shown below); with rice-vinegar–moistened hands, pat rice down to a thickness of about ½ inch, spreading it out to side and bottom edges of nori and to within 2 inches of top edge. Arrange a fifth each of the fish and vegetables (1 or 2 kinds) in rows across middle of rice.

Holding fish and vegetables down with your fingers, lift up mat with thumbs and roll over so that near edge of nori meets far edge of rice. Press mat around roll briefly; press in any loose ingredients at ends. Remove mat; cut roll into about eight 1-inch slices.

Repeat with remaining nori, rice, and fillings. Offer soy sauce and wasabi (let diners mix wasabi into soy sauce) for dipping; serve ginger alongside. Makes 30 to 40 pieces.

For Maki Sushi (recipe above), place nori on a bamboo rolling mat. Pat rice out to sides, bottom, and within 2 inches of top.

Holding filling in place with your fingers, roll mat over so near edge of nori meets far edge of rice; press mat around roll.

Slice roll firmly with a sharp knife (do not use a sawing motion), cutting into 1-inch-wide pieces.

■ **Sushi Rice.** In a 3- to 4-quart pan, cover 3 cups **short-grain rice,** such as pearl rice, with water and stir; drain. Rinse repeatedly until water is clear; drain again.

Add 3½ cups **water** to rice in pan. Cover and bring to a boil over high heat. Reduce heat to low and cook, without stirring, until water is absorbed (about 15 minutes).

Stir in ⅓ cup **seasoned rice vinegar** (or 4 teaspoons sugar dissolved in ⅓ cup distilled or white wine vinegar). Spread rice equally in 2 rimmed 10- by 15-inch baking sheets. Stirring, cool rice quickly until no longer steaming, fanning with a piece of cardboard or a hand-held hair dryer on cool setting. Let stand until rice reaches room temperature.

If made ahead, cover tightly and store at room temperature until next day. Makes 6 to 7 cups.

■ **Prepared Vegetables.** Choose 1 or 2 of the following:

Carrots. Cut 2 **carrots** into 3- to 4-inch-long julienne strips. Pour ⅓ cup **seasoned rice vinegar** (or 4 teaspoons sugar dissolved in ⅓ cup distilled or white wine vinegar) into a small pan. Bring to a boil over medium-high heat. Add carrots; cook just until tender-crisp (about 30 seconds). Drain.

Cucumber. Cut ½ **English cucumber** into 3- to 4-inch-long julienne strips.

Spinach. Discard stems from 1 pound **spinach;** rinse. Pour water to a depth of 1 inch into a 2- to 3-quart pan. Bring to a boil over high heat. Add spinach; cook just until limp (about 1 minute). Drain.

Mushrooms. Soak 2 ounces **Oriental dried mushrooms** in warm water to cover just until pliable; drain and rinse. Cut off and discard stems; cut caps into long, thin strips. Place in a small pan along with 2 tablespoons *each* **sugar, soy sauce,** and **water.** Cover and cook over medium heat, stirring occasionally, until liquid is absorbed (about 5 minutes).

Avocado. Pit and peel 1 medium-size firm-ripe **avocado.** Slice lengthwise into strips about ⅓ inch thick. Place in a bowl with ½ cup **lemon juice;** moisten each slice to prevent browning.

■ **Wasabi Paste.** In a small bowl, stir together 3 tablespoons **wasabi powder** and 3½ teaspoons **water** until smooth. To serve, divide into small portions.

Temaki Sushi (Hand-rolled Sushi)

1½ ounces toasted or untoasted nori
Sushi Rice (see above left)
Wasabi Paste (see above)
Sushi Toppings Tray (directions follow)
Toasted Sesame Seeds (directions follow)
Sesame Sauce (recipe follows)
Soy sauce
Pickled red ginger *(shoga)*

Toast untoasted nori as directed on facing page for Maki Sushi. With scissors, cut nori into 4- to 5-inch squares; stack on a plate or in a basket.

Prepare Sushi Rice, Wasabi Paste, Sushi Toppings Tray, Toasted Sesame Seeds, and Sesame Sauce and present in bowls or on platters or trays in center of table.

Let diners assemble their own hand-rolled sushi, laying a piece of nori in palm of hand and spooning a small amount of rice into center. Top with desired items from toppings tray; add wasabi or seeds and sauce to taste. Overlap 2 opposite corners of nori to enclose filling. Dip into soy sauce flavored with wasabi, if desired. Serve ginger alongside. Makes 6 servings.

■ **Sushi Toppings Tray.** Prepare **carrots, cucumber, spinach,** and **avocado** as directed for **Maki Sushi** (at left), except slice avocado ⅛ inch thick. Trim brown ends off 1 bag (3½ oz.) **fresh enoki mushrooms.**

Arrange vegetables separately on a large tray along with ½ pound shredded **crabmeat;** ½ pound medium-size or small **shrimp,** cooked, shelled, and deveined; ½ pound sashimi-grade **tuna** or frozen tilefish, mahi mahi, Pacific or Atlantic halibut, or salmon, boned, skinned, and thinly sliced; ¼ pound **smoked salmon,** thinly sliced; and ½ cup (2 oz.) **salmon caviar.**

Spoon rice and toppings onto nori to make Temaki Sushi (recipe at left) at the table. Serve with wasabi-flavored soy sauce and pickled ginger.

If made ahead, cover and refrigerate for up to 5 hours. Serve slightly cool or at room temperature.

■ **Toasted Sesame Seeds.** Toast ¼ cup **sesame seeds** in a 10- to 12-inch frying pan over medium-high heat, shaking pan frequently, until golden (3 to 5 minutes). Spoon into 1 or 2 small serving bowls. Makes ¼ cup.

■ **Sesame Sauce.** Stir together 1 cup **mayonnaise,** 4 teaspoons *each* **honey** and **toasted sesame seeds** (directions above), and 1½ teaspoons **sesame oil.** Spoon into 1 or 2 small serving bowls. Makes about 1 cup.

eat raw salmon—it may contain tapeworm larvae. The larvae are easily killed by cooking. To use for sashimi (page 54), freeze at below 0°F for at least 3 days to kill any tapeworm larvae.

Baby salmon can be boned and butterflied like trout (page 73).

■ **Cooking methods.** There are good salmon cuts for almost every cooking method. See individual species descriptions on page 53 for the best ways to cook each type. Baby salmon can be used in most recipes for trout (page 72).

Baking. Bake whole fish, roasts, steaks, or fillets in Piquant Vegetable Sauce. Bake whole fish with Almond-Rice or Toasted Bread Cube Stuffing. Oven-brown steaks or fillets or bake with a creamy topping. (See pages 82–86.)

Barbecuing and broiling. Barbecue steaks or small fillets over direct heat, supporting them on perforated foil. Barbecue whole fillets, roasts, and whole fish with indirect heat. Broil steaks and fillets with dry heat. Use Lemon-Butter or Sesame-Soy Baste for barbecuing or broiling. (See pages 86–88.)

Frying. Pan-fry steaks or fillets; no coating is needed for good browning. (See pages 90–92.)

Poaching and steaming. Steaks and fillets can be pan-poached, poached the classic way, steeped, or steamed Chinese-style. Whole fish and roasts can be poached the classic way or foil-steamed. (See pages 92–95.)

■ **Suggested recipes.** Gravlax Plus (page 47), Fish Fillets with Dill and Tangerine (page 91), Quenelles with Creamy Shallot Sauce (page 100), Quick Colorful Chowder (page 102), Puget Sound Salmon Gefilte Fish Soup (page 103), Salmon Salad with Tarragon Vinaigrette (page 107), Five-Spice Fish (page 111), Steamed Salmon with Sorrel (page 112), Grilled Salmon on Wilted Chicory Salad (page 113).

For baby salmon: Steamed Trout with Lettuce & Peas (page 96), Baby Salmon with Sautéed Leeks (page 113), Trout with Leeks & Vinegar (page 114), Calico Stuffed Trout (page 114).

For smoked salmon: Maki Sushi (page 54), Temaki Sushi (page 55), Smoked Salmon Mousse (page 116).

■ **Serving ideas.** Salmon is good hot or cold with a variety of sauces. Try Watercress Cream or Hot Ginger Sauce (page 94) or Basil Garlic Butter (page 125) with hot fish. Homemade Mayonnaise and any of its variations and Aïoli (page 123) are good with cold salmon.

Sardine See Herring, page 35

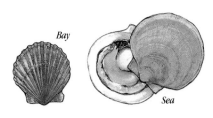

Bay

Sea

Scallops

Like clams and oysters, scallops are bivalves (two-shelled mollusks). Most are active swimmers, propelling themselves along the ocean floor by clapping their shells together using a well-developed muscle called the eye—the part of the scallop that is eaten.

Because scallops cannot close their shells tightly, they spoil quickly and are usually shucked at sea. The muscle is iced and the rest discarded (the cleaned shells are sometimes sold as decorative baking dishes). Sometimes, the coral-colored roe is left attached to be eaten with the muscle, a delicacy that is just beginning to be appreciated in the United States.

Of the hundreds of scallop species worldwide, three are of importance in the U.S. domestic harvest—sea, bay, and calico.

Sea scallops. These large scallops, the most widely available type, are dredged from deep waters off the Atlantic coast from the Gulf of Maine to North Carolina. New Bedford, Massachusetts, is the main scallop port in the United States. The shells of sea scallops can measure up to 8 inches across, their muscles up to 2 inches.

Bay scallops. The gourmet's favorite, these small scallops (also known as Cape Cod scallops) are in limited sup-

ply—and are expensive. They're found in inshore bays, harbors, and salt ponds from Long Island to Massachusetts. Other small scallops are often labeled "bay scallops" in markets, but there's only one real bay scallop.

Bay scallops generally grow to 4 inches, with ½-inch muscles.

Calico scallops. Although slightly larger and not as sweet and flavorful as bay scallops, calicos are often sold as "bay scallops." Most are taken from the coast of Florida and mechanically steam-shucked, so they're partially cooked. They get their name from the mottled look of their shells.

Other scallops. There's a small fishery on the Pacific Coast for the large *weathervane* species, a sea scallop found from Alaska to Oregon. A few frozen-at-sea weathervanes harvested off the Aleutians are available.

A major portion of the U.S. supply of scallops is imported from Canada, Japan, Peru, Iceland, New Zealand, and other countries. Some have the coral-colored roe attached.

■ **Size and forms.** See individual descriptions above for average sizes. Fresh and frozen scallops are considered equal in quality, so most are shipped frozen; markets usually defrost them to sell. Bay scallops are usually sold fresh.

High-quality scallops have a translucent clarity and a clean ocean smell with no sourness.

■ **Availability.** Peak season for fresh domestic scallops is November through March, but both fresh and frozen scallops are available all year.

■ **Taste and texture.** Scallops are sweet and mild in flavor, with tender-firm texture when cooked. The roe is mild flavored and firm textured.

■ **Preparation.** Thaw scallops if frozen. Some sea scallops still have a small piece of tough connective tissue attached to one side; pull it off and discard. Rinse scallops and dry well before cooking.

■ **Cooking methods.** Scallops need only brief cooking; overcooking or reheating cooked scallops will toughen them. The roe, if attached, can be cooked right along with the muscle.

Barbecuing and broiling. Barbecue or broil as for Fish or Shellfish Kebabs. Use Lemon-Butter or Sesame-Soy Baste. (See pages 86–88.)

Frying. *To pan-fry*, rinse ¾ to 1 pound **sea scallops** or bay scallops and dry thoroughly with paper towels. Place a 10- to 12-inch frying pan over medium-high heat until a drop of water sizzles and dances in pan. Add 2 tablespoons **olive oil** or salad oil and tilt pan to coat.

Adds scallops and, if desired, 1 large clove **garlic,** minced or pressed. Cook, turning often, until scallops are lightly browned and opaque inside when cut (about 5 minutes for sea scallops, about 3 minutes for bay scallops). If desired, serve with **Browned Butter** (page 92). Makes 3 or 4 servings.

Scallops can also be deep-fried; use British Beer or Japanese Tempura Batter. To stir-fry scallops, follow directions for Stir-fried Fish or Shellfish with Peas. (See pages 89–90, 95.)

Poaching. Rinse and drain 1 to 1½ pounds **scallops;** cut in half if over 1½ inches thick. In a 3- to 4-quart pan, bring 1½ inches **water** or Poaching Liquid (page 93) to a boil. Add scallops and return water to a simmer. Reduce heat, cover, and simmer until scallops are opaque inside when cut (4 to 5 minutes); drain. If made ahead, cover and refrigerate to use cold in salads or other preparations. Makes 3 or 4 servings.

■ **Suggested recipes.** Shrimp or Scallops and Pesto (page 91), Scallops & Shrimp in Béarnaise Cream (page 97), Scallops with Shallot Butter (page 102), Stir-fried Scallops & Asparagus on Cool Pasta (page 109), Skewered Fish, Northwest Style (page 118), Grilled Scallops with Red Pepper Sauce (page 118), Seafood Brochettes with Champagne Sauce (page 119).

■ **Serving ideas.** Good sauces to serve with scallops include Hollandaise, Béarnaise, and Mornay Sauce (page 124). Browned butter sauces (page 92) are good with pan-fried scallops.

Wrap sea scallops in bacon to broil and serve as an appetizer.

Scup *see Sea Bream, page 58*

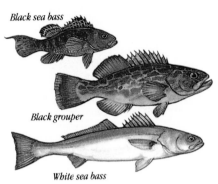

Black sea bass

Black grouper

White sea bass

Sea Bass/Grouper

No fish name causes more confusion at the fish market than sea bass. Because the name seems to sell well, many fish that are really something else are erroneously labeled "bass" or "sea bass." The sea bass family itself, which includes groupers, is the largest and most diverse group of fish in the world. Sea basses sold in U.S. markets that have a recognized identity are described here; also included is white sea bass, which is actually in the drum family (page 31) but is used more like sea bass.

For striped bass and freshwater white bass, see page 16.

Black sea bass. This fish seldom weighs more than 5 pounds; typical market size is between 1 and 2 pounds. Black sea bass is caught from Cape Cod to Florida, with heaviest landings off the mid-Atlantic states. It's sometimes called blackfish, confusing it with tautog (page 70); it's also different from the large grouper called black sea bass in California.

Small quantities of Atlantic black sea bass are available from April to November in New England and during the winter in the mid-Atlantic area. Most is sold fresh and whole, but some fillets are available. Black sea bass is popular in Chinese cuisine for deep-fried or steamed presentations of whole fish. The meat is lean and has extra-firm flakes.

Red and black groupers. These two similar fish are the most abundant of the groupers landed in the United States. They're found in the Atlantic from the Carolinas south to Brazil and throughout the Gulf of Mexico, where most are taken.

The red species (actually mottled brown) reaches 40 pounds, but most market fish are under 10 pounds. Black grouper is about twice the size of the red, weighing between 10 and 20 pounds when sold.

Grouper is landed year-round but is most plentiful in summer. Both fish, especially larger red groupers, may have parasites, harmless worms that are normally cut out of the flesh before it's sold.

Grouper is sold fresh, usually as steaks or fillets and sometimes as cleaned fish, with the head off. Whole fish have few small bones and are easy to fillet. The skin is tough and strong flavored; it should be removed from fillets before cooking. The meat is lean, white, and extra-firm.

White sea bass. Actually a member of the drum and croaker family, this "sea bass" is best known in California. It's caught along the Southern California coast and the west coast of Mexico, but most of the U.S. supply is now imported from Mexico, where it's called corvina. Though white sea bass can weigh 80 pounds, market fish average about 15 pounds. Never plentiful, it's most abundant in summer.

White sea bass is usually sold fresh, either whole and cleaned, with the head on, or as steaks or thick fillets. Small fish can be baked or poached whole. The meat is lean, with extra-firm flakes.

Other species. *Hapu'upu'u,* or Hawaiian black sea bass, is a reef fish taken off Hawaii and in the South Pacific. Though it grows to 50 pounds, 5 to 15 pounds is most common. The flavor is mild and sweet; the flesh is lean, white, and especially dense and meaty.

A fish sold in American markets as *Chilean sea bass* is a good-tasting fish, but it's much richer and softer than other sea bass.

Several New Zealand fish called sea bass are imported. One called *bluenose* is actually a sea bream, but it's an excellent, lean fish; its flavor is a little more pronounced than that of sea bass. Another fish, called *New Zealand groper,* is a true grouper. Both fish are sold as thick skinless fillets, and the flesh is dense and meaty.

A fish called *baquetta* or red grouper is actually Gulf coney grouper, especially popular in Southern California. It ranges from the Sea of Cortez to Central America and can reach 40 pounds. The skin is very thick and tough, but fillets are sold skinless. The meat is dense and meaty.

Small amounts of other large groupers appear in markets from time to time, including *yellowfin, Warsaw,* and *Nassau.* Their lean, white meat is mild in flavor, dense and meaty in texture.

■ **Size and forms.** Sea bass species vary widely in size; see individual descriptions above. Most sea bass is sold as skinless fillets. Small species, such as Atlantic black sea bass and small white sea bass, are sold whole and cleaned.

■ **Availability.** While some sea bass is in season at any time, demand usually exceeds supply.

■ **Taste and texture.** In general, sea bass meat is white, mild in flavor, and lean. Texture ranges from flaky and extra-firm to firm and meaty. One exception is Chilean sea bass (see page 57).

■ **Preparation.** Small whole fish may need to be cleaned. Fillet as for round fish, removing the skin from black sea bass or grouper fillets. For techniques, see pages 80–81.

■ **Cooking methods.** Cooking methods for sea bass depend on whether the fish can be described as having extra-firm flakes or as dense and meaty. The firm-flaked fish are Atlantic black sea bass, white sea bass, and Atlantic red and black groupers. Dense and meaty fish include Hawaiian hapu'upu'u, New Zealand bluenose, baquetta, giant sea bass, and other large groupers.

The oilier, softer Chilean sea bass fillets can be cooked much as you would salmon (page 53).

Baking. Any of the species are good baked in sauce. You can bake and stuff an Atlantic black sea bass or small white sea bass; use any of the suggested stuffings. Oven-brown Chilean sea bass fillets. Other sea basses are good baked with a creamy topping. (See pages 82–86.)

Barbecuing and broiling. Steaks and fillets of all the species except Chilean sea bass are firm enough to put directly on a well-greased grill and barbecue over direct heat. The dense and meaty fish are most dependable to skewer for kebabs; firm-flaked fish can be skewered, too, but set them on perforated foil. Use a mild baste, such as Lemon-Butter.

Broil Chilean sea bass with dry heat or with a crumb coating. Broil other sea basses with moist heat. (See pages 86–89.)

Frying. Pan-fry fillets of any of the species; they brown well without a coating. Both the firm-flaked and the dense and meaty fish work well for stir-frying. (See pages 90–92, 95.)

Poaching and steaming. Fillets of any of the species can be pan-poached, poached the classic way, foil-steamed, or steamed Chinese-style. Whole black sea bass can be poached the classic way or foil-steamed. (See pages 92–95.)

■ **Suggested recipes.** For all species: Fish Fillets with Dill and Tangerine (page 91), Burmese Fish with Sweet Onions (page 96), Faux Salmon Terrine (page 101), Quick Colorful Chowder (page 102), Fish Pot-au-Feu (page 103), Fish Pil-Pil in Red Sauce (page 104), Veracruz Fish Salad (page 107), Thai Fish & Watercress Salad (page 108), Fish Fillets with Sherry-Mushroom Sauce (page 111).

For black sea bass: Mr. Zhu's Steamed Fish (page 114), Pine Cone Fish (page 115).

For large, dense, and meaty fish: Skewered Fish, Northwest Style (page 118).

■ **Serving ideas.** Make a colorful summer salad with morsels of cold poached sea bass mixed lightly with Jalapeño Vinaigrette (page 100), sliced olives, fresh cilantro (coriander), slivered red or green bell pepper, and chopped yellow or red tomatoes. Complement barbecued steaks or fillets with Provençale or Diable Butter (page 125).

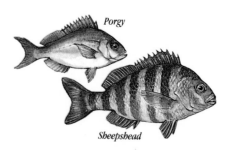

Porgy

Sheepshead

Sea Bream/Porgy/ Sheepshead

Several closely related species of fish along the Atlantic and Gulf of Mexico coasts of the United States are called either porgy or scup, strictly American names for members of a family known as sea breams. A fish called Atlantic sheepshead is another American sea bream, but a sports fish called California sheepshead is not related; it's a wrasse.

In the world of sea breams, the most renowned for their excellence are French *daurade,* or gilthead bream, and Japanese *ikijima tai,* the same fish confusingly sold elsewhere as New Zealand snapper, a Japanese favorite for sashimi. Almost as good tasting is *dentex,* caught off the western coast of Africa.

Porgy and scup. The common sea bream, usually called red or pink porgy in America, is plentiful on both sides of the Atlantic. Found from New York to Argentina and in the Gulf of Mexico, it usually weighs less than 5 pounds. The scup, fished from Nova Scotia to the Gulf of Mexico, is usually under 2 pounds; many weigh less than a pound.

These two fish are closely related, and the names are often interchanged. Both are good-tasting fish, but they have quite a few small, sharp bones and rather tough skin with large, heavy scales.

Sheepshead. Called convict fish because of its black and white stripes, sheepshead is caught from Nova Scotia to the Gulf of Mexico, with the bulk of the commercial catch coming from the gulf. Like porgy, it usually weighs less than 5 pounds and is a good-eating but bony fish.

Imported sea breams. The red-skinned *New Zealand snapper* (also called tai or red sea bream) is sold in American markets, especially on the West Coast; fish that are slightly below sashimi quality can be a good value. Some French *daurade* is imported, but it's very expensive. You may also find frozen-at-sea sea bream of various species, some of which can be both good tasting and inexpensive.

■ **Size and forms.** Sea breams range in size from under a pound to 20 pounds. Most, both fresh and frozen, are sold whole or headed and cleaned. Only limited amounts of fillets are sold, mainly sheepshead.

■ **Availability.** Porgy, scup, and sheepshead are caught year-round but in limited quantities, mainly because they're not popular in the United States. Most porgy and scup are sold in the East.

■ **Taste and texture.** The light-colored flesh is moist and coarse textured, with tender-firm flakes; it has a delicate, sweet flavor. These fish are quite lean (2 to 3 percent fat).

■ **Preparation.** Whole fish have many bones and heavy scales that are difficult to remove except right after the fish are caught. Larger fish have the highest ratio of meat to bones and are the easiest to fillet; follow directions for round fish. Remove the skin from fillets. Use tweezers or pliers to remove small bones. For techniques, see pages 80–81.

Small fish that have not been scaled can be skinned by sliding a knife under the tough skin and cutting outward; or

remove the skin with pliers as for catfish (page 21). You can also remove the skin, with scales, after cooking.

■ **Cooking methods.** Frying and poaching are popular ways to cook these mild-flavored fish, but other methods work, as well.

Baking. Bake skinned fillets or whole fish in Piquant Vegetable Sauce or oven-brown the skinned fillets or small fish. Bake larger fish with any of the suggested stuffings; skin the fish before or after cooking. (See pages 82–85.)

Barbecuing and broiling. Place skinned fillets or small fish in a hinged broiler or on perforated foil and barbecue over direct heat. Use indirect heat for larger fish—either skin the fish or cut several slashes through the skin on each side and remove the skin after cooking. Use Italian-style or Basil-Parmesan Marinade. Broil skinned fillets or small fish with moist heat; broil fillets with a crumb coating. (See pages 86–89.)

Frying. Deep-fry skinned fillets with British Beer or Lemon Batter. Pan-fry skinned fillets or skinned small fish; use flour or a crumb or cornmeal coating. (See pages 89–92.)

Poaching and steaming. Skinned fillets or skinned small fish can be pan-poached or steamed Chinese-style. Larger whole fish (with or without skin) can be poached the classic way or foil-steamed; remove the skin before serving. (See pages 92–95.)

■ **Suggested recipes.** Fish Fillets with Dill and Tangerine (page 91), Rockfish Florentine (page 96), Fish & Chard Pie (page 99), Quenelles with Creamy Shallot Sauce (page 100), Bourride (page 102), Fish Fillets with Sherry-Mushroom Sauce (page 111), Orange Roughy Maître d'Hôtel (page 112), Mr. Zhu's Steamed Fish (page 114).

■ **Serving ideas.** To bake a larger fish, add flavor by filling the cavity with orange and lemon slices and bay leaves; for a sauce, melt butter, flavor it with orange juice and grated orange peel, and drizzle over servings of the baked fish.

Accompany flour-dusted pan-fried fillets with Citrus Beurre Blanc (page 125) or any browned butter sauce (page 92).

Spotted seatrout

Seatrout/Weakfish

Spotted seatrout and gray weakfish are closely related to one another, but, despite the name, they're not related to true trout at all. Instead, they belong to a large family of fish that includes drums and croakers (page 31), as well as white sea bass (page 57).

Other fish in the seatrout/weakfish family are imported from Latin America and sold under the name "corvina." This name confuses them with two West Coast fish–the California corbina (reserved for sportfishing) and the shortfin corvina, an incidental catch; both are members of the extended weakfish family.

Slim, beautifully proportioned seatrout and weakfish are rather fragile and need to be handled carefully and kept well chilled. The "weak" label comes from a delicate mouth structure that permits a hook to tear out easily. The fish are susceptible to parasites, so they should never be used raw.

Large, silvery black spots on its sides distinguish spotted seatrout from gray weakfish, which may have small, indistinct silver spots. Of the two species, spotted seatrout has the firmer flesh and is considered better quality.

Spotted seatrout. Known also as speckled trout, this fish ranges from New York to the Gulf of Mexico, where most of the commercial catch is taken; "trout," as it's called in Louisiana, is especially popular there. Seatrout is available all year, with peak landings from October through February.

Gray weakfish. This migratory schooling fish (also called gray trout, gray squeteague, or yellowfin) ranges along the Atlantic coast from New York to Florida;

most of the catch is landed in Delaware and Chesapeake bays between April and November.

The supply is cyclical, so some years weakfish is more abundant than other years. The greenish skin of weakfish has colorful tints of purple, blue, green, copper, and gold.

■ **Size and forms.** Most commercially caught seatrout and weakfish are in the 1 to 3-pound range, though both fish can reach 8 pounds; some pan-size fish (about 8 oz. each) are also sold. Domestically caught fish are almost always sold fresh, whole and cleaned, usually with the head on.

Sometimes, large fish and imported frozen fish are sold as skin-on fillets. These species freeze well; they improve in texture, becoming firmer when frozen.

■ **Availability.** See individual species descriptions on page 59 and above.

■ **Taste and texture.** The flesh of spotted seatrout is fine grained, moist, and flaky. The flesh of gray weakfish is softer than that of seatrout. Both fish are moderately lean (about 3.5 percent fat) and have a mild, sweet flavor.

■ **Preparation.** Whole fish may need scaling. Large fish can be filleted as for round fish, but their soft flesh makes this rather difficult.

For techniques, see pages 79–80. Smaller fish can be boned through the belly and butterflied as for trout (page 73).

■ **Cooking methods.** Large fish are a good size to bake stuffed or to poach. Boned and butterflied fish can be broiled or baked to good advantage. The flesh tends to break apart easily when cooked.

Baking. Bake whole fish in Piquant Vegetable Sauce or with Almond-Rice or Spinach-Mushroom Stuffing. Oven-brown fillets. (See pages 82–85.)

Barbecuing and broiling. Barbecue fillets and small fish over direct heat; support fillets on perforated foil. Barbecue larger fish using indirect heat. Broil

fillets or butterflied fish with dry heat. Choose a mild baste, such as Lemon-Butter Baste, for barbecuing or broiling. Fillets can also be broiled with a crumb coating. (See pages 86–89.)

Frying. Pan-fry fillets or small fish; a crumb or cornmeal coating adds texture. (See pages 90–92.)

Poaching and steaming. Small fish and fillets can be pan-poached, steeped, or steamed Chinese-style. Larger fish can be poached the classic way or foil-steamed. (See pages 92–95.)

■ **Suggested recipes.** Steamed Trout with Lettuce & Peas (page 96), Bourride (page 102), Baked Fish & Ratatouille (page 112), Baby Salmon with Sautéed Leeks (page 113), Trout with Leeks & Vinegar (page 114), Calico Stuffed Trout (page 114), Mr. Zhu's Steamed Fish (page 114).

■ **Serving ideas.** Keep sauces mild so as not to overpower the fish's subtle flavor. Poached fish is good cold in salads, dressed with Dijon Vinaigrette Dressing (page 124); or serve cold fish with Homemade Mayonnaise or any of its variations (page 123).

A New Orleans classic is spotted seatrout meunière amandine—flour-dusted pan-fried fillets served with Almond Browned Butter (page 92).

Shad & Roe

Like salmon, shad is anadromous; after 2 to 5 years at sea, it ascends coastal rivers and streams to spawn. Only one species, the American shad, is harvested in the United States; it's a member of the herring family.

Abundant along the Atlantic Coast from the St. Lawrence River to Florida, shad is harvested in rivers where it spawns. Shad was introduced on the West Coast in the last century and can now be found from British Columbia to California; however, the only commercial harvest is in the Columbia River.

The succulent-tasting shad has one disadvantage—its many small bones, arranged so that it requires considerable skill to fillet one properly. (Shad has been described as an inside-out porcupine.) Thus, deboned shad fillets, considered a delicacy, are in short supply and in much demand, especially on the East Coast; shad meat is largely unutilized on the West Coast.

Another delicacy is shad roe. Female shad with roe commands the highest prices; females are also larger and therefore easier to fillet than bucks.

The sooner the roe is removed from the fish, the higher its quality; it should never remain in the fish more than 12 hours. The eggs should not be too mature; they should be small, crisp, and firm. Skeins should be intact.

■ **Size and forms.** Most fish weigh between 3 and 5 pounds, though shad grows to 11 pounds. It's sold whole, with or without roe, or as boned fillets weighing from ¾ to 1¼ pounds. The roe is also sold separately as pairs of skeins; a fairly large set, weighing more than 8 ounces, divides nicely into 2 servings.

■ **Availability.** The main season begins in January in Florida, moves north through the spring as waters warm, and ends in June in the Gulf of St. Lawrence. Late May and June is the spawning season in the West.

■ **Taste and texture.** Shad meat is soft and has a high oil content (almost 14 percent fat). Its flavor is rich, distinctive, and sweet.

■ **Preparation.** If you purchase a female shad with roe, handle it with care. Starting at the anal opening, make a shallow cut to avoid puncturing the roe; remove the roe gently. Scale and clean the fish. For techniques, see pages 79–80.

As an alternative to filleting shad, you can split the headed and cleaned fish in half along the back and simply remove the large bone. Split fish can be broiled or barbecued.

To prepare shad roe for cooking, wash the skein gently, being careful not to break the membrane covering. Pat dry with paper towels. Don't separate the set until after cooking.

■ **Cooking methods.** Its high oil content makes shad a good candidate for smoking (page 84), as well as barbecuing and broiling.

Baking. Oven-brown shad fillets. (See page 85.)

Barbecuing and broiling. Barbecue fillets over direct heat, placing them on perforated foil. Barbecue split fish with indirect heat. Broil fillets or split fish using dry heat. When barbecuing or broiling, use Lemon-Butter or Sesame-Soy Baste or Basil-Parmesan Marinade. You can also broil shad fillets with a crumb coating. (See pages 86–89.)

Frying. Pan-fry shad fillets, covering them with a crumb or cornmeal coating (pages 90–92).

To pan-fry shad roe, prepare 1 large set **shad roe** (about 8 to 12 oz.) as directed on facing page. Dust with about 2 tablespoons **all-purpose flour,** coating lightly. In an 8- to 10-inch frying pan, melt 2 tablespoons **butter** or margarine over medium heat. Add roe and cook, turning, until roe is browned on both sides and eggs are opaque white throughout (about 10 minutes total).

Remove from pan and divide skein. Arrange each serving on **buttered toast.** Season to taste with **salt** and **pepper.** Offer with **lemon wedges.** Serve with **Browned Butter** (page 92) or crisp bacon, if desired. Makes 2 servings.

Poaching and steaming. Fillets can be pan-poached, steeped, or steamed Chinese-style. (See pages 92–95.)

■ **Suggested recipes.** Fish Fillets with Dill and Tangerine (page 91), Orange Roughy Maître d'Hôtel (page 112), Grilled Salmon on Wilted Chicory Salad (page 113).

■ **Serving ideas.** Shad and shad roe are often served with bacon. To temper the oily taste of the fish, offer a tart accompaniment, such as Tomato-Caper Sauce (page 124) or Citrus Beurre Blanc (page 125).

Blacktip

Shark

In spite of its fearsome reputation, shark has finally become a popular food fish in the United States. The fact that it's essentially free of bones is one reason people like it; sharks don't have a bony structure like other fish.

There are as many as 300 species of shark, and they vary widely in size, habits, and edibility. Of the 20 or more species harvested commercially in the United States, six stand out for their superior eating qualities—common thresher, soupfin, and bonito, sold primarily on the West Coast, and blacktip, mako, and sandbar on the East Coast.

Discerning shoppers don't buy "shark"; instead, they buy "thresher" or "mako" or whatever is their choice of species.

The harvest method and proper handling of shark, beginning as soon as the fish is caught, determine quality; those caught with hook and line are best. Because of its unique elimination system, shark must be bled immediately; otherwise, the meat develops a strong ammonia odor. Once bled and cleaned, it must be kept well iced.

Common thresher. This large shark, growing to 20 feet and more than 1,000 pounds, is found in subtropical and temperate waters over much of the world, including offshore California.

Several subspecies of thresher are taken in the Atlantic, but none compares in quality with the common thresher. Its very long, sicklelike tail distinguishes this shark. Common thresher's very firm, dense flesh is pinkish beige when raw, turning light tan when cooked.

This shark is landed year-round, but peak season is April through summer.

Soupfin. A smaller Pacific shark, soupfin generally weighs between 50 and 100 pounds. Some consider it equal in quality to the common thresher, but it's not nearly as plentiful. Some soupfins are landed year-round. The fins of this fish are used by the Chinese for sharkfin

soup (they provide a gelatin base), which accounts for the fish's name.

Bonito. Unrelated to the bonito in the tuna family, this large Pacific shark is difficult to distinguish from Atlantic mako. Bonitos grow to 1,000 pounds and range from Southern California to Chile.

Peak season for California bonito is April through summer. Steaks cut from bonito look almost identical to swordfish steaks; they're equally firm and meaty.

Blacktip. This highly regarded small shark is one of the more common sharks in the warmer waters of the Atlantic, especially off Florida and in the Caribbean. Some are also found from Southern California to Peru. In the Atlantic, where most are harvested, the season is from November to April. Average size is 35 to 40 pounds.

Steaks of blacktip are fairly easy to recognize: they're white with distinctive ruby color around the outer edges.

Mako. Considered by many to be the best tasting of all sharks, mako is sometimes called bonito shark because it feeds on bonito tuna. Makos range in the Atlantic from Canada to the Caribbean, but most are taken in warm waters. Growing to 12 feet and 1,000 pounds, they're harvested year-round. Like Pacific bonito, mako yields steaks that look like swordfish. The meat is fine grained and moist.

Sandbar. Found in the Atlantic from New England to Brazil and also in the Gulf of Mexico, sandbars (also called brown shark) are taken in shallow water, hence, their name. Harvested all year, they can weigh up to 200 pounds. Sandbar meat resembles blacktip and, in fact, much of it is sold as blacktip.

■ **Size and forms.** The various species are sold as steaks or fillets, usually more than 1 inch thick.

■ **Availability.** See individual species descriptions above.

■ **Taste and texture.** Shark flesh is firm, dense, and meatlike in texture. It's lean and mild to moderately pronounced in flavor.

(Continued on next page)

■ **Preparation.** Avoid buying shark (or any fish) that has an unpleasant odor. However, if you detect a slight odor of ammonia in the shark you buy, it can be neutralized easily. Simply soak the pieces in milk, buttermilk, or ice water (if using water, add about 2 tablespoons lemon juice per quart) for 30 minutes before cooking.

■ **Cooking methods.** Shark's firm meat holds its shape very well in cooking, making it a good choice for kebabs and stir-frying.

Baking. Bake shark in Piquant Vegetable Sauce or with a creamy topping. (See pages 82–86.)

Barbecuing and broiling. Place steaks, fillets, or skewered cubes of shark directly on a greased grill and barbecue over direct heat; use Basil-Parmesan, Ginger-Soy, or Italian-style Marinade. Broil with moist heat. (See pages 86–89.)

Frying. Pan-fry steaks or fillets; they brown well without any coating. Shark can also be stir-fried. (See pages 90–92, 95.)

Poaching and steaming. Pan-poach shark, poach it the classic way, or steam it Chinese-style. (See pages 92–95.)

■ **Suggested recipes.** Burmese Fish with Sweet Onions (page 96), Fish Pot-au-Feu (page 103), Thai Fish & Watercress Salad (page 108), Five-Spice Fish (page 111), Swordfish Steaks with Mushrooms (page 117), Skewered Fish, Northwest Style (page 118).

■ **Serving ideas.** Shark takes well to spicy and assertive flavorings, including Mexican-style and Oriental seasonings. Over barbecued shark steaks, spoon tangy Cayenne Sauce (page 120) or Chilè-Cilantro Sauce (page 101). Tomato-Caper Sauce (page 124) and Provençale Butter and Diable Butter (page 125) are also good accompaniments.

Sheepshead *see Sea Bream, page 58*

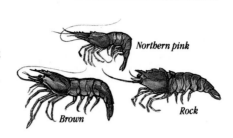

Northern pink

Brown

Rock

Shrimp

Shrimp is the most widely consumed seafood worldwide. And the harvest of both wild and farmed shrimp is increasing rapidly to keep pace with the soaring demand for this crustacean.

A large share of the shrimp sold in the United States is imported. Though hundreds of species are caught, shrimp can generally be classed by origin—either warm water or cold water. Most of the medium-size to large shrimp, often sold uncooked and unpeeled, come from warm waters. The familiar tiny pink shrimp sold cooked and peeled are cold-water species.

The term "prawn" is used in some areas to describe large shrimp, but worldwide the word is used for shrimp of any size. Especially when cooked in butter or in olive oil with garlic, shrimp are often called scampi, actually the name of a small lobsterlike crustacean found in the Atlantic and the Mediterranean.

Warm-water shrimp. These species, also known as tropical shrimp, are usually classified by shell color—mainly white, pink, or brown. However, the differences are subtle, so it's not easy to tell them apart. *White shrimp* have thin, pale shells and very mild flavor; *pink shrimp* have pale pink to deep rose shells; and *brown shrimp* have reddish brown shells and more flavor. Brown shrimp have an iodine odor, and some consider them less attractive; they usually cost less. When they're cooked, they look as pink as any shrimp.

In the United States, warm-water shrimp are caught along the South Atlantic and Gulf of Mexico coasts. Imported species come from South and Central America, Mexico, Australia, and much of Asia. Many, including the famed tiger prawns from Taiwan, are raised by aquaculture methods.

Rock shrimp are harvested in the South Atlantic and Gulf of Mexico. They have hard shells that are somewhat difficult to peel, but their meat is firm and sweet. There's also a small local fishery for tasty ridgeback, or Santa Barbara, shrimp, a rock shrimp caught along the California coast from Monterey south and sold fresh in local markets from October to May.

Freshwater shrimp, also called Malaysian prawns, inhabit coastal lakes and river deltas in southern Asia; they're also farmed in some other areas. These shrimp grow to 1 pound or more, but sizes from 4 to 10 per pound are typical. Oriental markets often sell them whole.

Freshwater shrimp are more perishable than other shrimp, and their supple flesh shrinks more in cooking.

Warm-water shrimp sold in the United States have their heads removed at sea. On shore, processors wash and sort them according to the number of tails in a pound, the "count." Larger shrimp generally cost more, but they don't necessarily taste better than smaller ones.

Cold-water shrimp. These shrimp, from northern waters, have firmer meat and sweeter, more delicate flavor than warm-water shrimp. The two most important species are almost identical, and both are very small—sometimes as small as 500 to a pound. *Ocean pink shrimp* range in Pacific waters from California to the Pacific Northwest. *Northern pink shrimp* are harvested in Alaskan waters and in the Atlantic from Maine to Scandinavia.

Most cold-water shrimp are cooked, machine-peeled, and sold as shrimp meat or salad shrimp; a few are sold whole and cooked. In general, larger ones are better, since peeling machines tend to damage them less.

Some large, choice cold-water shrimp are also found in Pacific waters. They include the *spot shrimp* (found from California to Alaska) and the *sidestripe* and *coonstripe shrimp* of the Pacific Northwest and Alaska. They're caught in limited amounts, usually in pots; much of the catch is sold fresh locally. Often, these shrimp have roe, which is delicious sucked off the cooked tail before it's shelled.

■ **Size and forms.** Warm-water shrimp are sold by the unpeeled tail count per pound. Sizes range from fewer than 10 to more than 70 per pound. Shrimp under 30 per pound are considered large; 30 to 50 count are medium-size. The headed shrimp (often called tails) are also sold peeled; peeled and deveined (with the sand vein removed); or cooked, peeled, and deveined. About 2 pounds unpeeled shrimp yield 1 pound of meat.

Almost all these shrimp are frozen at the processing stage, though they're usually sold thawed.

Cooked and peeled small cold-water shrimp are sold by the pound; they're frozen at the processing stage and are usually sold thawed. Large cold-water species, such as spot shrimp, are sold by count and are often available fresh.

■ **Availability.** Most species are sold year-round.

■ **Taste and texture.** All shrimp have mild, sweet flavor and a moderately firm texture. Cold-water varieties tend to be firmer, sweeter, and more delicate in flavor than warm-water shrimp.

■ **Preparation.** Remove the shells before or after cooking; shelled shrimp absorb more flavor from cooking juices, but shells add flavor if you plan to use the juices. To shell, remove the legs and peel off the shell, leaving the tail on, if you wish.

The sand veins of cold-water shrimp don't need to be removed (they come out with the heads if the shrimp are headed promptly upon landing). Deveining warm-water shrimp is optional; if you want to remove the vein, it's easiest to do it before cooking.

To devein shelled shrimp, use a sharp knife or scissors to cut ¼ inch deep along the back. Rinse out the vein under cool running water; or use a skewer to lift out the vein in several places along the back.

To devein unshelled shrimp, insert a pick or skewer between the shell segments to lift out the vein in several places along the back, as shown at right.

To devein rock shrimp, insert the blade of kitchen scissors in the sand vein opening and cut through the shell along the back from head to tail. Pull the sides of the shell apart to rinse out the sand vein. Remove the shell, if desired.

To butterfly shelled shrimp, split the shrimp along the vein, cutting almost all the way through until the shrimp lies flat.

■ **Cooking methods.** Shrimp cook very quickly and toughen if overcooked. To test, cut a shrimp in half; the flesh turns from translucent to opaque when cooked. Purchased cooked shrimp should be served as is or added to hot dishes only in the last few minutes to heat through.

Barbecuing and broiling. Barbecue over direct heat as directed for Fish and Shellfish Kebabs or broil shrimp kebabs with dry heat. Use any of the suggested bastes or marinades. (See pages 86–88.)

Frying. You can deep-fry shrimp, using Japanese Tempura or Lemon Batter, or stir-fry it. (See pages 89–90, 95.)

To pan-fry shrimp, have ready ¾ to 1 pound medium-size to large **shrimp** (thawed, if frozen); peel and devein as directed at left under "Preparation," if desired. Rinse and pat dry.

Place a 10- to 12-inch frying pan over medium heat until a drop of water sizzles and dances in pan. Add 1 tablespoon **butter,** margarine, or olive oil and swirl to coat. Add shrimp and, if desired, 1 large clove **garlic,** minced or pressed. Cook shrimp, stirring, until opaque when cut (4 to 8 minutes, depending on size). Makes 3 or 4 servings.

Simmering. To simmer shrimp, thaw, if frozen; devein as directed under "Preparation," if desired. Shell either before or after cooking.

For up to 2 pounds medium-size to large **shrimp,** pour enough **water** into a pan to generously cover shrimp. Add 2 teaspoons **salt,** if desired, for each quart water; bring to a boil over high heat.

Add shrimp; reduce heat, cover, and simmer until shrimp are opaque when cut (for large shrimp, 4 to 5 minutes if shelled, 5 to 6 minutes if unshelled; for medium-size shrimp, 3 to 4 minutes if shelled, 4 to 5 minutes if unshelled).

Remove shrimp immediately and immerse briefly in cold water. Allow ¼ to ⅓ pound shrimp per serving.

■ **Suggested recipes.** Temaki Sushi (page 55), Shrimp or Scallops and Pesto (page 91), Scallops & Shrimp in Béarnaise Cream (page 97), Spiced Shrimp Appetizer (page 101), Thai Seafood Firepot (page 105), San Francisco-style Cioppino (page 105), Chile, Shrimp & Corn Salad (page 108), Mexican-style Squid Salad (page 110), Seafood Linguine (page 119), Seafood Brochettes with Champagne Sauce (page 119), Shrimp with Green Onions (page 120), Orange Risotto with Shrimp (page 120).

■ **Serving ideas.** Heap cold simmered shrimp on a bed of shredded lettuce and accompany with Remoulade Sauce (page 123). Or mix lightly with diced avocado and Tarragon Vinaigrette Dressing (page 107).

For a quick casserole, combine shrimp with bite-size pieces of cooked fish, top with Mornay Sauce (page 124) and buttered crumbs, and broil until golden brown.

Warm tiny, cooked cold-water shrimp in butter to serve as a sauce over pan-fried fish fillets; add a squeeze of lemon or lime.

To devein unshelled shrimp, insert a pick or skewer between shell segments and lift out vein. Repeat in several places if necessary.

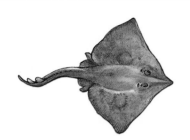

Skate

A rising star on the American seafood scene, skate is a member of the ray family and a cousin of the shark. This unusual-shaped fish has a broad, flat body, triangular "wings" (the edible part), and a whiplike tail. Found in temperate waters worldwide, it's harvested in the United States along both the Atlantic and Pacific Coast.

Skate is more perishable than some fish, so use it as soon as possible after purchase. It does freeze well; use it within 4 months.

■ **Size and forms.** Skate ranges from several inches to several feet across, but most market skate is under 10 pounds. The edible wings from East Coast species average 1½ pounds; wings from some Pacific species weigh more than 10 pounds.

Each wing yields 2 fillets divided by cartilage; there are no bones. Both whole wings (skinned or unskinned) and skinless fillets are sold, either fresh or frozen.

■ **Availability.** Most of the catch is incidental, so skate is found in markets intermittently year-round; peak season in New England is September to April.

■ **Taste and texture.** When cooked, the deeply ridged fillets are tender and somewhat gelatinous. The meat is lean and ranges in color from cream to deep red. The taste is sweet and delicate.

■ **Preparation.** If you buy unskinned whole wings, remove the skin before cooking. Poach in gently boiling water to cover until the skin loosens (about 2 minutes); cool quickly under cool running water and scrape off the skin. Skinned wings can be cooked whole or cut into fillets. Some connoisseurs believe the flavor is enhanced by cooking skate with the cartilage intact, especially if it's to be served cold.

To fillet, start at the thick side of the wing and run a sharp knife between the flesh and cartilage; repeat on the other

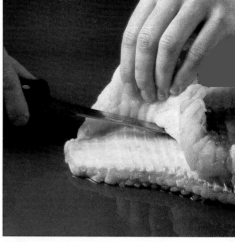

To fillet skate, run a knife between flesh and cartilage, starting at thick end of wing. Repeat on other side.

side (see above right). Lift off the fillets and discard the cartilage. Divide the fillets into serving-size pieces.

■ **Cooking methods.** Check doneness at the thickest part; the meat should no longer look translucent. To eat skate with the cartilage attached, anchor the fish with a fork and scrape off the cooked meat.

Baking. Bake filleted or unfilleted skate in Piquant Vegetable Sauce; or oven-brown. (See pages 82–85.)

Broiling. Broil filleted or unfilleted skate, using the dry-heat method and basting with Lemon-Butter Baste; or broil with a crumb coating. (See pages 87–89.)

Frying. Pan-fry filleted or unfilleted skate, using flour or a light crumb coating. (See pages 90–92.)

Poaching and steaming. Filleted or unfilleted skate can be pan-poached or poached the classic way. (See pages 92–94.)

■ **Suggested recipes.** Mackerel with Tart Onion Sauce (page 112), Pan-fried Skate with Cucumbers & Capers (page 117).

■ **Serving ideas.** Serve hot skate with Caper Butter or another browned butter sauce (page 92), or with Mornay or Tomato-Caper Sauce (page 124). Skate is also good cold in a salad with Dijon Vinaigrette Dressing (page 124).

Whole skate wing is easy to identify by its unique shape and ridged appearance. This wing has been skinned; it's ready to cook whole or filleted.

Smelt

These small, silvery fish, highly esteemed in Europe, are underutilized by American cooks. Of the nine species in North America, two are harvested commercially in volume: rainbow smelt and eulachon. Others of minor importance include capelin in the Pacific and North Atlantic and longfin, night, whitebait, and surf (silver) smelt on the Pacific Coast.

Other smeltlike fish include silversides and grunion.

Most smelt enter fresh water to spawn, but others spawn on sandy beaches or in shallow estuaries.

Rainbow smelt. As is typical of most smelt, rainbow enters fresh water in the spring to spawn. But there are also land-locked populations in Canada and the Great Lakes; most commercially harvested smelt are now caught on the Canadian side of Lake Erie. Maine also has a small harvest of rainbow smelt. Almost all the production is frozen.

Surf or silver smelt taken commercially in Puget Sound is similar to rainbow smelt.

Eulachon. Also called candlefish or Columbia River smelt, eulachon ranges from Northern California to the Bering Sea, but almost the entire commercial production is taken in the Columbia River and its tributaries. All is sold fresh; quality varies according to how it's harvested and handled. Because of its high oil content, freshness is the key to quality.

■ **Size and forms.** Rainbow smelt averages 6 inches in length and is sold headed, cleaned, and frozen, mostly in 1-pound bags. (Although soft fleshed, smelt freezes well.) Eulachon varies from 3 to 8 inches in length and is sold fresh and whole.

■ **Availability.** Fresh eulachon is sold in winter, beginning in December and usually peaking in February or March. Frozen smelt is sold year-round.

■ **Taste and texture.** Eulachon has tender, soft flesh; the flesh of other smelt is firmer. Smelt has a delicate flavor and a cucumberlike odor.

■ **Preparation.** Some people like to eat the whole smelt—head, bones, and all. If you prefer, cut or twist off the head, slit open the belly, and remove the innards.

If you're planning to cook smelt whole, most species are easy to debone. First pinch the fish gently but firmly along the length of the backbone and stomach; then twist the head below the gills and pull to lift out the skeleton and entrails. Or open up the belly cavity and lift out the head, bones, and tail in one piece.

■ **Cooking methods.** The all-time favorite way to cook smelt is to fry it in shallow fat, but other methods also work.

Baking. Try oven-browning smelt. (See page 85.)

Barbecuing and broiling. Barbecue smelt over direct heat; support the fish on perforated foil or in a hinged broiler. Broil with dry heat. Use Lemon-Butter Baste or Italian-style Marinade. (See pages 86–89.)

Frying. You can deep-fry smelt, using Japanese Tempura Batter. (See pages 89–90.)

To fry smelt in shallow fat, rinse 1 pound **smelt** well and pat dry with paper towels. Dip or shake fish in about ½ cup **all-purpose flour** to coat lightly; shake off excess.

Heat ¼ to ½ inch **salad oil** in a 10- to 12-inch frying pan over medium-high heat. When oil is hot, add fish, a few at a time, and cook, turning, until golden brown and crisp on both sides (2 to 3 minutes total). Drain on paper towels and keep warm until all are cooked. Makes 2 or 3 servings.

■ **Suggested recipes.** Mackerel with Tart Onion Sauce (page 112).

■ **Serving ideas.** Offer fried smelt with a browned butter sauce (page 92), with Tartar Sauce (page 123), with Tomato-Caper Sauce (page 124), or simply with orange or lemon wedges to squeeze over. To complement fried smelt, serve Jicama Salad (page 111).

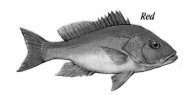

Red

Snapper

Genuine red snapper is both beautiful to look at and delicious tasting, and demand always exceeds supply. True red snapper is found from North Carolina to the Gulf of Mexico, but most is landed in Florida. Fish weighing between 2 and 4 pounds have metallic pink skin; larger fish are redder.

Actually, much of what's sold as *red snapper* today is some other species of snapper. Of several other Florida and Caribbean snappers, the *mutton snapper* and the *silk snapper* most closely resemble red snapper in appearance and edibility. Other snappers from those waters include the *yellowtail, vermilion,* and *gray.*

Throughout the world, approximately 250 species of tropical reef fish are called snapper. Hawaii harvests about 14 different snapper species. They include *ta'ape* (also called blue-lined snapper), a golden pan-size fish with handsome blue horizontal stripes; a pink snapper called *opakapaka;* a red snapper called *onaga;* and a gray snapper called *uku.*

Other snappers are imported from Indonesia, Thailand, the Philippines, Central and South America, and Mexico; they're often sold as frozen fillets.

The fish commonly sold as Pacific red snapper in California is not a snapper at all but rather a rockfish (page 51). For New Zealand snapper, see Sea bream, page 58.

■ **Size and forms.** Red snapper grows to 35 pounds, but 4- to 6-pound fish are most common. Most market fish from Florida and Caribbean waters weigh less than 5 pounds. Hawaii's ta'ape runs from ½ to 1 pound; other Hawaiian snappers range from 3 to 10 pounds.

True red snapper is always sold in a form that allows buyers to identify it: either as cleaned whole fish or as skin-on fillets. Fillets from other species with reddish skin are sometimes sold skin-on, but most are sold skinned.

■ **Availability.** True red snapper is scarce and expensive, but it is sold year-round; heaviest landings in Florida are in summer.

■ **Taste and texture.** The flesh of snapper is tender-firm, moist, and lean (about 1.3 percent fat), with mild but distinctive, sweet flavor.

■ **Preparation.** Trim off the spiny fins of whole fish before scaling them; fillet as for round fish. For techniques, see pages 79–80.

■ **Cooking methods.** Their appearance and size make snappers ideal for baking with a stuffing or poaching whole.

Baking. Bake fillets or whole fish in Piquant Vegetable Sauce, or bake whole fish stuffed with Almond-Rice or Toasted Bread Cube Stuffing. Fillets can be oven-browned or baked with a creamy topping. (See pages 82–86.)

Barbecuing and broiling. Though smoke doesn't actually enhance their flavor, fillets can be barbecued over direct heat, supported on perforated foil; use Lemon-Butter Baste or another mild baste. Broil fillets with moist heat or a crumb coating. (See pages 86–89.)

Frying. Pan-fry fillets or whole Hawaiian ta'ape, using flour or a light crumb coating. (See pages 90–92.)

Poaching and steaming. Fillets and pan-size whole fish can be pan-poached, steeped, or steamed Chinese-style. Larger fish can be pan-poached, poached the classic way, or foil-steamed. (See pages 92–95.)

■ **Suggested recipes.** Fish Fillets with Dill and Tangerine (page 91), Rockfish Florentine (page 96), Bourride (page 102), Veracruz Fish Salad (page 107), Orange Roughy Maître d'Hôtel (page 112), Mr. Zhu's Steamed Fish (page 114), Pine Cone Fish (page 115).

■ **Serving ideas.** A browned butter sauce (page 92), especially one with nuts, is a good accompaniment, as are Citrus Beurre Blanc and Diable Butter (page 125). Serve snapper cold in salads with Homemade Mayonnaise (page 123) or Dijon Vinaigrette Dressing (page 124).

Snook

Found in tropical waters from southern Florida and the Gulf of Mexico to Central and South America, snook is no longer fished commercially in the United States. However, some is imported from Mexico and Latin American countries, where it's called *ro'balo*.

Snook can grow to 50 pounds, but fish that weigh between 2 and 6 pounds are best—flavor is distinctively mild and sweet, and the flesh is firm and moist, like that of mahi mahi (page 41) and red and black Atlantic groupers (page 57). Use snook as you would those fish. For best flavor, remove the skin from fillets, as it can impart an off-flavor to the meat.

Sole *see Flounder, page 32*

Spot *see Croaker, page 31*

Squid

Sometimes called: Calamari

Squid is a mollusk, but instead of an external shell, it has a thin, transparent interior cuttlebone, or quill. The head (with eyes) has legs and tentacles attached. A tube-shaped section, sometimes called the mantle, contains a quill and ink sac (ink is discharged when a predator nears). Formerly underutilized in this country, squid is now earning its deserved respect in the culinary world.

Three species of squid are caught for food along North American coastlines—*California* (or Monterey) from the Pacific (mostly caught in California) and *longfin* (or winter) and *shortfin* (or summer) from the Atlantic. About 75 percent of the catch is Monterey squid. Longfin has a thinner body wall and tends to be slightly larger than the other two, but all three can be used interchangeably.

Giant squid (averaging about 5 lbs.) is imported from Mexico and Argentina and generally sold as frozen thick steaks that have already been tenderized; these are sometimes called grande calamari steaks.

■ **Size and forms.** Squid is sold fresh or frozen whole, as cleaned tubes (mantles only), tubes and tentacles, or in rings (sliced tubes). The cleaned tubes range from 3 to 12 inches in length. Giant squid is sold as tenderized steaks.

■ **Availability.** Squid is available year-round, both fresh and frozen. The Atlantic species are caught in largest numbers in spring and early summer; the best are those caught in traps. Squid freezes extremely well—properly cleaned and frozen squid is often superior to fresh because freezing breaks down some of squid's fiber. It can even be thawed and refrozen without affecting its quality.

To clean squid, gently pull tube and head apart; pull out and discard long, clear quill. Scoop out and discard material in tube.

Cut in front of eyes to sever tentacles; discard eyes and attached material. Squeeze tentacles near cut end to pop out hard, dark beak.

With your fingers, pull off and discard thin speckled membrane covering tube. Rinse and drain tubes; they're now ready to cut or stuff.

■ **Taste and texture.** Squid's mildly sweet taste is often compared to abalone. The lean flesh, if cooked properly, is firm and tender.

■ **Preparation.** Whole squid needs to be cleaned before cooking. If a recipe calls for whole tubes or rings, gently pull to separate the tube from the head and pull out and discard the long, clear quill inside the tube (shown above). With your fingers or a spoon, scoop out and discard the interior of the tube. Rinse well.

With a sharp knife, cut in front of the eyes to sever the tentacles; discard the eyes and attached material. Squeeze the tentacles near the cut end to pop out the hard, dark beak; discard it, rinsing and reserving the tentacles. With your fingers, pull off and discard the thin speckled membrane covering the tube.

Rinse and drain the tubes. For rings, cut the tube crosswise into desired widths.

To make cleaning easier when you're preparing squid steaks or strips, slip a knife inside the tube and slit it lengthwise. Finish cleaning as for whole tubes; for strips, cut crosswise in desired width.

If you're planning to pan-fry steaks, you'll need to tenderize them first to keep them from curling up in the pan. Cut and clean the tubes as directed at left. Place, membrane side up (outside), on a board; if wider than 4 inches, cut in half lengthwise. Make ¾-inch-deep cuts at about 1-inch intervals all around the edges.

With a metal tenderizing mallet, pound gently until paper-thin, starting in the center and working all the way out and over edge (be careful not to tear the meat). Or use a single-edge razor blade or sharp knife to score the membrane side at about ½-inch intervals, making a crosshatch pattern; cut all the way through the tough outer surface, but take care not to cut through the meat.

■ **Cooking methods.** The secret to tender squid is to cook it quickly; overcooking makes it tough and rubbery.

Baking. To oven-brown, clean 1 pound **squid tubes** as directed under "Preparation"; slit lengthwise and open flat. Prepare a half recipe of **crumb coating** as directed at right for frying. Brush one side of each squid piece with **olive oil** or salad oil and coat with crumb mixture, pressing in well. Roll up, crumb side out, and fasten with a wooden pick.

Arrange squid about 1 inch apart in a greased baking pan. Bake, uncovered, in a 450° oven until browned (about 10 to 12 minutes). Transfer to a serving platter. Makes about 4 servings.

Frying. You can deep-fry or stir-fry squid. (See pages 89–90, 95.)

To pan-fry, tenderize 1 pound cleaned **squid tubes** as directed under "Preparation."

For crumb coating, combine on wax paper 1 cup **fine dry French bread crumbs** or seasoned bread crumbs, 1½ tablespoons **grated Parmesan cheese,** and, if desired, 1 tablespoon finely chopped **parsley.**

In a shallow bowl, beat 1 **egg** with 2 tablespoons **milk** until blended. Dip each tube into egg mixture, drain briefly, and dredge in crumb mixture; shake off excess. Arrange in a single layer on wax paper.

Pour enough **olive oil** or salad oil into a wide frying pan to cover bottom. Place over medium-high heat. When oil is hot, add squid, without crowding, and cook, turning once, until browned on both sides (about 1 minute total). Remove from pan, drain on paper towels, and keep warm.

Continue until all are cooked, adding oil as needed. Makes about 4 servings.

Poaching. Cut whole tubes into ½-inch rings. For 1 to 1½ pounds **squid rings,** bring about 1½ inches **water** to a boil in a 4- to 5-quart pan. Add rings and, if desired, **tentacles.** Reduce heat, cover, and simmer for 30 seconds. Drain and cool quickly under cool running water. Use in salads or appetizers. Makes 4 to 6 servings.

■ **Suggested recipes.** Mexican-style Squid Salad (page 110), Mushroom-stuffed Calamari (page 122).

■ **Serving ideas.** Offer squid with Tartar Sauce (page 123) or Cocktail Sauce (page 124). Deep-fried whole squid tubes, slit and opened flat to cook, make a hearty San Francisco-style sandwich on a toasted, split French roll with Tartar Sauce and lemon wedges.

Sturgeon

This prehistoric survivor of the ice age is the largest freshwater fish in the world (a 1,500-pounder was caught in the Snake River in 1928). Sturgeon was once abundant in North America, but of the seven native species, only two— white and green—survive in sufficient quantities to support commercial fishing. The reason for sturgeon's extreme vulnerability is its valuable roe—the source of caviar.

Sturgeon was fished almost to extinction in the late 1800s. Though still not plentiful, it has slowly come back, and production is increasing. And there is

good news on the aquaculture front: small farmed white sturgeon from Northern California is now available in some markets, and prospects for increased production are good.

Wild sturgeon sometimes migrates to the sea, but these fish are usually found in the big rivers and estuaries that empty into the Pacific. It's illegal to fish sturgeon commercially in California, so most market sturgeon comes from the Columbia River system. Like shark, sturgeon has no bones, only cartilage.

White sturgeon is the larger and finer eating of the two kinds. Only fish between 4 and 6 feet long are legal, a size limitation that protects egg-bearing females. These slow-growing fish may be 19 years old before spawning. Only a tiny amount of the roe is harvested (page 19). It's possible to produce farmed sturgeon weighing 8 to 10 pounds in 2 years.

The smaller *green sturgeon* tends to inhabit brackish waters of river mouths. Green sturgeon meat is generally, but not always, stronger tasting than white. Some is substituted for white in markets, but most is smoked; smoked sturgeon is on a par with smoked salmon.

The flesh of green sturgeon is usually red or yellow-orange; the white species has lighter-colored flesh.

■ **Size and forms.** Wild sturgeon ranges from 15 to 80 pounds; farmed fish in markets runs about 10 pounds. Sturgeon is sold fresh (as thick boneless chunks, steaks, or fillets) or smoked.

■ **Availability.** Though some is taken as an incidental catch throughout the year, sturgeon is most plentiful in late summer and fall.

■ **Taste and texture.** The flesh is firm and meaty, almost like veal. It's moderately oily, with mild but distinctive flavor.

■ **Preparation.** No preparation necessary.

■ **Cooking methods.** Sturgeon is good smoked (page 84), barbecued, or stir-fried. Don't overcook it—the meat easily becomes dry.

Baking. Bake in Piquant Vegetable Sauce, or bake pieces with a creamy topping. (See pages 82–86.)

Barbecuing and broiling. Barbecue sturgeon over direct heat, placing pieces directly on a greased grill, or use for kebabs. Broil with dry or moist heat. Use any of the suggested bastes or marinades for barbecuing or dry-heat broiling. (See pages 86–89.)

Frying. Fillets or thin slices can be pan-fried; they brown well without any coating, or you can dust them with flour. The pieces hold their shapes well when stir-fried. (See pages 90–92, 95.)

Poaching and steaming. Fillets or steaks can be pan-poached, poached the classic way, or foil-steamed. (See pages 92–94.)

■ **Suggested recipes.** Burmese Fish with Sweet Onions (page 96), Salmon Salad with Tarragon Vinaigrette (page 107), Thai Fish & Watercress Salad (page 108), Five-Spice Fish (page 111), Grilled Salmon on Wilted Chicory Salad (page 113), Grilled Tuna with Teriyaki Fruit Sauce (page 117), Swordfish Steaks with Mushrooms (page 117), Skewered Fish, Northwest Style (page 118).

■ **Serving ideas.** For a French touch, pan-poach (page 92) steaks or chunks, using champagne or another sparkling wine in place of broth and wine; melt an additional 1 to 2 tablespoons butter into the reduced poaching liquid to thicken.

Aïoli (page 123), Tomato-Caper Sauce (page 124), and Citrus Beurre Blanc (page 125) are all complementary to sturgeon.

Surimi:
Shellfish
Look-Alikes

They look like the real thing— pink, perfectly arched shrimp; snow-white shreds of crabmeat tinged with red; meaty scallops. But a closer inspection reveals that they're actually imitations: surimi-base products that offer an economical, year-round alternative to real shellfish.

Introduced in the late 1970s, these "seafood analogs," as they're known in the trade, are based on an age-old Japanese method of food preservation. Lean, white-fleshed fish—most commonly Alaskan pollock—is minced and rinsed repeatedly in cool water until a tasteless, odorless, gelatinous paste called surimi is formed. This is then stabilized with sugar and sorbitol to keep moisture in.

The Japanese have enjoyed small cakes of surimi, called *kamaboko,* for years. Recently, fluctuating market conditions for fresh seafood have taken surimi a step further: combined with starch, egg white, and artificial and/or natural flavors and colors, then pressed through an extruder, it forms shellfish clones that look and taste very much like the real thing. These are then cooked and frozen.

All surimi-base products are required by U.S. law to be labeled "imitation," so there should be no confusion when purchasing them. Their reasonable price tags—most surimi products cost less than fresh shellfish—are another clue that this is not true shellfish.

Look for surimi in freezer cases alongside other fish products; thawed surimi is often sold with fresh fish.

Surimi products have a longer shelf life than real shellfish. Purchased frozen, they can be kept in the freezer for months. If bought thawed, most imitation seafood lasts for up to 5 days in the refrigerator. Check for stale, sour odors before using; surimi products do not develop strong fish odors.

Quality and flavor vary, so if you don't like the first brand you try, sample another. Surimi products have a sweeter taste than natural shellfish, and some are a bit saltier.

Read the package carefully; many manufacturers are now using some real shrimp or crabmeat in their surimi products. Though this may be good news in terms of flavor, it's bad news for people who have chosen imitation shellfish because they cannot eat the real thing.

Surimi products are available both unbreaded and breaded. The unbreaded type can simply be thawed (if frozen) and used cold in salads, sandwiches, or other cold dishes. To use it in cooked dishes, add it to the pan in the last minutes of cooking, leaving just enough time for it to heat through (it toughens if overcooked). Or quickly sauté or broil unbreaded surimi and serve with any sauce you would normally choose for shellfish.

To prepare breaded surimi, pour salad oil into a pan to a depth of 1½ inches and heat to 375°F on a deep-frying thermometer. Add surimi, a few pieces at a time, and cook until breading is golden brown. Serve with your favorite dipping or cocktail sauce.

Choose one or more surimi shapes to use in the mild seafood curry below.

Seafood in Curry Cream

- ¼ cup butter or margarine
- 1 medium-size onion, thinly sliced
- 1 tablespoon *each* curry powder and all-purpose flour
- 1 teaspoon *each* ground cumin, ground coriander, and minced fresh ginger
- 1 clove garlic, minced or pressed
- 1 cup sour cream
- ½ cup *each* plain yogurt and regular-strength chicken broth
- 1 *each* medium-size green and red bell pepper (or 2 of one color), seeded and chopped
- 1 pound (about 2¾ cups) unbreaded surimi, cut into bite-size pieces
- 1 large tomato, halved, seeded, and cut into ½-inch pieces
  About 4 cups hot cooked rice
- ¼ cup thinly sliced green onion tops

In a 10- to 12-inch frying pan, melt butter over medium heat. Add onion and cook, stirring occasionally, until soft (about 10 minutes). Reduce heat to low; add curry, flour, cumin, coriander, ginger, and garlic. Cook, stirring, for 2 to 3 minutes. Add sour cream, yogurt, and broth; mix well. Stir in bell peppers. Simmer, uncovered, until peppers are slightly softened but still tender-crisp (6 to 8 minutes).

Add surimi and simmer, covered, until hot (about 5 minutes). Stir in tomato. Serve over rice and garnish with green onion tops. Makes 4 servings.

Per serving: 622 calories, 26 g protein, 70 g carbohydrates, 26 g total fat, 92 mg cholesterol, 462 mg sodium

Imitation seafood, known as surimi, closely resembles the real thing. Available forms include lobster tails, breaded and unbreaded scallops and shrimp, and crab.

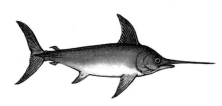

Swordfish

There's only one species of swordfish, but this powerful swimmer roams the tropical and temperate seas of the world. Swordfish is taken in U.S waters off the California and New England coasts in summer and fall, and in the Gulf of Mexico and off Florida's east coast in winter.

In addition, more and more swordfish (both fresh and frozen) is now being imported, especially from Japan, Latin America, Taiwan, and Spain.

Flesh color varies from pink to beige, but it all turns the same light color when cooked. Quality depends largely on how the fish are caught and handled; it's important that they be cleaned, bled, and iced immediately. Fish caught domestically tend to be more consistently high in quality than imported fish, and they're usually more expensive.

Because of their large size, whole fish are difficult to freeze properly. Loins and chunks are successfully frozen, and some high-quality frozen-at-sea swordfish is available.

■ **Size and forms.** Most commercially-caught swordfish range from 50 to 200 pounds, but occasionally, 1,000-pounders are landed. Swordfish has few bones. The meat is sold in chunks or boneless loins, which are cut into steaks in markets. Domestically-caught fish are usually sold fresh.

■ **Availability.** Year-round.

■ **Taste and texture.** The firm, meat-like flesh has mild but distinctively rich flavor; it's moderately oily (about 4 percent fat).

■ **Preparation.** No preparation necessary.

■ **Cooking methods.** Swordfish is the classic choice to skewer for fish kebabs. The meatlike steaks are excellent barbecued, broiled, or baked. They're also good smoked (page 84).

Baking. Bake in Piquant Vegetable Sauce or with a creamy topping. (See pages 82–86.)

Barbecuing and broiling. Barbecue steaks or kebabs over direct heat. Broil steaks or kebabs with dry heat. Use Lemon-Butter Baste or Italian-style or Basil-Parmesan Marinade. Steaks are also good broiled with moist heat. (See pages 86–89.)

Frying. Pan-fry steaks; they brown well without any coating. You can also stir-fry swordfish. (See pages 90–92, 95.)

Poaching and steaming. Steaks or chunks can be pan-poached, poached the classic way, foil-steamed, or steamed Chinese-style. (See pages 92–95.)

■ **Suggested recipes.** Burmese Fish with Sweet Onions (page 96), Thai Fish & Watercress Salad (page 108), Five-Spice Fish (page 111), Grilled Salmon on Wilted Chicory Salad (page 113), Grilled Tuna with Teriyaki Fruit Sauce (page 117), Swordfish Steaks with Mushrooms (page 117), Skewered Fish, Northwest Style (page 118).

■ **Serving ideas.** The rich flavor of swordfish stands up to sauces with pronounced flavor, such as Tomato-Caper Sauce (page 124) or Basil Garlic or Diable Butter (page 125). The meat is good cold in a salad with a dressing; try Basil Vinaigrette Dressing (page 109), Creamy Horseradish Sauce (page 123), or Aïoli (page 123).

Tautog

Sometimes called: Blackfish, Cape blackfish

The first appearance of tautog in the shallow coastal waters of New England is a harbinger of spring. This stout-bodied fish spends the winter in deeper water in an inactive state. It's found from spring to fall in rocky-bottom areas from Nova Scotia to South Carolina but is most common from Cape Cod to Delaware Bay.

■ **Size and forms.** Tautog can grow to 25 pounds, but average size is about 3 pounds. It's usually sold whole or as skin-on fillets.

■ **Availability.** Tautog is available from spring into fall, mostly in the Northeast.

■ **Taste and texture.** Tautog's lean flesh is extra-firm and keeps its shape well when cooked. The flavor is mild but distinctive.

■ **Preparation.** The skin is tough and best removed before or after cooking. Fillet or cut into steaks as for round fish; remove skin from fillets. For techniques, see pages 80–81.

To skin a whole fish before cooking, freeze it just until the skin stiffens; then remove the skin with a sharp knife.

■ **Cooking methods.** Because it holds its shape so well, tautog is a favorite for stews and chowders; it's also good stir-fried.

Baking. Bake fillets, steaks, or whole fish in Piquant Vegetable Sauce, or bake whole fish with any of the suggested stuffings. Fillets or steaks can be oven-browned or baked with a creamy topping. (See pages 82–86.)

Barbecuing and broiling. Fillets or steaks can be barbecued on a greased grill over direct heat. Barbecue whole fish using indirect heat. Use any of the suggested bastes or marinades. Broil fillets or steaks with moist heat or with a crumb coating. (See pages 86–89.)

Frying. Deep-fry fillets, using British Beer or Lemon Batter. To pan-fry, coat with flour or a crumb coating. Use also for stir-frying. (See pages 89–92, 95.)

Poaching and steaming. Fillets can be pan-poached, steeped, or steamed Chinese-style. Whole fish can be poached the classic way or foil-steamed. (See pages 92–95.)

■ **Suggested recipes.** Fish Fillets with Dill and Tangerine (page 91), Burmese Fish with Sweet Onions (page 96), Seviche with Kiwi Fruit (page 100), Faux Salmon Terrine (page 101), Quick Colorful Chowder (page 102), Fish Pot-au-Feu (page 103), Fish Pil-Pil in Red Sauce (page 104), Veracruz Fish Salad (page 107), Thai Fish & Watercress Salad (page 108), Fish Fillets with Sherry-Mushroom Sauce (page 111), Orange Roughy Maître d'Hôtel (page 112), Grilled Salmon on Wilted Chicory Salad (page 113), Grilled Tuna with Teriyaki Fruit Sauce (page 117).

■ **Serving ideas.** Present pan-fried or pan-poached tautog fillets with small red thin-skinned potatoes, steamed baby carrots, and hot melted butter seasoned with grated lemon peel and ground white pepper to drizzle over all.

Serve hot cooked tautog with a browned butter sauce (page 92), Citrus Beurre Blanc (page 125), or Diable Butter (page 125). Offer Homemade Mayonnaise or Radish Tartar Sauce (page 123) with cold fish.

Tilapia

Native to Africa, this little fish can thrive just about anywhere, in either fresh or salt water. It's been farmed since ancient times in the Middle East. Tilapia breeds

fast and can easily be interbred to produce new hybrids to suit specific environments or market needs.

Today, various tilapia hybrids are cultured in many areas of the world, including the United States. The future promises increasing supplies in American markets.

Quality depends on the water in which tilapia grows. Fed on fish meal and grain and raised in clean water, it tastes delicious; but a fish harvested in dirty water tastes like the water.

In the past, tilapia hasn't had a good reputation and has often been passed off as "sunshine bass," "sunfish," or some kind of snapper. However, top-quality farmed tilapia is available today; buy it from a reliable market and you won't be disappointed.

■ **Size and forms.** Most tilapia is in the 1- to 1½-pound range, but some hybrids grow to 5 pounds or more. Their skin color ranges from black to brilliant red. Tilapia is sold whole, both cleaned and uncleaned, as fresh or frozen fillets, and sometimes live. Fillets are usually small and thin (2 to 5 oz.)

■ **Availability.** Year-round.

■ **Taste and texture.** The cooked meat has moist, tender flakes. The flavor is mild and sweet, but can be slightly earthy. Tilapia is quite lean (about 2.3 percent fat).

■ **Preparation.** Whole fish may need scaling and cleaning; fillet as for round fish. For techniques, see pages 79–80.

■ **Cooking methods.** These mild-flavored fish are best baked, fried, or poached.

Baking. Bake whole fish with Piquant Vegetable Sauce or stuffed with any of the suggested stuffings. Oven-brown fillets. (See pages 82–85.)

Barbecuing and broiling. Small fish can be placed on a well-greased grill and barbecued over direct heat; use Lemon-Butter or Sesame-Soy Baste. Broil fillets with moist heat or a crumb coating. (See pages 86–89.)

Frying. To deep-fry fillets, dip them first in British Beer or Lemon Batter. Pan-fry fillets or small fish, using flour or a crumb coating. (See pages 89–92.)

Poaching and steaming. Fillets and whole fish can be pan-poached, poached the classic way, steeped, foil-steamed, or steamed Chinese-style. (See pages 92–95.)

■ **Suggested recipes.** Fish Fillets with Dill and Tangerine (page 91), Rockfish Florentine (page 96), Fish & Chard Pie (page 99), Faux Salmon Terrine (page 101), Bourride (page 102), Quick Colorful Chowder (page 102), Fish Pil-Pil in Red Sauce (page 104), Veracruz Fish Salad (page 107), Orange Roughy Maître d'Hôtel (page 112), Baked Fish & Ratatouille (page 112), Calico Stuffed Trout (page 114), Mr. Zhu's Steamed Fish (page 114).

■ **Serving suggestions.** Accompany this mild-flavored fish with a sauce, such as one of the browned butters on page 92, Watercress Cream (page 94), Tartar Sauce (page 123), or Basil Garlic or Diable Butter (page 125).

Tilefish

Of the two species of tilefish harvested in the United States, *golden tilefish* is by far the more important. This colorful, heavy-bodied fish is found from Nova Scotia to the Gulf of Mexico.

Fish that dwell in deep offshore canyons on the edge of the continental shelf are considered superior to those caught in shallower waters; a diet of red crabs gives the deep-water fish firmer texture and sweeter taste.

Slightly smaller and softer-fleshed *gray tilefish,* also called blackline tilefish, is caught along with golden tilefish off the coast of Florida. Increasing amounts of imported tilefish are now beginning to appear in U.S. markets:

golden and gray tilefish from Mexico and an excellent-tasting, black-spotted silvery tilefish from Argentina.

■ **Size and forms.** Tilefish grows to 80 pounds, but most is in the 4- to 15-pound range; fish over 8 pounds are considered large, have firmer flesh, and are the choicest.

Tilefish is sold whole and cleaned, with the head on, or as fillets. Golden tilefish fillets are usually sold with the skin on (look for yellow spots on the skin); gray tilefish fillets are marketed skinless. Most domestic fish is sold fresh; imported fish comes both fresh and frozen.

■ **Availability.** Tilefish is available all year, but demand usually exceeds the supply. The harvest of domestic golden tilefish peaks in the spring.

■ **Taste and texture.** Tilefish's light-colored meat turns white when cooked; it's lean (about 2.3 percent fat), tender-firm, and moist, with a mild, nutlike flavor.

■ **Preparation.** Scale whole fish and fillet as for round fish—a row of pin-bones extends at a right angle all along the backbone, so fillets will not be boneless. Skin fillets, if desired. For techniques, see pages 79–81.

■ **Cooking methods.** Tilefish holds its shape well in soups and stews.

Baking. Bake fillets or thick chunks in Piquant Vegetable Sauce. Fillets may also be oven-browned or baked with a creamy topping. (See pages 82–86.)

Barbecuing and broiling. Fillets can be barbecued over direct heat; place on perforated foil. Use Lemon-Butter Baste or Italian-style or Basil-Parmesan Mari-nade. Broil with moist heat or with a crumb coating. (See pages 86–89.)

Frying. Deep-fry fillets, using Japanese Tempura or Lemon Batter. Pan-fry with flour, a light crumb coating, or Golden Egg Wash. (See pages 89–92.)

Poaching and steaming. Fillets can be pan-poached, steeped, or steamed Chinese-style. Fillets or whole fish can be poached the classic way or foil-steamed. (See pages 92–95.)

■ **Suggested recipes.** Gravlax Plus (page 47), Maki Sushi (page 54), Temaki Sushi (page 55), Fish Fillets with Dill and Tangerine (page 91), Fish & Chard Pie (page 99), Quenelles with Creamy Shallot Sauce (page 100), Seviche with Kiwi Fruit (page 100), Quick Colorful Chowder (page 102), Fish Pot-au-Feu (page 103), Fish Pil-Pil in Red Sauce (page 104), Veracruz Fish Salad (page 107), Seviche Salad (page 108), Fish Fillets with Sherry-Mushroom Sauce (page 111), Orange Roughy Maître d'Hôtel (page 112), Mr. Zhu's Steamed Fish (page 114).

■ **Serving ideas.** Accompany cooked tilefish with buttery or creamy sauces, such as a browned butter sauce (page 92), Hollandaise (page 124), or Citrus Beurre Blanc (page 125). Tilefish is good cold in salads with Tarragon Vinaigrette Dressing (page 107), Dijon Vinaigrette Dressing (page 124), or Homemade Mayonnaise (page 123).

Rainbow

Trout

The numerous species of trout are all freshwater members of the extended salmon family; however, trout can also be raised in salt water. Just as baby salmon is used like trout, so can large trout be used like salmon.

A favorite of anglers, rainbow trout is the most universally cultivated fish. In the United States, only farm-raised rainbows can be sold. Other market species include steelhead trout, Arctic char, and lake trout.

Rainbow trout. Native to western North America, this species has been transplanted all over the world. Wild trout and trout raised in earthen ponds usually have a red band that runs the length of their body, which accounts for their name; they also have pale orange to deep red flesh.

Most farmed trout, raised in concrete raceways in fresh water, are olive green with black speckles; their flesh is white. Market fish are usually harvested under 2 pounds; cleaned fish range between 8 and 10 ounces.

Saltwater rainbows, imported from Norway and Finland, can grow to 10 pounds or more; these fish are usually sold as salmon-trout.

Steelhead trout. This oceangoing rainbow trout has adopted the anadromous life-style of salmon. Steelhead, like Atlantic salmon, can spawn more than once. It has pink flesh and looks and tastes much like Atlantic salmon.

Steelhead is usually considered a sportfish, but a few are taken commercially by Indians in Washington State. Steelhead is also farmed now and sold young, about the size of rainbow trout or baby salmon.

Arctic char. This circumpolar fish, closely related to brook trout and lake trout, is found in scattered populations throughout the Northern Hemisphere. Most wild chars are oceangoing fish that spawn in fresh water, much like salmon, but there are also some landlocked and nonmigratory char.

Wild fish grow to 25 pounds, but market size ranges from 4 to 10 pounds. In general, the larger the fish and the redder its flesh, the higher the quality.

The supply of char is limited; most is imported from Canada. But char can also be farmed successfully in either fresh or salt water, and char farming is now underway in Canada, Scandinavia, and the United States. Farmed fish will be sold at sizes comparable to rainbow trout.

Lake trout. Also called togue (in the eastern United States) or gray trout (in Canada), the lake is the largest char in North America; it can grow to 100 pounds, though market size is 1½ to 10 pounds. Lake trout is found in deep, clear lakes from Maine to Vancouver Island and Alaska. Most of the commercial catch is taken in the Great Lakes.

The meat ranges in color from white to red and is usually oilier than that of other trout, though its fat content varies widely from area to area. The larger the fish, the higher its fat content.

■ **Size and forms.** Market fish range from 1½ to 10 pounds; see individual species descriptions above. Pan-size fish 6 to 9 inches long are sold whole and cleaned; some are also boned and butterflied. Larger fish may be whole and cleaned or cut into fillets or steaks.

Trout is sold fresh, frozen, or smoked.

■ **Availability.** Farmed fish and lake trout are available the year around; wild Arctic char and steelhead are available fresh in summer.

■ **Taste and texture.** In general, trout has tender, flaky flesh and mild flavor; the oil content varies widely from about 3.5 percent to more than 20 percent for some lake trout. The oiliest fish have the richest taste.

■ **Preparation.** Trout has thin skin and minute scales, so scaling or skinning is not necessary. Fish 12 to 14 inches long can be filleted as for round fish; fish 4 pounds or larger can be filleted or cut into steaks. For techniques, see page 80.

Trout has a simple bone structure, and small fish are easily boned through the belly; you'll need fairly sharp kitchen scissors and a small, sharp-pointed knife. Use the scissors to snip out the belly (pelvic) fins from a cleaned fish. Then cut through the flesh on both sides of the dorsal and anal fins and pull them out (shown at right). Cut close to the collarbones to remove the head.

Open the belly cavity and, from the inside, cut through the fine rib bones on both sides of the backbone. With a knife, scrape away the meat on both

To bone uncooked trout, snip off belly fins with scissors. With a sharp knife, slice flesh along both sides of dorsal and anal fins and pull them out.

Open belly cavity of trout and, using scissors, cut through fine rib bones on both sides of backbone almost to tail, extending opening if necessary.

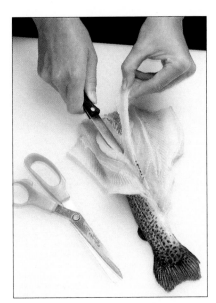

Using a small sharp knife, carefully scrape meat away from backbone on both sides to free it. Sever backbone at tail end.

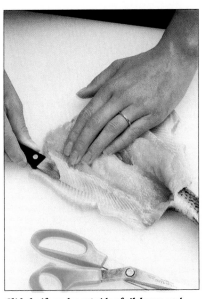

Slide knife under cut side of rib bones and gently lift them off. Run your fingers over flesh to be sure all bones are removed.

sides under the backbone as you pull it free. Snip it off at the tail end. Slide the knife under the cut ends of the rib bones and gently pull them away. Rinse the fish and pat dry.

To cook butterflied, simply spread the sides apart.

■ **Cooking methods.** Size determines the most appropriate ways to cook trout. Small fish (6 to 9 inches long) are ideal for pan-frying. Fish 12 to 14 inches long can be baked or poached whole or filleted. Trout over about 4 pounds— whole, fillets, or steaks—can be cooked as for salmon (page 53). All trout species are delicious smoked (page 84).

For best flavor, cook whole fish with the head and tail on.

Baking. Steaks, fillets, or whole fish can be baked in Piquant Vegetable Sauce. Cleaned bone-in or boned trout can be baked with Almond-Rice, Almond–Wild Rice, or Spinach-Mushroom Stuffing. Oven-brown small fish, steaks, or fillets. (See pages 82–85.)

Barbecuing and broiling. Barbecue small fish, steaks, or fillets over direct heat, placing steaks or fillets on perforated foil and whole fish directly on a well-greased grill. Barbecue fish weighing more than 2 pounds with indirect heat. Broil small fish, steaks, fillets, or boned and butterflied small fish with dry heat. Use Lemon-Butter or Sesame-Soy Baste or Italian-style or Ginger-Soy Marinade when barbecuing or broiling.

You can also broil steaks or fillets with a crumb coating. (See pages 86–89.)

Frying. Pan-fry small fish, steaks, or fillets using flour or a crumb or cornmeal coating. (See pages 90–92.)

Poaching and steaming. Small fish, steaks, or fillets can be pan-poached, steeped, or steamed Chinese-style. Small or large trout can be poached the classic way or foil-steamed. (See pages 92–95.)

■ **Suggested recipes.** Gravlax Plus (page 47), Steamed Trout with Lettuce & Peas (page 96), Salmon Salad with Tarragon Vinaigrette (page 107; use whole fish), Orange Roughy Maître d'Hôtel (page 112; use lake trout fillets), Grilled Salmon on Wilted Chicory Salad (page 113; use whole fish), Baby Salmon with Sautéed Leeks (page 113), Trout with Leeks & Vinegar (page 114), Calico Stuffed Trout (page 114), Mr. Zhu's Steamed Fish (page 114).

■ **Serving ideas.** Browned butter sauces (page 92) are good with trout. Keep seasonings mild so as not to mask trout's delicate flavor. Poached trout is good cold in a salad with Homemade Mayonnaise (page 123) or Dijon Vinaigrette Dressing (page 124).

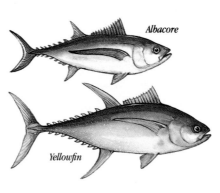

Albacore

Yellowfin

Tuna

The world's biggest consumers of tuna are the Japanese, who usually eat tuna raw, and Americans, who still eat most of their tuna from a can. But with more and more fresh and frozen tuna available in U.S. markets, tastes are changing.

These large members of the mackerel family roam the world's seas. Of the 13 species of tuna, four are important in the marketplace: albacore, bluefin, yellowfin, and bigeye. Of less importance is the small bonito, which can't legally be sold as tuna because it's of lesser quality.

Tuna varies widely in quality, depending on how it's caught and handled. When fish struggle hard after they're hooked, quality diminishes. It's important that tuna be bled properly and refrigerated quickly after landing.

In markets, two grades are sold. The best is called sashimi grade, suitable to be eaten raw; the second is called grill or fry grade, usually from tuna that struggled longer on the line. The grade is critical for fish to be eaten raw, but not for cooked meat.

Tuna that has been mishandled can cause scombroid poisoning (page 13); avoid any that looks brown and opaque.

Albacore. This long-distance swimmer, called tombo in Hawaii, is found in both the Atlantic and Pacific. It's most abundant on the West Coast from early summer through fall. One of the smaller tunas, albacore taken on the West Coast ranges from 10 to 30 pounds; fish taken in Hawaii run larger—up to 50 pounds. The smaller Atlantic albacore fishery is centered in the eastern part of the ocean.

Albacore is the only species that can be labeled "white meat tuna" when canned. Its beige-colored meat turns white when cooked. The meat is quite soft when raw but firms quickly when cooked.

Bluefin. The largest tuna, this nomad circumnavigates the globe. It's harvested off both the East and West coasts of the United States. Though bluefin can grow to 1,500 pounds, most market fish weigh less than 150 pounds. The meat of smaller fish is medium red and can be labeled "light tuna" when canned; larger fish have deeper red meat.

Oil content depends on whether fish are migrating, feeding, or spawning. For sashimi, the oiliest meat is preferred for its mild flavor and lack of fish odor, but the flavor becomes quite strong when cooked. For cooking, leaner bluefin is preferred because it's milder in taste. Bluefin meat can also be soaked overnight in salt water for milder flavor.

The bulk of the catch is canned or used raw, but fresh bluefin is sold on the East Coast during the summer.

Yellowfin. Known as ahi in Hawaii, the yellowfin is the most abundant of the tuna species, ranging throughout the world's tropical and subtropical waters. In the United States, it's caught off California, Hawaii, and Florida.

Most market fish are in the 20- to 100-pound range, though they can reach 400 pounds. The meat of cooked yellowfin is usually lighter than that of bluefin but not as light as albacore; it's less oily than any of the other species. Yellowfin has firm flesh and is good both raw and cooked. The cooked meat tastes flavorful but not strong.

Bigeye. Though not abundant in North American catches, some bigeyes are taken in Hawaii, the Gulf of Mexico, and the Atlantic. They can reach 500 pounds, but average weight is 100 pounds.

Valued second only to bluefin for sashimi, bigeyes are also good cooked.

Bonito. This miniature "tuna" swims in large schools and is taken from Baja to Southern California from late fall to early winter. Most is taken inshore and young, weighing 3 to 12 pounds. The flesh is red and fairly pronounced in flavor. Quite soft before cooking, bonito is easiest to handle if cooked whole or cut into steaks.

■ **Size and forms.** Tuna ranges from 3 to more than 1,000 pounds, depending on the species. Its unique bone structure divides the meat into four long, triangular boneless sections called loins (see below).

The meat from larger tunas is sold as boneless chunks or slices called steaks or fillets. Albacore and bonito are sold whole or cut into loins or steaks.

(Continued on next page)

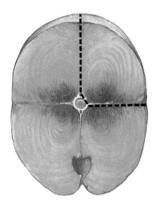

Cross section of albacore shows back, stomach, and lateral bones radiating from central backbone. Cutting along bones (as shown by dotted lines) frees loins.

To cut albacore into loins, cut on an angle from pectoral fin to top of head, slicing down to backbone.

Following line visible on side of fish, cut along lateral bones from head to tail, again slicing to backbone.

Cut through meat at tail end; then, with knife parallel to back bones, cut along side of dorsal fin all the way to lateral bone.

Slide your fingers along cut edges to loosen, gently pulling loin free. Continue cutting along bones to remove remaining loins.

■ **Availability.** Tuna is landed all year, but supplies of fresh tuna are most reliable in summer. Some excellent frozen-at-sea tuna is also available.

■ **Taste and texture.** All tunas have oilier and stronger-tasting dark red streaks of meat running down both sides; when those streaks of meat are removed before cooking, the tuna tastes milder. Tuna meat, especially albacore and bonito, tends to be soft before cooking, but it firms and becomes meaty when cooked.

Fat content varies from 1 percent for yellowfin to nearly 8 percent for some bigeyes.

■ **Preparation.** To cut a small albacore or bonito into steaks, scale and clean it (pages 79–80); then cut it into thick steaks, slicing through the body and using a saw to cut through the large center bone.

Albacore's unique anatomy allows whole fish to be cut into four boneless loins. Work with skin-on whole fish. Scale the fish first unless you plan to skin the loins later.

To cut the fish into loins, follow the bone lines shown in the drawing on page 75, being sure to cut all the way to the backbone.

To remove the first loin, make a deep cut at an angle from the pectoral fin to the top of the head on one side of the fish (shown on page 75). Make another cut along the lateral bones, working from the head to the tail. Then cut along the back bones, starting at the tail end and cutting toward the head. Carefully pull the loin free with your fingers. Turn the fish over and repeat on the other side.

To remove the belly loins, make a cut along the belly side of the lateral bones. Starting below the pectoral fin, make a shallow cut around the belly cavity; then follow the line of meat with your knife, cutting down to the tail (be careful to avoid cutting into the viscera). Free the loin with your hands. Repeat on the other side. Cut away the dark red streaks of meat that run along one edge of the loins, if desired.

To skin, place the loin skin side down and, holding the knife parallel to the skin, cut between the flesh and skin.

For steaks, cut the loin crosswise into 1- to 2-inch-thick slices. For sashimi, cut into ¼-inch-thick slices down to the skin; then slide the knife between the flesh and skin to remove the skin, if not already done.

■ **Cooking methods.** Avoid overcooking tuna, which makes the meat dry and tasteless. At its best barbecued or smoked (page 84), tuna is good cooked by other methods, too.

Baking. Bake steaks (slices) or loins in Piquant Vegetable Sauce. Oven-brown slices. (See pages 82–85.)

Barbecuing and broiling. Barbecue thick steaks or slices over direct heat, placing them directly on a greased grill (if pieces seem soft, hold them together with wooden picks—they'll firm quickly). Barbecue chunks or whole loins with indirect heat. Broil steaks or slices with dry heat. Use any of the suggested bastes or marinades. (See pages 86–88.)

Frying. Pan-fry tuna slices; they brown well without any coating. (See pages 90–92.)

Poaching and steaming. Slices can be pan-poached or steamed Chinese-style. Thick slices, chunks, whole loins, or whole bonito can be poached the classic way or foil-steamed. (See pages 92–95.)

■ **Suggested recipes.** Gravlax Plus (page 47), Maki Sushi (page 54), Temaki Sushi (page 55), Burmese Fish with Sweet Onions (page 96), Thai Fish & Watercress Salad (page 108), Five-Spice Fish (page 111), Mackerel with Tart Onion Sauce (page 112), Grilled Salmon on Wilted Chicory Salad (page 113), Grilled Tuna with Teriyaki Fruit Sauce (page 117), Swordfish Steaks with Mushrooms (page 117), Skewered Fish, Northwest Style (page 118).

■ **Serving ideas.** Tuna is especially good with assertive seasonings or paired with fruit or bacon.

For a colorful accompaniment to marinated, barbecued tuna steaks, stir-fry Chinese pea pods, red bell pepper strips, and fresh corn kernels in a little salad oil; season with a few drops of Oriental sesame oil.

Use cold cooked tuna in salads with Homemade Mayonnaise or Aïoli (page 123).

Turbot see Flounder, page 32; Halibut, page 34

Walleye see Perch, page 49

Weakfish see Seatrout, page 59

Whitefish

Although the word sounds ambiguous and is often used incorrectly for some other fish, whitefish is the correct name for this family of freshwater fish. Though these fish are related to salmon and trout, they're quite different from salmon in appearance and eating qualities. Whitefish inhabits deep-water lakes and rivers from New England to Minnesota and north to the Canadian Arctic, as well as in northern Europe.

Lake whitefish is the most important species in North America, but several species of cisco are also harvested commercially.

Lake whitefish. This fish is taken all year in the Great Lakes and other deep lakes in the northern United States and Canada. In winter, ingenious anglers cut holes through the thick ice and use nets to catch the fish, which are then hauled to the surface by snowmobiles. The best whitefish is taken by trap rather than net, which tends to bruise the fish; check for bruise marks (dark coloration), especially around the belly.

Whitefish has delicious roe, sold as golden whitefish caviar.

Cisco. Several species of cisco are sold by the name chub; they're also called lake herring and, in Canada, tullibee. Smaller and bonier than lake whitefish, most ciscoes are sold smoked, but they're also available fresh near where they're caught. Ciscoes have excellent small, dark roe.

Size and forms. Lake whitefish grows to 20 pounds, but most commercial fish weigh from 1 to 4 pounds. Ciscoes are usually under a pound. Whitefish is sold fresh or frozen as whole fish or fillets; it's also available smoked.

Availability. Whitefish is sold year-round, though fish caught in winter when they're fatter and firmer are generally considered superior to those caught in summer.

Taste and texture. These are oily fish, averaging 6 to 9 percent fat. The snow-white flesh is tender and flaky, the flavor rich and mild, almost sweet.

Preparation. Whole fish should be scaled and cleaned; fillet as for round fish. For techniques, see pages 79–80.

Cooking methods. The size and mild flavor of lake whitefish make it ideal for poaching or baking whole. Because of its high oil content, it's also good broiled, barbecued, or smoked (page 84). Prepare fresh roe as for shad roe (page 60).

Baking. Bake fillets or whole fish in Piquant Vegetable Sauce. Bake whole fish with any of the suggested stuffings. Small fish or fillets can also be oven-browned. (See pages 82–85.)

Barbecuing and broiling. Barbecue fillets or small fish over direct heat, supporting fillets on perforated foil. Barbecue whole fish weighing more than 2 pounds with indirect heat. Broil fillets or small fish with the dry-heat method. Use Lemon-Butter or Sesame-Soy Baste or Basil-Parmesan Marinade for broiling or barbecuing. Fillets can also be broiled with a crumb coating. (See pages 86–89.)

Frying. Pan-fry fillets, using a crumb coating. (See pages 90–92.)

Poaching and steaming. Fillets or small fish can be pan-poached, steeped, or steamed Chinese-style. Larger fish can be poached the classic way or foil-steamed. (See pages 92–95.)

Suggested recipes. Puget Sound Salmon Gefillte Fish Soup (page 103), Salmon Salad with Tarragon Vinaigrette (page 107), Five-Spice Fish (page 111), Braised Sablefish (page 112), Grilled Salmon on Wilted Chicory Salad (page 113).

For small whole fish: Steamed Trout with Lettuce & Peas (page 96), Calico Stuffed Trout (page 114).

Serving ideas. Use cold, poached whitefish like salmon. Keep sauces simple and not too rich to avoid overpowering the delicate flavor of the fish; try Radish Tartar Sauce (page 123) or Tomato-Caper Sauce (page 124). Or serve simply with a squeeze of orange or lemon.

Whiting see Cod, page 26

Wolffish

Sometimes called: Ocean catfish, Sea cat, Loup de mer

A fierce-looking fish with a thick, tapering body, a craggy head, and a mouthful of sharp canine teeth, wolffish is well adapted to feeding on shellfish. Of the several nearly identical species found in northern waters of the Atlantic and Pacific, the Atlantic wolffish is the only one landed in commercial quantities.

It ranges in the North Atlantic as far south as Cape Cod and in Europe from the North Sea west to Iceland; the bulk of the catch is harvested by Iceland, Norway, and Canada. A solitary dweller in the sea, wolffish is almost always taken as an incidental catch with other fish.

Size and forms. Wolffish sometimes reaches a length of 5 feet and a weight of 40 pounds. It's almost always sold as skinless fillets, fresh or frozen.

Availablility. Sold mainly in New England, wolffish is available all year but in limited quantities.

Taste and texture. When cooked, the lean (2.4 percent fat) white flesh has moist, tender-firm flakes; the flavor is very mild.

Preparation. No preparation necessary.

Cooking methods. This versatile fish can be cooked in many ways.

Baking. Fillets are good baked in Piquant Vegetable Sauce, oven-browned, or baked with a creamy topping. (See pages 82–86.)

Barbecuing and broiling. Barbecue over direct heat, supporting fillets on perforated foil; use any of the suggested bastes or marinades. Broil with moist heat or with a crumb coating. (See pages 86–89.)

Frying. Deep-fry, using any of the suggested batters. To pan-fry, coat with flour, crumbs, or Golden Egg Wash. (See pages 89–92.)

Poaching and steaming. Fillets can be pan-poached, poached the classic way, steeped, foil-steamed, or steamed Chinese-style. (See pages 92–95.)

Suggested recipes. Fish Fillets with Dill and Tangerine (page 91), Rockfish Florentine (page 96), Fish & Chard Pie (page 99), Seviche with Kiwi Fruit (page 100), Faux Salmon Terrine (page 101), Quick Colorful Chowder (page 102), Puget Sound Salmon Gefillte Fish Soup (page 103), Fish Pot-au-Feu (page 103), Fish Pil-Pil in Red Sauce (page 104), Veracruz Fish Salad (page 107), Seviche Salad (page 108), Fish Fillets with Sherry-Mushroom Sauce (page 111), Orange Roughy Maître d'Hôtel (page 112), Baked Fish & Ratatouille (page 112), Mr. Zhu's Steamed Fish (page 114).

Serving ideas. Offer wolffish with a browned butter sauce (page 92) or with Aïoli (page 123), Citrus Beurre Blanc, Basil Garlic Butter, or Diable Butter (page 125). Wolffish can also be used in fish stews.

Yellowtail see Jack, page 35

Basic Techniques

From market to table, step-by-step instructions for perfectly prepared seafood, including best—and easiest— cooking methods

Preparation

Most fish today is sold ready to cook as steaks or fillets. Whole fish available in markets is often cleaned and scaled. But if you buy a whole fish that has not been cleaned or scaled, or you catch one yourself, you'll need to know how to prepare it for cooking.

The preparation required depends on the kind of fish and how you intend to cook it. The buying guide beginning on page 15 tells you which of the following steps are needed for each fish. Procedures unique to a particular kind of fish are also described there.

Shellfish preparation varies from species to species; look under the individual listings in the buying guide.

Cleaning Whole Fish

The following section describes preparation techniques if you're dealing with an uncleaned whole fish. Not every step may be necessary; follow the preparation guidelines for the particular fish. The way you plan to cut, cook, and present a fish may change the order of these procedures.

■ **Scaling.** Most fish have scales that should be removed before cooking, unless you plan to fillet and skin the fish or remove the skin after cooking. If your fish hasn't already been cleaned, it's easiest to scale it first. Some fish, such as catfish and eel, have such tough skin that it should be removed altogether (page 21).

Place the fish in the sink under cool running water and grasp the head firmly (hook your thumb inside the gill area, if necessary). With a fish scaler (available in cookware stores), a short serrated knife, or another small, dull knife, scrape off the scales, using short, firm strokes and working from the tail toward the head (shown at right). Rinse well.

■ **Removing the head and tail.** It's generally easiest to remove the head before cleaning the fish. (If you're planning to fillet the fish, however, the job will be easier if you leave the head on.)

With the fish on its side, use a sturdy knife to slice through the flesh just behind the gill covering. If the fish is small, you'll be able to slice through the spine, severing the head. For a large

To remove scales, scrape skin with a serrated fish scaler or knife under cool running water, working from tail toward head.

fish, slice to the spine from both sides. Then, positioning the knife blade between two vertebra, tap the back of the knife with a mallet; or cut through the bone with a small saw. Reserve the head (without gills), if you wish, to use in Fish Stock (page 93).

If you want to remove the tail, simply cut it off.

Trout coated with cornmeal sizzle to golden perfection when pan-fried. This basic cooking method is an easy way to prepare many kinds of fish. A squeeze of lemon and some fresh parsley are all the embellishments you'll need.

■ **Cleaning.** Regardless of how a fish will be cut, it must first be eviscerated, or cleaned—have its internal organs removed. This should be done as soon as possible after the fish is caught, since bacteria in the viscera may cause fish to spoil quickly. Most fish sold in markets has already been cleaned; if not, the market may clean it for you.

To clean a fish yourself, make a shallow cut with a sharp knife or scissors the length of the belly to the vent opening, being careful not to cut into the entrails. Remove the contents of the belly cavity. (If the head is on, slice the belly open from the vent to the chin; lift the gill covering and remove the gills

To cut steaks from a whole fish, use a sharp, heavy knife and firmly cut crosswise through fish.

To fillet a round fish, start by slicing in an arc behind gills from belly flap to top of head; cut down just to backbone.

along with the viscera.) Run a knife down both sides of the backbone inside the fish to remove any remaining material.

You can also eviscerate the fish through the gills; this method preserves the shape better for stuffing or cooking a fish whole. Lift the gill covering, reach inside, and pull gently to remove the accordion-shaped gills and attached viscera.

■ **Bones and fins.** On flatfish, you can trim both edges deeply to get rid of the small fin bones and still retain almost all of the flesh.

On round fish, many of the small bones are attached to fins. Before cooking, you can cut the flesh on both sides of the dorsal and anal fins and simply pull them out, with the bones attached. If you plan to cook and present the fish whole, leave the fins on—they help maintain the fish's shape and are easy to pull out of a cooked fish before serving.

Before cooking a fillet or a steak, run your fingers over the surface to locate small bones; pluck them out with tweezers or pliers.

Then turn knife blade toward tail and slice under flesh, using ribs as a guide; sever fillet at tail to remove.

Cutting Fish

Basic bone structure determines how you can cut a fish. See page 7 for an explanation of the skeletal differences between round fish and flatfish.

■ **Cutting steaks.** Steaks (usually ¾ to 1½ inches thick) can be cut from round fish or from such large flatfish as halibut. Cut down firmly, perpendicular to the spine (shown at left); tap the knife with a mallet to cut through the bone, if necessary, or use a saw.

■ **Filleting round fish.** To do this job cleanly, you'll need a knife with a thin, sharp blade that's flexible enough to ride over the bones as you slice off the flesh above them. Place the cleaned fish on its side on a board. Insert the knife at an angle behind the gills at the belly flap and, continuing in an arc to the top of the head, cut just to the spine (shown above left).

Cleaning and filleting fish is simplified when you invest in the right tools: a large, nonporous board that's easy to clean thoroughly, a serrated fish scaler with an attached gutting blade, and a filleting knife with a long, sharp, flexible blade.

To skin a fillet, slide a knife under flesh about ½ inch from tail, grasp skin firmly, and slice off fillet.

Without lifting the knife, turn the blade so it faces the tail. Keeping the knife parallel to the board and using the ribs as a guide, slice off the fillet (shown on facing page, top right). Sever at the tail end and lift off the fillet; repeat on the other side. Remove any small bones remaining in the fillets with needle-nose pliers.

Filleting flatfish. For large flatfish, such as petrale sole, you can cut two fillets from each side.

Place the fish on a board. Using a knife with a thin, sharp, flexible blade, cut to the bone in an arc behind the head; then score through the flesh along the sides where you can feel the ribs and fin bones meet; also score across the tail end (shown below left). Cut to the backbone in the center of the fish from head to tail. Starting at the head end on one side, insert the knife at an angle behind the head. Using long, smooth strokes, cut the fillet away from the ribs (shown below right).

Repeat to remove the second fillet; then turn the fish over and repeat.

To cut one fillet from each side of a smaller fish, cut in an arc behind the head and score the sides and tail as directed above. Then remove the fillet from each side as described above for a round fish.

Skinning fillets. To skin a fillet, place it, skin side down, on a board. Using a long knife with a stiff blade, cut to the skin about ½ inch above the tail end. Then grasp the end firmly and slide the knife between the flesh and the skin; with one continuous cut, remove the fillet in a single piece (shown above).

To fillet a flatfish, first score through flesh behind head, along sides where ribs and fin bones meet, and across tail.

To remove 2 fillets from a side, score down middle of backbone, insert knife behind head on 1 side, and cut off fillet.

Basic Techniques **81**

Cooking Methods

You need master only a few basic techniques to cook any fish or shellfish well. Using the simple cooking methods described on the following pages, you can prepare a wide range of dishes. Whether you need a hurry-up meal with fish from the freezer or a fine dish you can present to company, you'll find answers here. (For further elaborations on these basic cooking methods, see "A Repertoire of Recipes," pages 99–125.)

Each of the basic cooking techniques explains the types of fish best cooked by that method. Before deciding how to cook any fish, find it on the chart on pages 8–9. This chart groups fish according to their density, flavor, and fat content—the most important factors in determining the best ways to cook fish.

The buying guide beginning on page 15 gives more specific suggestions on how to cook each type of fish. Basic methods of cooking shellfish are also described there.

■ **Judging doneness.** The key to success in cooking fish and shellfish is learning to judge when it's done. Seafood cooks so quickly that it's easily overcooked, losing moisture and flavor in the process. Many recipes recommend cooking fish until the flesh flakes easily when prodded with a fork, but this is usually too long for optimum flavor and juiciness. Another often-used guide is to cook fish 10 minutes for each inch of thickness; but our testing indicates that this, too, may be too long.

As fish cooks, the flesh changes from translucent to opaque. To test, cut a small slit in the center of thicker fillets, steaks, and whole fish; when the flesh looks just slightly translucent or wet inside (shown below), remove the fish from the heat. It will cook a little more from the retained heat.

Pan-fry thin fillets on one side just until the tops look milky white; turn them over and begin removing them from the pan at once. When cooking large fish, you can insert a meat thermometer into the thickest part, parallel to the backbone; cook to an internal temperature of 135° F.

The flesh of crab, crayfish, lobster, scallops, and shrimp turns from translucent to opaque when cooked. Cut into the center of a lobster tail, scallop, or shrimp to test. Remove oysters, clams, and mussels from the heat as soon as the shells open. Shucked oysters are cooked when the edges curl.

Abalone and squid cook too quickly to test by cutting; follow the guidelines in the buying guide.

Cut into thickest part to check doneness of fish; flesh should look just slightly translucent or wet (it will continue to cook a bit).

Baking

Fish cooks more slowly in the oven than by other methods, so timing isn't as critical, and there's less chance of overcooking. In each of our baking methods, moisture is introduced in the form of a sauce, stuffing, or coating; each adds flavor and texture as well as protects the fish from drying out.

There's a good way to bake most types of fish, lean or oily. The buying guide beginning on page 15 suggests which methods are best for each fish.

■ **Fish Baked in Sauce.** This baking method is recommended for whole fish up to about 6 pounds or for fish steaks or fillets at least ¾ inch thick. After baking, spoon the colorful vegetable sauce around the fish on the serving platter. For whole fish over 4 pounds, double the quantity of sauce.

> 1 or 2 fresh or thawed frozen whole fish (2 to 4 lbs. total), scaled and cleaned (pages 79–80); 1½ to 2 pounds fresh or thawed frozen fish steaks or fillets; or 4 to 6 cleaned small fish, such as trout or mackerel
> Piquant Vegetable Sauce (recipe follows)

Rinse fish and pat dry. Remove head and tail from whole fish, if desired. Place fish in a greased baking pan large enough for fish and sauce. Prepare Piquant Vegetable Sauce and spoon over fish.

Bake, uncovered, in a 400° oven until fish looks just slightly translucent or wet inside when cut in thickest part (for whole fish, about 10 minutes for each inch of thickness, measured in thickest part; for fillets and steaks, 15 to 25 minutes).

Transfer fish to a warm platter and spoon sauce around fish. For large fish, use 2 wide spatulas to lift out of pan. Lift off top layer of skin and pull out fins, if desired. To serve, cut to bone and slide a spatula between flesh and ribs to lift off each serving. To serve bottom half, remove backbone (sever from head, if neccessary) and cut down to skin. Makes 4 to 6 servings.

Piquant Vegetable Sauce. Heat 2 tablespoons **butter**, margarine, or olive oil in a wide frying pan over medium heat. Add 1 medium-size **onion**, finely chopped, and 2 large cloves **garlic**, minced or pressed. Cook until soft.

Spoon Piquant Vegetable Sauce over fish and bake for juicy, flavorful results.

Stir in 1 large **carrot,** finely chopped; ¼ cup minced **parsley;** ¾ teaspoon each **dry basil** and **oregano leaves;** 1 teaspoon **sugar;** 1 small **bay leaf;** and ½ cup regular-strength **chicken broth** or Fish Stock (page 93). Bring to a boil; reduce heat, cover, and simmer until carrot is soft (about 10 minutes).

Add 1 can (about 14 oz.) **pear-shaped tomatoes** (break up with a spoon) and their juice, 2 tablespoons **capers,** and 1 tablespoon **red wine vinegar.** Cook, uncovered, over medium heat, stirring often, until most of the liquid has evaporated. Season to taste with **salt** and **pepper.** If made ahead, reheat to simmering before using.

■ **Baked Stuffed Fish.** Whole fish that weigh up to about 6 pounds are good candidates for baking with a stuffing. Use this method also for small fish, such as trout or baby salmon, whole or boned. Most of the whole fish in Groups IIa, IIb, and III (pages 8–9) can be baked this way.

1 **whole fish (3 to 6 lbs.) or 4 to 6 small fish (6 to 8 oz. *each*), scaled and cleaned (pages 79–80)
   Stuffing (recipes follow)**
2 **tablespoons melted butter or margarine
   Parsley sprigs and lemon wedges (optional)**

Rinse fish inside and out; pat dry. Remove head and tail, if desired (fish stay more moist if baked whole). Prepare stuffing of your choice. Lightly pack stuffing into fish cavity; sew opening with heavy thread or close with picks. (Wrap any extra stuffing in foil and bake in pan alongside fish.)

Arrange stuffed fish in a greased baking pan just large enough to hold fish. Brush top with some of the butter. If desired, insert a meat thermometer into thickest part of large fish.

Bake, uncovered, in a 400° oven, basting several times with remaining butter, until just slightly translucent or wet inside when cut in thickest part or until thermometer registers 135°F (about 10 minutes for each inch of thickness, measured in thickest part).

Carefully transfer fish to a warm platter. Lift off top layer of skin and pull out fin bones, if desired. Drizzle any remaining cooking juices from pan over fish. Garnish with parsley and lemon wedges, if desired. To serve, cut to bone and slide a spatula between flesh and ribs to lift off each serving. To serve bottom half, lift and remove backbone (sever from head, if necessary) and cut down to skin. Accompany each serving with some of the stuffing. Makes 4 to 8 servings.

Almond-Rice or Almond–Wild Rice Stuffing. In an 8- to 10-inch frying pan, melt 2 tablespoons **butter** or margarine over medium heat. Add ¾ cup *each* sliced **onion** and **celery** and ½ cup **sliced or slivered almonds.** Cook, stirring, until vegetables are soft (about 5 minutes).

Remove from heat and add ¼ teaspoon **dry thyme leaves,** 2 teaspoons grated **lemon peel,** 3 tablespoons **lemon juice,** and 2 cups cooked **long-grain white rice** (or 1 cup *each* cooked wild rice and long-grain rice). Season to taste with **salt** and **pepper.** Makes about 3 cups.

Spinach-Mushroom Stuffing. Have ready 4 cups chopped **fresh spinach** (about 1 pound), lightly packed, or 2 packages (10 oz. *each*) thawed frozen spinach, with moisture squeezed out. In a wide frying pan, melt 3 tablespoons **butter** or margarine over medium-high heat. Add ⅓ cup thinly sliced **mushrooms** and cook, stirring, until limp (about 2 minutes). Add 1 small **onion,** chopped; 2 teaspoons **dill weed;** a dash of **pepper;** and fresh spinach (if used). Cook until onion is limp and spinach is wilted but still bright green. If using frozen

spinach, add after onion is limp; do not cook. Stir in ⅓ cup **fine dry bread crumbs.** Season to taste with **salt** and **pepper.** Makes about 3 cups.

Toasted Bread Cube Stuffing. Have ready 2 cups **toasted bread cubes** or unseasoned croutons. (To prepare toasted cubes, cut part of a loaf of sourdough or crusty Italian bread into ½-inch cubes to make 2 cups. Spread in a single layer on a baking sheet and bake in a 400° oven, stirring occasionally, until dry and crisp, about 10 minutes.)

In a bowl, combine bread cubes; 2 tablespoons finely chopped **parsley;** ½ cup thinly sliced **green onions,** including some of the tops; 1 medium-size **red or green bell pepper,** seeded and finely chopped; 3 tablespoons **dry white wine** or regular-strength chicken broth; and 3 tablespoons melted **butter** or margarine. Season to taste with **salt** and **pepper.** Makes about 3 cups.

Whole Pacific rockfish filled with Toasted Bread Cube Stuffing makes an elegant main dish. Sew cavity closed with a sturdy needle and thread, or close with picks.

Smoking Fish on the Barbecue

Smoking brined fish is an ancient technique that preserves fish and, in the process, turns it into a delicacy. With just a few hours' time and minimal equipment, you can smoke either fresh-caught or purchased fish at home.

Two steps are involved. The first is to cure the fish (to help prevent spoilage) either by soaking it in a brine or by packing it in a dry cure. With a wet brine, it's easier to control the amount of salt penetration and the moistness of the fish. The dry method is good if you want to cure your own catch right at the fishing site.

Smoking, the second step, can be done in any type of covered barbecue (including commercial smokers). Cooked slowly over low heat that's carefully monitored with an oven thermometer, the fish stays moist and has time to absorb the swirling smoke of the wood chips.

Almost any type of fish can be smoked, but such moderately fat to fatter types as salmon, steelhead, trout, sturgeon, sablefish, tuna, mackerel, bluefish, and lake whitefish retain the moistest texture.

Serve smoked fish warm or at room temperature as an appetizer, an entrée, or a breakfast treat. The flavor is rich, so portions can be modest. For ideas on using smoked fish, see page 116.

■ Preparation and curing. You can use whole fish or 1- to 1½-inch-thick steaks or fillets. Scale and clean whole fish (pages 79–80). Leave small fish, such as trout or mackerel, whole; fillet large fish (page 80), leaving the skin on.

Cure by either the wet brine or the dry pack method. Each mixture makes enough to cure 10 pounds of fish.

Wet brine cure. In a noncorrodible container (such as glass or stainless steel) just large enough to hold fish, combine 3 quarts **cold water**, 1½ cups **salt**, ¾ cup firmly packed **brown sugar**, 1½ cups **granulated sugar**, 1 tablespoon **whole white peppercorns**, 6 **bay leaves**, 1½ teaspoons *each* **whole allspice** and **cloves**, 2 teaspoons **ground ginger**, and 2 cloves **garlic**, peeled and split. Stir until salt and sugar are dissolved.

Add fish, making sure all surfaces are covered (if fish floats, turn skin side up so flesh is submerged). Cover and let stand at room temperature for 2 hours or refrigerate for up to 6 hours.

Dry pack cure. In a large container, mix together 1 cup *each* **rock salt** and firmly packed **brown sugar**, ¾ teaspoon **ground white pepper**, ½ teaspoon *each* **ground allspice** and **ginger**, ½ teaspoon **cracked bay leaf**, and 1 clove **garlic**, minced or pressed.

Arrange pieces of wax paper on a flat surface. Sprinkle about ⅓ of the salt mixture in center of paper and set fish, skin side down, on top. Pat remaining mixture onto flesh. Cover and let stand at room temperature for 2 hours or refrigerate for up to 6 hours.

■ Smoking. Lift fish from wet or dry salt mixture; rinse thoroughly under a slow stream of cold water, gently rubbing flesh, if necessary, to release salt. Place fish, skin side down, on several layers of paper towels. Blot to dry. Let dry, uncovered, at room temperature until flesh feels tacky (about 30 minutes).

Ignite 20 charcoal briquets in a covered barbecue. Meanwhile, soak

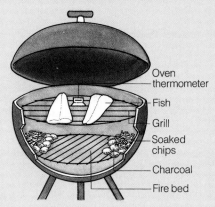

Oven thermometer
Fish
Grill
Soaked chips
Charcoal
Fire bed

4 cups hickory chips in water to cover for at least 20 minutes.

In a small bowl, mix ⅓ cup **maple syrup**, 1½ tablespoons **soy sauce**, and ¼ teaspoon **ground ginger**. Set baste aside.

When coals are completely covered with gray ash (about 30 minutes), arrange as shown below: in a small (about 18-inch) barbecue, push 5 coals to each side; in a medium-size (about 22-inch) barbecue, push 6 coals to each side; and in a large (about 26-inch) barbecue, push 8 coals to each side. Using long-handled tongs, transfer remaining coals to a small metal pan; add 4 to 6 new coals to these so they will ignite for later use.

Grease grill. (For fish fillets, lightly grease skin to prevent sticking.)

Drain wood chips; sprinkle about ½ cup of the chips over each stack of coals in barbecue. Set grill about 6 inches above coals. Position fish (skin side down for fillets) side by side in center of grill so no part of fish extends over coals. Place oven thermometer in center of grill, on top of fish if necessary. Cover grill. If barbecue is vented, adjust to maintain low heat (check manufacturer's directions).

When fish has smoked about 20 minutes, check thermometer; it should read 160° to 180°. If temperature is below 160°, add a hot coal or 2 to each side of barbecue; remove 1 or 2 coals if too hot. Sprinkle each pile of coals with ½ cup more wet hickory chips. Pat surface of fish with a paper towel to keep dry; brush lightly with baste.

About every 20 to 30 minutes, check barbecue. Add coals as needed to maintain temperature between 160° and 180°; add wood chips as needed to produce a steady stream of smoke. Each time you check barbecue, blot fish with a paper towel and brush with baste.

Continue smoke-cooking until fish flakes easily when prodded with a fork in thickest part (about 1 hour for small fish, 2 to 3 hours for 1- to 1½-inch-thick fish steaks or fillets). To remove from grill, loosen edges with a wide spatula and slide gently onto a baking sheet; serve hot or let cool to room temperature. If made ahead, wrap airtight and refrigerate for up to 2 weeks; freeze for up to 6 months.

Insert a thermometer deep into center of thickest part parallel to backbone; when thermometer registers 135°F, remove fish from heat.

Rinse fresh or individually frozen fish and pat dry. Thaw packaged frozen fish at room temperature for 15 minutes or just until soft enough to cut crosswise into 3 or 4 pieces; rinse and pat dry. Prepare Cheese-crumb Coating.

Pour butter into a shallow bowl. Dip fish in butter and then in coating to coat thickly. Place at least an inch apart in a foil-lined shallow rimmed baking pan. Bake, uncovered, in a 425° oven until browned and just slightly translucent or wet inside when cut in thickest part (10 to 20 minutes for fresh fish, 30 to 40 minutes for frozen fish). Transfer to a warm platter. Makes 3 or 4 servings.

Cheese-crumb Coating. Crumble 1 slice **firm-textured bread** into a blender or food processor and whirl to make soft crumbs. On wax paper, mix crumbs with ½ tablespoon **grated Parmesan cheese**, ¼ teaspoon **dry thyme leaves**, and ½ teaspoon **paprika**.

■ Baked Fish with a Creamy Topping.
Fish steaks and fillets baked by this method come out of the oven with a creamy coating that enhances their flavor and keeps them moist. This is a good treatment for lean fish in Groups IIa, III, and IVa (pages 8–9) and makes a wonderful entrée for guests. The topping can be made ahead and added just before baking.

> 1½ to 2 pounds **fish steaks or fillets** (¾ to 1¼ inches thick)
> ¼ cup **lemon juice**
> **Topping** (recipes follow)

Rinse fish and pat dry. Arrange in a single layer in a greased 8- by 12-inch baking pan or dish. Pour lemon juice evenly over fish. Prepare topping of your choice and spoon over fish, covering tops completely.

Bake, uncovered, in a 400° oven until just slightly translucent or wet inside when cut in thickest part (10 to 20 minutes). Using a wide spatula, transfer fish to a warm platter or individual dinner plates. Makes 4 to 6 servings.

Creamy Vegetable Topping. Combine 1 cup *each* finely grated **carrots** and chopped seeded **tomatoes**, ⅓ cup *each* chopped **green onions** (including tops) and **mayonnaise**, ¼ cup **cream cheese** (mash to soften), 2 tablespoons minced **parsley**, and ¼ teaspoon **pepper**. Using a fork, mix until well blended. Season to taste with **salt**.

Sour Cream–Cheddar Topping. Stir together ½ cup *each* **mayonnaise** and

■ Baked Large Whole Fish.
Rinse **large whole fish** inside and out; pat dry. Remove head and tail, if desired. Arrange fish in a greased baking pan (to make fish easier to handle, line bottom side with heavy-duty foil and lay in pan foil side down). If fish is too long to fit, cut in half crosswise and bake halves side by side in pan (or use 2 pans, if necessary).

Melt ¼ cup **butter** or margarine and brush some inside fish cavity; if desired, tuck in some **parsley sprigs** and **lemon slices**. Brush top of fish with more of the butter. If desired, insert a meat thermometer into thickest part.

Bake as directed for Baked Stuffed Fish (page 83), baking without stuffing. If necessary, reassemble cut fish on platter, disguising cut with parsley. Serve with a sauce, if desired.

■ Oven-browned Fish.
A cheese-crumb coating keeps fish moist while it bakes to a crusty brown. This is a good way to bake steaks, fillets, and small whole fish with flaky textures in Groups II and III (pages 8–9). Start with fresh or frozen fish.

> 1 to 1½ pounds fresh or individually frozen **fish steaks or fillets** (½ to 1 inch thick), or packaged frozen fish, or 3 or 4 cleaned small fish, such as **trout**
> **Cheese-crumb Coating** (recipe follows)
> 3 tablespoons **butter** or margarine, melted

Coat fresh or frozen fillets with melted butter and a cheese-crumb mixture for oven-browning.

To lock in moisture and add flavor and richness, bake fillets or steaks with a creamy topping, such as this version with vegetables.

sour cream and 2 teaspoons **all-purpose flour** until smooth. Add 1 tablespoon minced **onion** and ⅛ teaspoon **ground red pepper** (cayenne). When fish is almost done, remove pan from oven and sprinkle ½ cup **shredded Cheddar cheese** over fish; continue to bake just until cheese is melted (about 2 more minutes).

Barbecuing

Fish that are both full flavored and at least moderately oily—fish in Groups IIb, IIc, and IVb (pages 8–9)—benefit the most from barbecuing, because the smoke enhances their flavor. Smoke overpowers lean, delicately flavored fish, such as those in Groups I and IIa. The fish in Groups III and IVa have a strong enough flavor for barbecuing but are not usually enhanced by the smoke.

Shrimp and scallops are easily barbecued when skewered for kebabs. And for delicious appetizers, you can place live oysters, clams, and mussels directly on the hot grill until their shells open.

To help keep them moist while they barbecue, brush fish and shellfish with a basting sauce or with butter or oil. Bastes also add mild flavor. Soaking fish in a marinade before cooking gives it even more flavor; intensity depends on the length of time you let it soak.

Since air temperature and other conditions can affect cooking time, test fish for doneness often to avoid overcooking.

■ **Barbecued Seafood: Direct-heat Method.** Use this method to barbecue fish steaks, fillets, small whole fish, kebabs, and certain kinds of shellfish.

Steaks, Fillets, and Small Whole Fish. Ignite 25 to 30 briquets 30 to 45 minutes before cooking. For a gas or electric grill, follow manufacturer's directions.

Meanwhile, rinse and pat dry 1½ to 2½ pounds **fresh or thawed frozen fish steaks** or fillets (½ to 1½ inches thick) or cleaned small fish, such as trout. Have ready a mixture of 2 tablespoons melted **butter** or margarine and 2 tablespoons **salad oil,** or prepare a baste or marinade (facing page). Soak fish in

marinade (if used) for length of time suggested.

When coals are just covered with grey ash (you can hold your hand near grill for only 2 to 3 seconds), spread them in a solid layer. Place grill 4 to 6 inches above coals and grease grill. Lay firm fish (Groups III and IV) directly on grill. For all other fish, place a sheet of greased foil (just large enough to hold fish pieces without crowding) on grill; with a skewer, poke holes in foil and arrange fish on it. Or enclose fish in a greased hinged broiler.

Cover grill with hood and adjust dampers as directed by manufacturer. Or cover entire grill with foil, crimping pieces together, if necessary, and tucking edges inside rim of barbecue. Cook fish, turning once and brushing often with butter-oil mixture, baste, or reserved marinade, until just slightly translucent or wet inside when cut in thickest part (6 to 8 minutes for fish less than 1 inch thick, 10 to 15 minutes for fish 1 to 1½ inches thick). Transfer to a warm platter. Makes 4 to 8 servings.

Fish or Shellfish Kebabs. Choose fish with firm, dense flesh (Group 1V, pages 8–9) or fish that are nonflaky, such as monkfish, so pieces won't fall off skewers. Or use large scallops (1 to 1½ inches thick) or medium-size to large shrimp.

Prepare barbecue as directed at left. If using wood skewers, soak them in water for 30 minutes. For 1 to 2 pounds **fish** or shellfish, have ready a mixture of 2 tablespoons melted **butter** or margarine and 2 tablespoons **salad oil,** or prepare a baste or marinade (facing page)

Rinse fish, pat dry, and cut into 1-inch cubes. If using scallops, rinse and pat dry. To use shrimp, shell and devein (page 63). Soak fish or shellfish in marinade (if used) for length of time suggested.

When fire is hot, string about 5 pieces fish or shellfish on each skewer (run skewer twice through shrimp, near head and tail ends). If desired, alternate on skewers with **onion,** cut into 1-inch cubes; **green or red bell peppers,** seeded and cut into 1-inch pieces; **cherry tomatoes;** cooked **thin-skinned potatoes** (1 to 2 inches in diameter); or small **zucchini** or other summer squash, cut 1 inch thick.

Place kebabs on greased grill. Cook, turning to brown all sides and brushing often with butter-oil mixture, baste, or reserved marinade, until fish looks just slightly translucent or wet inside when cut (8 to 10 minutes) or until scallops or shrimp look opaque inside (5 to 8 minutes for scallops, 3 to 5 minutes for shrimp). Remove to a warm platter. Makes 3 to 6 servings.

Rich sablefish fillets cook over direct heat on barbecue. Perforated foil supports fish and allows fat to drain off; rosemary-infused Lemon-Butter Baste adds delicate flavor.

For large fish and whole fillets, barbecue by indirect heat. Method allows fish to cook slowly while a foil pan catches drippings.

Bastes

&

Marinades

You can add flavor and moisture to barbecued or broiled fish with a baste or marinade. To determine which of the following choices enhances a particular type of fish, see the buying guide starting on page 15. Each recipe makes enough for 4 to 6 servings.

Lemon-Butter Baste

Melt ¼ cup **butter** or margarine; mix in ¼ cup **lemon juice** and 1 teaspoon **dill weed** or crushed dry rosemary, or omit herbs and add 2 cloves garlic, minced or pressed.

Per tablespoon: 54 calories, 0 g protein, 1 g carbohydrates, 6 g total fat, 16 mg cholesterol, 61 mg sodium

Sesame-Soy Baste

Stir together ⅓ cup **soy sauce;** 3 tablespoons *each* **Oriental sesame oil** and minced **green onions** (including tops); 1 tablespoon *each* **vinegar** and minced **fresh ginger;** 2 teaspoons **sugar;** 2 cloves

garlic, minced or pressed; and a dash of **ground red pepper** (cayenne).

Per tablespoon: 46 calories, 1 g protein, 2 g carbohydrates, 4 g total fat, 0 mg cholesterol, 543 mg sodium

Italian-style Marinade

Stir together 2 tablespoons **olive oil;** ½ cup **white wine vinegar;** 1 clove **garlic,** minced or pressed; ¼ cup chopped **parsley;** and ¼ teaspoon **dry oregano leaves.** Soak fish in marinade for 15 to 30 minutes, turning several times. Lift out fish, reserving marinade to use as a baste.

Per tablespoon: 27 calories, 0 g protein, 1 g carbohydrates, 3 g total fat, 0 mg cholesterol, 1 mg sodium

Ginger-Soy Marinade

Combine 1 teaspoon minced **fresh ginger** or ½ teaspoon ground ginger;

1 clove **garlic,** minced or pressed; 1 tablespoon **sugar;** and ½ teaspoon grated **lemon peel.** Stir in ⅓ cup **soy sauce,** 2 tablespoons **dry sherry** or sake, 2 tablespoons **salad oil,** and 2 teaspoons **lemon juice.** Soak fish in marinade for 10 to 15 minutes, turning several times. Lift out fish, reserving marinade to use as a baste.

Per tablespoon: 36 calories, 1 g protein, 3 g carbohydrates, 3 g total fat, 0 mg cholesterol, 544 mg sodium

Basil-Parmesan Marinade

In a food processor or blender, combine ⅔ cup chopped **fresh basil leaves,** or 2 tablespoons dry basil leaves and ¼ cup chopped parsley; ¼ cup **salad oil;** ⅓ cup **white wine vinegar;** 3 tablespoons **grated Parmesan cheese;** 2 cloves **garlic;** and ⅛ teaspoon **pepper.** Whirl until puréed. Soak fish in marinade for 20 to 30 minutes, turning several times. Lift out fish, reserving marinade to use as a baste.

Per tablespoon: 50 calories, 1 g protein, 1 g carbohydrates, 5 g total fat, 1 mg cholesterol, 24 mg sodium

---

Oysters, Clams, and Mussels. Scrub live medium-size **oysters** with a stiff brush in running cold water; rinse. Rinse hard-shell clams. Pull off beards and scrub mussels, if necessary; rinse.

Prepare barbecue as directed on facing page. When fire is hot, put as many oysters, clams, or mussels on grill as fit in one layer. Cook, turning once, until oyster shells open slightly (about 4 minutes) or clam or mussel shells open wide (about 3 minutes).

To eat, pluck out meat with a fork. If desired, serve with Warm Garlic Butter (page 125) for dipping. Allow about 6 to

8 oysters or 1 pound clams or mussels per serving.

■ **Barbecued Seafood: Indirect-heat Method.** Use this method for whole fillets of large fish, such as salmon, and for chunks and steaks over 1½ inches thick, as well as for large whole fish.

Whole Fillets, Chunks, and Steaks. Ignite about 50 long-burning briquets 40 to 45 minutes before cooking. For a gas or electric grill, follow manufacturer's directions for indirect cooking.

Meanwhile, rinse 1½ to 2½ pounds **fish** and pat dry. Line skin side of a whole fillet with heavy-duty foil; press smoothly to fit. Have ready ¼ cup

melted **butter** or margarine, or prepare a baste (recipes above).

When coals are just covered with grey ash, bank about half the briquets on each side of fire grate; place a metal drip pan in center. Set grill 4 to 6 inches above pan and grease grill.

Lay fillets, foil side down, on grill over drip pan; place chunks or steaks directly on grill above drip pan. Brush with butter or baste. Cover grill with hood and adjust dampers as directed by manufacturer. Or cover entire grill with foil, crimping pieces together, if necessary, and tucking edges inside rim of barbecue.

Cook, turning steaks and chunks once (do not turn fillets) and brushing often with butter or baste, until just slightly translucent or wet inside when cut in thickest part (8 to 10 minutes for each inch of thickness). Remove to a warm platter and cut into serving-size pieces. Makes 4 to 8 servings.

Large Whole Fish. Prepare barbecue as directed for whole fillets. Remove head, if desired, from scaled and cleaned **whole fish** (2 to 8 lbs.). Rinse inside and out; pat dry. Lightly season cavity with **salt** and **pepper** and tuck in slices from 1 **lemon** and 1 small **onion.** If desired, add a few **parsley sprigs.** Fit a doubled piece of heavy-duty foil against one side of fish from head to tail. For each 2 to 4 pounds fish, have ready ¼ cup melted **butter** or margarine, or prepare a baste (recipes on page 87).

When fire is hot, place fish on grill over drip pan; you may want to wad some foil under tail to protect it from heat. Brush with butter or baste. If

Lean fish, such as shark, benefit from moist-heat broiling. For maximum flavor, baste once or twice while fish cooks.

desired, insert a meat thermometer into thickest part of fish. Cover grill as directed above. Cook, brushing often with butter or baste, until just slightly translucent or wet inside when cut in thickest part or until thermometer registers 135°F (8 to 10 minutes for each inch of thickness).

Slide a wide metal spatula carefully under foil-lined fish and ease onto a warm platter (it's easier to have a helper hold platter while you use 2 spatulas to move fish). Lift off top layer of skin and pull out fins, if desired. To serve, cut to bone and slide a spatula between flesh and ribs to lift off each serving. To serve bottom half, lift and remove backbone (sever from head, if necessary) and cut down to skin. Allow ½ to 1 pound whole fish per serving.

Broiling

Like baking and barbecuing, broiling is usually considered a dry-heat method of cooking fish. Its intense dry heat is best reserved for fish with enough natural oil to keep it moist. However, we offer two other methods of broiling that produce delicious results with many lean fish as well.

Our buying guide, which begins on page 15, tells which broiling methods are best for each fish and suggests bastes, marinades, coatings, and sauces that complement individual choices.

■ Broiled Seafood: Dry-heat Method.
Fish that are moderately oily and at least ½ inch thick fare best with dry-heat broiling; included in this category are fish in Groups IIb, IIc, and IVb (pages 8–9). You can use one of the bastes or marinades on page 87 to flavor and moisten them. Kebabs and boned and butterflied trout and baby salmon also broil easily and well with dry heat.

After the fish is broiled, especially if it's basted simply with butter or oil, offer it with a browned butter (page 92) or sauce (pages 123–125).

1½ **to 2½ pounds fish steaks or fillets (½ to 1¼ inches thick) or fish, shrimp, or scallop kebabs; or 4 to 6 cleaned small fish, such as trout, or boned and butterflied trout or baby salmon**
¼ **cup melted butter or margarine, salad oil, or olive oil; or 1 recipe baste or marinade (page 87)**
Salt and pepper (optional)

Place fish in a 12- by 14-inch broiler pan. Adjust oven rack for proper distance from top of fish to heat source: 3 inches for pieces ½ to ¾ inch thick, 4 inches for pieces 1 to 1¼ inches thick. Remove fish from pan and preheat broiler pan.

Rinse fish and pat dry; cut into serving-size pieces. Prepare kebabs as directed on page 86. Soak fish or kebabs in marinade (if used) for length of time suggested. Brush broiler pan rack with oil and place fish, skin-on fillets and butterflied trout skin side down, on hot pan without crowding. Brush tops of fish with butter or baste.

Broil, basting once or twice and turning once, if needed, to lightly brown both sides (don't turn skin-on fillets or butterflied trout), until just slightly translucent or wet inside when cut in thickest part (3 to 6 minutes for pieces ½ to ¾ inch thick, 6 to 10 minutes for pieces 1 to 1¼ inches thick). Transfer fish to a warm platter and, if desired, season to taste with salt and pepper. Makes 4 to 6 servings.

■ Broiled Seafood: Moist-heat Method.
Broil lean fish by this method, which protects them from drying out while cooking; fish in Groups IIa, III, and IV (pages 8–9) are good choices. Use fish fillets, steaks, or small whole fish between ½ and 1¼ inches thick.

1½ **to 2½ pounds lean fish steaks or fillets (½ to 1¼ inches thick) or 4 to 6 cleaned small fish, such as trout**
About 1 cup Fish Stock (page 93), dry white wine, or regular-strength chicken broth
About 2 tablespoons melted butter or margarine
1 **teaspoon dill weed or dry thyme leaves**
Salt and pepper (optional)

Rinse fish and pat dry; cut into serving-size pieces. Arrange fish in a single layer in a greased 11- by 13-inch baking pan that can be used under broiler. Adjust oven rack for proper distance from top of fish to heat source: 3 inches for pieces ½ to ¾ inch thick, 4 inches for pieces 1 to 1¼ inches thick. Remove pan from oven and preheat broiler.

Pour fish stock around fish to a depth of ⅛ inch. Combine butter and dill; brush tops of fish with some of butter mixture. Broil fish, basting once or twice with remaining butter mixture (do not turn), until just slightly translucent or wet inside when cut in thickest part (3 to 6 minutes for fish ½ to ¾ inch thick, 6 to 10 minutes for fish 1 to 1¼ inches thick).

Transfer fish to a warm platter and, if desired, season to taste with salt and pepper. Makes 4 to 6 servings.

■ Broiled Fish or Oysters with Crumb Coating.
This method is good with both lean and oily fish and also with shucked oysters.

> 1 to 2 pounds fish steaks or fillets (½ to 1¼ inches thick) or 16 to 20 ounces shucked oysters
> ¾ cup fine dry French bread crumbs
> 1 tablespoon grated Romano or Parmesan cheese
> 1 small clove garlic, minced or pressed
> ½ tablespoon finely chopped parsley
> ⅛ teaspoon pepper
> ¼ cup melted butter or margarine, olive oil, or salad oil

Place fish in a 12- by 14-inch broiler pan. Adjust oven rack for proper distance from top of fish to heat source: 3 inches for pieces ½ to ¾ inch thick or for oysters, 4 inches for fish 1 to 1¼ inches thick. Remove fish from pan and preheat broiler pan.

Rinse fish and pat dry; or drain oysters and pat dry. Combine bread crumbs, cheese, garlic, parsley, and pepper. Dip each piece of fish in melted butter to coat, drain briefly, and then roll in crumb mixture; shake off excess. Arrange fish on hot broiler pan.

Broil, turning once, until browned and fish is just slightly translucent or wet inside when cut in thickest part (3 to 5 minutes for fish ½ to ¾ inch thick or for oysters, 6 to 10 minutes for fish 1 to 1¼ inches thick). Transfer to a warm platter. Makes 3 to 6 servings.

Deep-frying

Deep-fried fish and shellfish remain among the most popular seafoods. No cooking method other than deep-frying produces quite the same contrast of crisp crust and tender fish. Though preparing fish this way adds calories, careful attention to temperature can

Use tongs to lower batter-coated fish into hot oil for deep-frying. Cook only a few pieces at a time to keep oil hot for even browning.

minimize the amount of oil absorbed by the fish as it cooks.

The best choices for deep-frying are lean, mild-flavored fish that are moderately firm to firm, nonflaky fish, shrimp, and squid. Choose fillets or boneless chunks of fish in Groups IIa, IIb, and III (pages 8–9).

You'll need a deep-fat fryer, a wok, or another deep pan large enough to hold at least 1½ inches of oil (pan shouldn't be more than half full). A deep-frying thermometer will help you maintain the best temperature for frying. A small wire strainer is useful for removing crumbs from the oil so they won't burn. Have on hand tongs or a slotted spoon for dipping fish in batter and another slotted spoon, wire strainer, or tongs for turning and removing pieces from the fat.

Serve the fried fish simply with lemon wedges and a shaker of salt. Or offer Tartar Sauce or any of the other cold sauces on page 123. For fish fried in beer batter, you may want to follow the British tradition of offering malt vinegar to shake over. Japanese tempura has its own dipping sauce.

■ Deep-fried Fish or Shrimp.
To ensure that the fish is evenly cooked and nicely browned without being overcooked, the pieces should be uniform in size and not too large or thick. Use clean, fresh salad oil for frying.

> Tempura Dipping Sauce (for tempura batter only; recipe follows)
> 1 to 2 pounds fish fillets or boneless pieces, or medium-size to large shrimp
> Salad oil
> Frying batter (recipes follow)
> Salt (optional)

Prepare Tempura Dipping Sauce (if used); set aside..

Rinse fish and pat thoroughly dry. Cut ½- to 1-inch-thick fillets into pieces about 1½ by 3 inches; cut thicker fish pieces into 1¼- to 1½-inch cubes; for tempura, cut fish into thin strips about ¼ by 1½ by 3 inches. Shell and devein shrimp (page 63; you may leave shrimp tails on). In a deep pan, heat 1½ to 2 inches oil to 375°F on a deep-frying thermometer (at that temperature, a drop of batter sinks halfway in oil and then quickly rises to surface).

Prepare batter of your choice. Dip fish, a piece at a time, into batter to coat; drain briefly and then slip gently into hot oil (add only 4 or 5 pieces at a time to pan to avoid lowering temperature of oil). Cook, turning occasionally, until golden brown outside and just slightly translucent or wet inside when cut; shrimp should look opaque inside (4 to 5 minutes). Cook pieces dipped in tempura batter until lightly browned (2 to 3 minutes). Remove from oil and drain briefly on paper towels; remove any bits of batter from oil before adding more fish.

Serve immediately or keep warm until all pieces are fried. Season to taste with salt, if desired. Offer dipping sauce for tempura. Makes 3 to 6 servings.

Tempura Dipping Sauce. In a small pan, mix ½ cup **regular-strength chicken broth**, 2 tablespoons **soy sauce**, ⅓ cup **water**, 1 teaspoon **sugar**, and, if desired, ½ teaspoon grated **fresh ginger**. Bring to a boil; remove from heat and let cool to room temperature.

■ Deep-fried Squid.
Clean **whole squid** (page 67), separating tubes (mantles) from heads (with legs). Cut tubes crosswise into ½-inch-wide rings. Rinse pieces and pat thoroughly dry. For 1 to 2 pounds squid, shake pieces in about ½ cup **all-purpose flour** in a plastic bag to coat lightly; shake off excess. Then dip in a mixture of 2 **eggs** lightly beaten with 2 tablespoons **milk;** drain briefly. Dredge pieces in a mixture of ½ cup *each* **fine dry bread crumbs** and **all-**

purpose flour. Let dry on a wire rack for 15 to 30 minutes.

Cook as directed for Deep-fried Fish or Shrimp (page 89), frying squid just until lightly browned (about 30 seconds; do not overcook or squid will become tough). Squid, if not thoroughly dry, may spatter oil when frying; if necessary, loosely cover pan. Drain on paper towels and season to taste with **garlic salt** or salt. One pound squid makes 3 or 4 servings.

■ **Batters.** Any of these batters can be used for deep-frying fish. Shrimp is best coated with Japanese Tempura Batter or Lemon Batter. Each recipe makes enough for up to 2 pounds of fish or shrimp.

British Beer Batter. Combine 1 cup **all-purpose flour,** ½ teaspoon **paprika,** and ⅛ teaspoon **pepper.** Gradually stir in ¾ cup **beer;** beat until smooth.

Japanese Tempura Batter. Just before frying, beat 1 **egg** in a small bowl. Remove half the egg (about 2 tablespoons) and reserve for other uses. To remaining egg in bowl add 1 cup *each* **ice water** and **all-purpose flour;** mix lightly with a fork—batter should still have lumps of flour. To keep cold while frying fish, place bowl inside a larger one half-filled with ice.

Lemon Batter. Combine 1 cup **all-purpose flour,** 1½ teaspoons **baking powder,** and ¼ cup **cornstarch;** mix until well blended. Add 2 tablespoons **lemon juice** and 1 cup **water;** mix until blended.

Pan-frying

You can pan-fry, or sauté, almost any fish fillet, steak, or small whole fish. With slight variations on our basic method, you can pan-fry frozen fish without defrosting it; and for company dinners, you can prebrown fish ahead of time and then finish cooking it in the oven just before serving.

Tiny fish, such as smelt and whitebait, call for a special frying technique—see page 65. Many shellfish are also good candidates for pan-frying; for directions, look under the individual listings beginning on page 15 for abalone, some clams, soft-shell crab, oysters, scallops, shrimp, and squid.

For even browning, make sure the fish or shellfish is dry and use a frying pan that heats evenly. Covering fish with a light dusting of flour or other coating before frying helps keep it dry and aids in browning—especially helpful for fish

that cook very quickly. A coating of seasoned crumbs or cornmeal also adds flavor and texture to mild, soft-fleshed fish. Most thick, firm-fleshed fish brown well without a coating and may even overbrown if coated before frying.

■ **Pan-fried Fresh Fish.** If your pan has a good nonstick surface, you can use the minimum amount of oil called for. To add flavor and richness to fish after it's cooked, use a quickly prepared browned butter or serve with a sauce (pages 123–125).

> 1 to 2 pounds fresh fish steaks, fillets, or cleaned small fish
> Coating (optional; recipes on page 92)
> ½ to 2 tablespoons *each* salad oil and butter or margarine, or 1 to 4 tablespoons salad oil
> Salt and pepper (optional)
> Browned butter sauce (optional; recipes on page 92)

Rinse fish and pat thoroughly dry. Cut fillets into serving-size pieces. If desired, prepare coating of your choice and cover pieces with coating.

Place a 10- to 12-inch frying pan over medium heat. Add oil (starting with minimum amount) and heat until oil ripples when pan is tilted. Add butter (starting with minimum amount) and heat just until melted. Arrange fish, without crowding, in pan (lay fillets, both skinned and skin-on, skin side up).

For pieces less than ½ inch thick, cook until tops look milky white (2 to 4 minutes); turn pieces and immediately begin transferring them from pan onto a warm platter. For pieces ½ to ¾ inch thick, cook on both sides until browned and just slightly translucent or wet inside when cut in thickest part (4 to 8 minutes total). For pieces 1 to 1½ inches thick, cook on both sides until fish is browned and tests done as above (10 to 15 minutes total).

Repeat for any remaining pieces, adding more oil and butter as needed. If desired, season to taste with salt and pepper. Prepare browned butter of your choice, if desired, and pour over fish. Makes 3 to 6 servings.

■ **Pan-fried Frozen Fish.** Rinse individually **frozen steaks** or fillets and pat dry. Or thaw a 1-pound package of frozen fish at room temperature for 15 minutes or just until soft enough to cut crosswise into 3 or 4 pieces; pat dry.

Continued on page 92

Pan-fry thin fillets, such as sole, just until tops are milky white; turn over and then start removing from pan.

Finish pan-fried fish with Almond Browned Butter, quickly prepared in same pan in which fish was cooked.

Parchment

Packets

of Flavor

A brown-tinged paper packet arrives on your plate. When you slash it open, out puffs the steamy aroma of deliciously seasoned seafood, baked to exceptional moistness in its own juices.

Seafood baked in parchment, or *en papillote* as it's called in French, is impressive, delicious, and not difficult to make; the filled packets can be assembled ahead of time. You simply place each serving of fish or shellfish on buttered parchment, top it with an herb or vegetable seasoning mixture, wrap it up, and bake.

Look for parchment in well-stocked supermarkets, specialty food shops, or cookware stores.

Seafood Baked in Parchment

**Seafood and seasonings
(recipes follow)
Cooking parchment
About 3 tablespoons melted butter
or margarine
Salad oil**

Prepare seafood and seasonings of your choice. Set aside.

Cut parchment into 4 pieces, each about 6 inches longer than seafood portion and 4 times as wide as narrow side. About 1 inch from a long edge, brush each piece with about 2 teaspoons of the melted butter, covering an area the same size as a serving of seafood. Center a portion of fish on buttered area; add seasonings as directed.

Fold long edge of parchment closest to filling over seafood; then fold forward so filling is wrapped in parchment. With cut end of parchment down, double-fold each end of packet, pressing lightly to crease and tucking ends under. (At this point, you may cover and refrigerate packets until next day.)

Place packets slightly apart, folded ends down, on large baking sheets; brush lightly with oil. Bake in a 500° oven until fish looks just slightly translucent or wet inside or shellfish is opaque (7 to 10 minutes); cut a tiny slit through parchment into seafood to test.

Immediately transfer to dinner plates. To serve, cut packets open with a sharp knife or scissors just enough to expose contents without letting juices run out. Makes 4 servings.

■ Fish Fillets with Dill and Tangerine.
Mix 3 tablespoons *each* **olive oil, white wine vinegar,** and chopped **green onions** (including tops); 1 teaspoon chopped **fresh dill** or ½ teaspoon dill weed; and 1 teaspoon shredded **tangerine or orange peel.** Set aside.

Cut 1½ pounds **fish fillets** (1 inch thick) from Group IIa, IIb, IIc or III (pages 8–9) into 4 equal pieces. Pull out any bones with pliers or tweezers. For each serving, place 1 piece fish on buttered section of parchment, drizzle with a quarter of the oil mixture, and season to taste with **salt** and **pepper.** Fold and bake as directed.

■ Sole Fillets with Peas and Sesame Oil.
Cut 1½ pounds large **sole fillets** (about ¼ inch thick) lengthwise into 12 strips. Roll each strip from narrow end into a loose coil. For each serving, place 3 sole rolls on buttered section of parchment and spoon about ½ cup **fresh or frozen peas** evenly over fish. Season to taste with **salt** and **pepper.**

In a small bowl, blend ¼ cup *each* **sesame oil** and **lemon juice,** 2 teaspoons grated **orange peel,** and ¼ teaspoon **Dijon mustard;** for each serving, spoon a quarter of the oil mixture over fish and peas. Fold and bake as directed.

■ Shrimp or Scallops and Pesto.
In a food processor or blender, combine ¾ cup lightly packed **fresh basil leaves** (or 2 tablespoons dry basil leaves and ¾ cup lightly packed parsley), ⅓ cup grated **Parmesan cheese,** and 3 tablespoons *each* **olive oil** and **lemon juice;** whirl until well blended. Set aside.

Peel and devein 1½ pounds **large shrimp** (under 30 per lb.); or rinse 1½ pounds scallops and pat dry. Arrange shellfish in 4 equal portions on buttered sections of parchment. Top each portion with a quarter of the basil mixture, 1 thin **lemon slice,** and 1 **Niçoise or ripe olive.** Season to taste with **salt** and **pepper.** Fold and bake as directed.

Salmon baked in parchment with dill and tangerine is exceptionally flavorful. To serve, slash open packets at the table. Accompany with boiled red potatoes and fresh asparagus for a simple, elegant meal.

Dredge fish in **all-purpose flour** to coat both sides, or dip one side at a time first in milk and then in Light Crumb Coating (recipe follows).

Cook as directed for Pan-fried Fresh Fish (page 90), but for pieces less than ½ inch thick, increase heat to medium-high and cook for 5 to 6 minutes; for pieces ½ to ¾ inch thick, cook over medium heat for 6 to 8 minutes; for pieces 1 to 1½ inches thick, cook over medium-low heat for 20 to 25 minutes.

◼ Prebrowned Fish.

Rinse and pat dry **fish steaks** or fillets at least ½ inch thick. Coat pieces with **Golden Egg Wash** (above right). Cook as directed for Pan-fried Fresh Fish (page 90), but increase heat to medium-high and cook fish (any thickness) until golden brown (about 1 minute on each side). Remove fish from pan and arrange, slightly overlapping any thin edges, in a shallow rimmed baking pan. Cover and set aside for up to 1½ hours.

Shortly before serving, uncover and bake in a 375° oven until just slightly translucent or wet inside when cut in thickest part (about 8 minutes for pieces ½ inch thick, about 10 minutes for pieces ¾ to 1 inch thick, about 15 minutes for pieces 1 to 1½ inches thick).

◼ Coatings.

For suggestions on which coating is best for a particular fish, see the buying guide beginning on page 15. Each recipe makes enough to coat up to 2 pounds of fish.

Flour Coating. Dredge fish in ½ cup **all-purpose flour** to coat all over; shake off excess.

Light Crumb Coating. Dip fish, one piece at a time, in ½ cup **milk;** drain briefly and then dredge in ½ cup finely crushed **seasoned croutons** or cracker crumbs, or use a mixture of ¼ cup *each* all-purpose flour and yellow cornmeal. Shake off excess.

Heavy Crumb Coating. Dip fish, one piece at a time, in ½ cup **all-purpose flour** to coat lightly; shake off excess. Then dip in a mixture of 2 **eggs** lightly beaten with 2 tablespoons **milk;** drain briefly. Dredge pieces in 1 cup **crumbs** (choose from finely crushed seasoned croutons, cornmeal, fine dry bread crumbs, cracker crumbs, wheat germ, or a mixture of ⅓ cup fine dry bread crumbs and ⅔ cup finely minced or ground almonds or walnuts). Place fish pieces on a wire rack and refrigerate for 15 to 30 minutes.

Golden Egg Wash. Beat together 2 **eggs,** 1½ tablespoons **grated Parmesan cheese,** and 1 tablespoon minced **parsley;** set aside. Just before frying, dredge fish in ½ cup **all-purpose flour;** shake off excess. Coat pieces in egg mixture.

◼ Quick Browned Butter Sauces.

Drizzle one of the following sauces over cooked fish to add flavor. Each recipe makes enough for up to 2 pounds of fish.

Browned Butter. In an 8- to 10-inch frying pan, heat ¼ cup **butter** or margarine over medium-high heat until it foams and begins to brown. Remove from heat and stir in 2 tablespoons **lemon juice** and, if desired, 1 tablespoon finely chopped **parsley.**

Almond or Filbert Browned Butter. Follow directions for **Browned Butter** (above), adding ¼ cup **sliced or slivered almonds** or coarsely chopped filberts when butter foams; stir until nuts begin to brown. Remove from heat and add **lemon juice.** Omit parsley.

Caper Butter. Follow directions for **Browned Butter** (above), adding 2 tablespoons rinsed and drained **capers** when butter foams. Heat just until capers are hot. Omit lemon juice and parsley.

Poaching, Steaming & Steeping

Fish cooks quickly and gently when it's simmered or steeped in liquid or cooked over steam. Choose the method best suited to the size and type of fish you have. All fish can be cooked by one or another of these moist-heat methods.

Live crab, lobster, or crayfish or uncooked shrimp is easily cooked by either simmering or steaming. Steaming is also the technique most often used to cook live clams, oysters, and mussels. See the individual listings beginning on page 15 for directions.

◼ Pan-poached Fish.

Our short-cut pan-poaching technique is one of the easiest ways to cook fresh or frozen fish steaks, fillets, or small whole fish. The fish steams in a small amount of seasoned liquid inside a covered pan. After

Pan-poaching in a small amount of seasoned liquid is a quick way to produce deliciously cooked fish.

Cooking liquid from pan-poached salmon steaks is reduced to make a succulent glaze.

To poach the classic way, lower fish into liquid in an oval fish poacher straddling 2 burners.

the fish is cooked and removed from the pan, the cooking liquid is reduced to make a succulent sauce.

1 to 2 pounds fresh or individually frozen fish fillets or steaks, packaged frozen fish, or cleaned small fish

1½ tablespoons butter or margarine

3 shallots or 3 green onions (with about 4 inches tops), finely chopped

1 clove garlic, minced or pressed

½ cup regular-strength chicken broth or ¼ cup *each* broth and dry white wine

Rinse fresh fish and pat dry; rinse frozen fish just to remove ice glaze. Set fish aside. In a wide frying pan, melt butter over medium heat. Add shallots and garlic and cook, stirring, until limp (about 3 minutes). Add broth and bring to a boil.

Arrange fish in pan in a single layer or set frozen block of fish in pan. Reduce heat, cover, and simmer until just slightly translucent or wet inside when cut in thickest part (3 to 4 minutes for fresh fish ¼ to ⅓ inch thick, 4 to 6 minutes if frozen; 4 to 6 minutes for fresh fish ½ to ¾ inch thick, 6 to 9 minutes if frozen; 8 to 12 minutes for fresh fish 1 to 1½ inch thick, 13 to 22 minutes if frozen; 15 to 18 minutes for a 1- to 1¼-pound package frozen fish).

With a wide spatula, lift out fish and arrange on a warm platter; cover and keep warm. Boil pan juices (with any liquid that accumulates on platter) over high heat until reduced to desired consistency. Makes 3 to 6 servings.

■ **Classic Poached Fish.** The classic method of poaching fish by immersing it in a flavorful liquid best suits whole fish, steaks or boneless chunks at least ½ inch thick, and rolled sole fillets. Any fish can be poached this way, but steaks and fillets from Groups IIa, IIb, and IIc (pages 8–9) require careful handling to keep them intact.

If you poach large whole fish often, consider purchasing a fish poacher. Long, oval-shaped pans, poachers come in a range of sizes and are equipped with a rack for lowering and raising the fish from the liquid. If you don't have a special pan, you can improvise by using a roasting pan large enough to allow the fish to lie flat (the tail can turn up) and deep enough for the liquid to just cover the fish. In place of a rack, you can use cheesecloth to help lower and raise the fish from the liquid.

Serve hot or cold with a browned butter (facing page), serve hot or cold with a sauce (pages 123–125), or use cold in salads and sandwiches.

Fish steaks or boneless chunks (½ to 1½ inches thick), thin sole fillets, or a whole fish (up to about 8 pounds) Poaching Liquid or Fish Stock (recipes follow)

Rinse fish and pat dry. If using sole, roll and fasten with a pick or tie with string. If pieces are much larger than surface area of your spatula, wrap fish in cheesecloth, folding edges together on top, to make handling easier after cooking.

Prepare enough Poaching Liquid to cover fish in pan. Bring liquid to a boil in poaching pan; you may need to use two burners at once for a large poaching pan. Lower fish into pan. Reduce heat, cover, and simmer very gently until just slightly translucent or wet inside when cut in thickest part; lift out of liquid to test (6 to 10 minutes for each inch of thickness, about 4 minutes for rolled sole fillets).

Lift fish out of pan, gently remove from rack or cheesecloth, and arrange on a warm platter. For whole fish, lift off top layer of skin and pull out fins, if desired. To serve, cut to bone and slide a spatula between flesh and ribs to lift off each serving. To serve bottom, lift

and remove backbone (sever from head, if necessary) and cut down to skin.

Serve hot, or refrigerate to serve cold.

Poaching Liquid (or Court Bouillon). In a large pan, combine 1 medium-size **onion**, sliced; 8 **whole black peppercorns**; 4 **whole allspice**; ½ **lemon**, sliced, or 3 tablespoons white wine vinegar; 1 **bay leaf**; 1 teaspoon **salt**; about ½ cup **dry white wine** (optional); and 2 to 5 quarts **water** (enough to cover fish pieces). For more than 5 quarts water, double amount of seasonings. Cover and simmer for at least 20 minutes. To reuse poaching liquid, refrigerate for up to 2 days; freeze for longer storage.

Fish Stock (or Fish Fumet). Thoroughly rinse 2 to 3 pounds **fish heads** and **carcasses** (do not use fish entrails, gills, or pieces of skin) and break into pieces (you can also use shrimp or crab shells). In a 6- to 8-quart pan, combine trimmings with 1 large **onion**, chopped; 1 **carrot**, sliced; ½ cup chopped **parsley**; 1 **bay leaf**; 1 cup **dry white wine** or 3 tablespoons lemon juice; and 2 quarts

To serve a whole fish, gently peel off top skin and pull out fins; slice down to backbone and lift off portions with a spatula. Remove backbone to serve bottom half.

water. Bring to a boil, skimming off any scum on surface. Reduce heat, cover, and simmer for 45 minutes. Strain and discard fish and seasonings. If made ahead, cover and refrigerate for up to 3 days; for longer storage, freeze for up to 3 months. Makes about 2 quarts.

■ Steeped Fish.
Steeping works best for mild-flavored fish steaks, fillets, and small whole fish. Adapted from a classic Chinese cooking method, steeping involves bringing a large quantity of water to a boil, removing the pan from the heat, and adding the fish. At this low temperature, fish cook very gently and evenly, retaining their natural juices and flavor. Use steeped fish in salads or sandwiches, or serve as suggested below.

> **Watercress Cream or Hot Ginger Sauce (optional; recipes follow)**
> 1 **to 2 pounds fish steaks or fillets (¾ to 1 inch thick) or thin sole fillets, or 2 to 4 cleaned small fish**
> **Seasonings: 2 or 3 slices lemon, fresh ginger, or onion; or 3 or 4 parsley or thyme sprigs**

Prepare Watercress Cream, if desired.

If using sole, roll fillets and fasten with a pick or tie with a cord. Place fish in a pan with a tight-fitting lid and pour in enough water to cover fish 1 to 2 inches; depending on size and shape of fish, you may need a deep frying pan or 5- to 6-quart pan. (Pieces can overlap, but water needs to flow between them.) Lift out fish; add 1 or more of the suggested seasonings to water in pan.

Cover pan and bring water to a rolling boil over high heat. Remove from heat and quickly immerse fish in water. Cover pan and let stand. Do not open lid until you are ready to check for doneness (6 to 8 minutes per inch of thickness). Lift out fish to check; it should look just slightly translucent or wet inside when cut in thickest part. If not done, return to hot water, cover, and let steep slightly longer.

Drain fish. Serve hot with sauce, if desired. Or plunge fish into ice water, drain, cover, and refrigerate; serve with one of the cold sauces on page 123, or use in salads or sandwiches. Makes 3 to 6 servings.

Watercress Cream. In a blender or food processor, combine ½ cup lightly packed **watercress sprigs,** 2 tablespoons coarsely chopped **green onion** (including top), 1 teaspoon **anchovy paste,** 1 tablespoon **lemon juice,** ¼ teaspoon **dry tarragon,** and 2 tablespoons **whipping cream.** Whirl until puréed.

In a separate bowl, beat 6 more tablespoons whipping cream until stiff. Fold into watercress mixture to blend. Cover and refrigerate for up to 1 hour. Pass at the table to spoon over individual servings.

Hot Ginger Sauce. Arrange hot fish on a warm platter. Drizzle with 1 tablespoon **soy sauce** and sprinkle with ¼ cup thinly sliced **green onions** (including some of the tops). Heat 3 tablespoons **salad oil** in a small pan over medium heat. When oil is hot, add 1 large clove **garlic,** minced, and 1½ tablespoons **fresh ginger slivers** (about 1 inch long). Cook, stirring, just until garlic is light golden (about 1 minute). Pour over fish.

■ Foil-steamed Fish.
You can steam fish pieces or any whole fish that fits into your steamer or a large roasting pan. You enclose the fish with its seasonings in foil, and it steams inside the foil wrapper. The result is much like poached fish, but without the fuss. Foil-steaming is also a good way to cook a whole package of frozen fish without having to defrost it first.

Foil-steamed fish is an excellent choice when you want cold cooked fish

Chilean sea bass and aromatic ingredients are enclosed in foil for steaming. Moist results are much like poaching.

for salad or sandwiches. Since no oil or butter is used in the preparation, you'll want to serve the fish with a sauce. Use one of the browned butters on page 92 or a sauce (pages 123–125). Allow ½ to 1 pound cleaned fish or ⅓ to ½ pound fish steaks or fillets per serving.

> **Fresh fish steaks, fillets, or cleaned fish, or 1- to 1½-pound package frozen fish, unthawed**
> **Chopped green onions (including tops), chopped parsley, and bay leaves (optional)**

Rinse fish and pat dry. Place on a sheet of foil large enough to enclose it, with shiny side of foil inside; arrange steaks or fillets to make a compact, evenly thick package. For each pound of fish, sprinkle top and, if using whole fish, cavity with about 1 tablespoon onion, ½ tablespoon parsley, and ½ bay leaf, if desired. Wrap fish in foil, securing at top to keep in juices.

Place on a rack in a steamer over about 1 inch boiling water (to improvise a steamer, place a rack over boiling water in any large pan that can be tightly covered). Or arrange in a baking pan slightly larger than package. If cooking a large whole fish, insert a meat thermometer through foil into thickest part of fish, if you wish.

Cover and steam, or bake in a 425° oven, until just slightly translucent or wet inside when foil is opened and fish is cut in thickest part, or until thermometer in a large fish registers 135°F (12 to 15 minutes for each inch of thickness for fresh fish; 25 to 30 minutes for a 1-pound package frozen fish).

Open foil and drain off any liquid inside; discard seasonings. Transfer fish to a warm platter. If desired, remove fins and lift off skin from top side of whole fish.

■ Chinese-style Steamed Fish.
The Chinese often steam fish on a serving plate placed over boiling water. Use this technique for small quantities of fish— steaks, fillets, or such small whole fish as trout. You can use a wok fitted with a rack and lid, or a bamboo steamer. Or you can improvise a steamer using any covered pan fitted with a rack that will support the plate of fish over about 1 inch of boiling water.

To lift the hot plate from the steamer, use wide-opening tension tongs, available in Oriental hardware stores. Otherwise, use thick potholders. If you're

Wide-opening tongs are handy for removing a plate of fish from a bamboo steamer for Chinese-style cooking.

using a bamboo steamer, you can serve the plate of fish from the steamer rack.

About 1 pound fish steaks or fillets (½ to 1 inch thick) or 2 cleaned small fish (about 8 oz. each)
1 **piece fresh ginger (1 inch long), thinly sliced**
1 **whole green onion (including top)**
1 **teaspoon salad oil or ½ teaspoon Oriental sesame oil**
2 **teaspoons soy sauce**
1 **teaspoon dry sherry**
1 **tablespoon chopped green onion (including top)**

Rinse fish and pat dry. Arrange, slightly overlapping thin edges, on a heatproof 8- to 10-inch rimmed plate at least ½ inch smaller in diameter than steamer. Arrange ginger and whole green onion on fish. Place on a rack in a wok or steamer over 1 inch boiling water. Cover and steam until just slightly translucent or wet inside when cut in thickest part (8 to 10 minutes for each inch of thickness).

Remove plate and pour off any liquid from fish; discard ginger and whole green onion. Combine oil, soy sauce, and sherry; pour over fish. Garnish with chopped green onion. Makes 2 or 3 servings.

Stir-frying

Stir-frying involves rapid stirring and tossing of fish cubes or shellfish over high heat in a wok or large frying pan. Nonflaky fish, such as monkfish, cusk, or ocean pout, or any of the firm-textured fish in Groups III and IV (pages 8–9) can be cooked this way without breaking up. Scallops, shrimp, and squid are good shellfish choices for stir-frying.

You'll need to have everything ready to add to the pan—there's no time to assemble ingredients once the cooking begins. Fish and vegetables should be cut into uniform-size pieces and all the ingredients placed within reach.

■ Stir-fried Fish or Shellfish with Peas. This basic stir-fry recipe can be made with asparagus or broccoli instead of peas.

Cooking Sauce (recipe follows)
2 **teaspoons sesame seeds**
1 **to 1¼ pounds monkfish or other firm-fleshed fish, scallops, medium-size shrimp, or squid**
1 **clove garlic, minced or pressed**
1 **tablespoon minced fresh ginger**
½ **pound edible pea pods or ¾ pound asparagus or broccoli**
2 **tablespoons salad oil**

Prepare Cooking Sauce; set aside.

Toast sesame seeds in a small frying pan over medium-high heat, shaking pan frequently, until golden (about 2 minutes); set aside.

Remove membrane from monkfish (page 42). Rinse fish, pat thoroughly dry, and cut into 1-inch chunks. If using scallops, rinse and pat thoroughly dry. If using shrimp, shell and devein (page 63). To use squid, clean (page 67); then cut tubes (mantles) crosswise into 1-inch strips. In a bowl, combine fish or shellfish, garlic, and ginger; set aside.

Remove ends and strings from peas. If using asparagus, remove tough ends and cut into ½-inch slanting slices. To use broccoli, remove tough ends, peel stems, and cut crosswise into ¼-inch slices; cut flowerets ½ inch thick. Cook vegetable in about 1 quart boiling salted water just until tender (about 1 minute for peas, about 2 minutes for asparagus or broccoli). Cool quickly in ice water, drain, and set aside.

Heat a wok or wide frying pan over high heat. Add 1 tablespoon of the oil. When oil is hot, add half the fish or shellfish mixture; cook, turning and stirring gently with a wide spatula, until fish looks just slightly translucent in center when cut (about 2 minutes) or shellfish looks opaque inside (about 2 minutes for scallops or shrimp, 30 seconds for squid). Slide out and set aside. Add remaining 1 tablespoon oil and cook remaining fish or shellfish; slide out and set aside.

Stir sauce with any accumulated juices from fish, add to pan, and bring to a boil, stirring. Add vegetable and fish or shellfish and stir gently until hot (about 1 minute). Transfer to a warm platter and sprinkle with sesame seeds. Serve immediately. Makes about 4 servings.

Cooking Sauce. Combine ¼ cup regular-strength **chicken or beef broth,** 2 tablespoons *each* **dry sherry** and **soy sauce,** 1 tablespoon *each* **lemon juice** and **Oriental sesame oil,** and 2 teaspoons **cornstarch.**

For an all-purpose stir-fry, quickly cook shellfish or firm fish chunks and combine with blanched snow peas and sauce.

Fish & Shellfish in the Microwave

Microwave cooking, like steaming, brings out the natural flavor of fish and shellfish and produces moist, tender results. You can use your microwave to cook seafood perfectly plain—if you wish, accompany servings with a flavored butter or sauce (pages 123–125) or with a browned butter (page 92). Or try one of the following recipes, using your microwave every step of the way.

Let the chart guide you when cooking seafood in the microwave. If you're using frozen seafood, thaw it completely before microwaving. To judge doneness, follow the guidelines on page 82.

Since microwaved seafood continues to cook after it's removed from the oven, be sure to let it stand for the recommended time before you check doneness. Then, if necessary, continue to microwave in 30-second increments. It's better to undercook delicate seafood and add more cooking time later than to overcook it.

Use heavy-duty plastic wrap to cover chile-seasoned Burmese Fish with Sweet Onions (recipe at right) as it completes cooking in microwave oven.

Rockfish Florentine

- ¾ cup sour cream
- ⅓ cup mayonnaise
- 2 tablespoons *each* all-purpose flour and lemon juice
- ¼ teaspoon dill weed
- 2 bunches spinach (1½ to 2 lbs. *total*), rinsed and stemmed
- 1 pound rockfish fillets (about ½ inch thick) or other skinless fillets from Group IIa (pages 8–9)
  Salt and pepper
  Paprika

Combine sour cream, mayonnaise, flour, lemon juice, and dill weed. Stir with a wire whisk until smoothly blended; set aside.

Place spinach in a 3-quart microwave-safe casserole. Cover and microwave on HIGH (100%) for 4 to 5 minutes, stirring once. Let stand, covered.

Rinse fish and pat dry. Place in a 7- by 11-inch or 10-inch round microwave-safe baking dish, with thickest portions toward outside of dish; season to taste with salt and pepper. Microwave, uncovered, on HIGH (100%) for 3 minutes. Rotate each fillet a half-turn and spread with sour cream mixture. Microwave on HIGH (100%) for 3 more minutes; let stand for 3 minutes.

Meanwhile, drain spinach and arrange on a warm platter. Top with fish; spoon any sauce remaining in baking dish over fish. Sprinkle with paprika. Makes 4 servings.

Per serving: 380 calories, 29 g protein, 12 g carbohydrates, 25 g total fat, 92 mg cholesterol, 333 mg sodium

Pictured at left
Burmese Fish with Sweet Onions

- 2 tablespoons salad oil
- 1 large onion, thinly sliced
- 1 tablespoon minced fresh ginger
- ¼ teaspoon ground turmeric
  About 4 teaspoons seeded, minced fresh hot chile, such as jalapeño
- 1½ tablespoons soy sauce
- 1 teaspoon sugar
- ⅛ teaspoon pepper
- 1½ pounds swordfish steaks (about 1 inch thick) or other steaks from Group III or IV (pages 8–9)

In a 7- by 11-inch or 10-inch round microwave-safe baking dish, stir together oil, onion, ginger, turmeric, and 3 teaspoons of the chile (more, if you like its heat). Microwave, uncovered, on HIGH (100%) for 10 to 12 minutes, stirring every 4 minutes, or until onion is limp. Stir in soy sauce, sugar, and pepper.

Rinse fish and pat dry. Push onion mixture aside and lay fish in dish. Spoon onion mixture in a band over fish. Cover and microwave on HIGH (100%) for 2 minutes; rotate dish a half-turn and microwave on HIGH (100%) for 2 more minutes. Let stand for 3 minutes. If desired, sprinkle remaining chile over fish. Makes 3 or 4 servings.

Per serving: 268 calories, 31 g protein, 5 g carbohydrates, 13 g total fat, 59 mg cholesterol, 524 mg sodium

Steamed Trout with Lettuce & Peas

- 3 tablespoons chopped fresh mint
- 1 tablespoon finely shredded lemon peel (yellow part only)
- 1 clove garlic, minced or pressed
- 1 cup frozen petite peas, thawed
- 3 cups shredded romaine lettuce leaves
  Salt and pepper
- 4 cleaned whole trout or baby salmon (about 8 oz. *each*)
- 1 tablespoon lemon juice
- 8 to 12 lemon wedges

Mix mint, lemon peel, garlic, peas, and romaine; season to taste with salt and pepper. Pat mixture gently into a

Microwave Cooking Guidelines

Fish	Preparation	Cooking Time (CT) Standing Time (ST)
Fish steaks or fillets (½ to ¾ inch thick), 1 pound	Rinse and pat dry. In a greased 7- by 11-inch baking dish, arrange fish in an even layer, with thickest portions toward outside of dish. Season to taste with melted butter or margarine, paprika, dill weed, or lemon juice. Cover with heavy-duty plastic wrap.	CT: 3 to 5 minutes per pound Microwave on HIGH (100%), turning after 2 minutes. ST: 3 minutes, covered
1 or 2 cleaned small fish, 8 to 10 ounces *each*	Rinse and pat dry. Fill cavity with thin lemon or green onion slices, if desired. In a greased 7- by 11-inch baking dish, arrange fish lengthwise, backbones toward outside of dish. Brush with melted butter or margarine. Cover with heavy-duty plastic wrap.	CT: 1 fish: 2½ to 3½ minutes 2 fish: 5 to 7 minutes Microwave on HIGH (100%), turning fish and bringing cooked portion to inside of dish halfway through cooking. ST: 3 minutes, covered
Shellfish		
Hard-shell clams or mussels in shell, 1 dozen	Scrub well. In a 10-inch pie dish or serving plate, arrange shells in a circle, hinge side toward outside of dish. Cover loosely with heavy-duty plastic wrap.	CT: 3 to 4 minutes Microwave on HIGH (100%) until shells open. ST: 1 minute, covered
Oysters in shell, 10 to 12 Eastern or 8 medium-size Pacific	Same as clams or mussels in shell	CT: 4 to 5 minutes Microwave on HIGH (100%) until shells open. ST: 2 minutes, covered
Scallops, 1 pound	Rinse well; cut in half if large. Place in a 1½-quart casserole. Season to taste with melted butter or margarine or lemon juice. Cover with lid or heavy-duty plastic wrap.	CT: 2½ to 3½ minutes Microwave on HIGH (100%), stirring after 1½ minutes. ST: 2 to 3 minutes, covered
Shrimp, medium-large (30 to 35 per lb.), 1 pound	Shell and devein, if desired. On a flat 10- to 12-inch plate, arrange shrimp in a single layer with meaty portion toward outside of plate. Cover with heavy-duty plastic wrap.	CT: 4 to 5 minutes Microwave on HIGH (100%), bringing cooked portion toward inside of plate after 2 minutes. ST: 3 to 5 minutes, covered

mound on an 8- to 10-inch rimmed microwave-safe plate.

Rinse fish and pat dry. Neatly arrange trout, cavity sides down and heads in same direction, over lettuce, leaning fish against each other.

Cover and microwave on HIGH (100%) for 4 minutes. Turn trout end over end. Microwave, covered, on HIGH (100%) for 5 to 7 more minutes or until trout look just slightly translucent or wet inside when cut in thickest part. Let stand, covered, for 3 minutes. Sprinkle with lemon juice. Transfer trout to individual plates and spoon lettuce mixture alongside. Garnish with lemon wedges. Makes 4 servings.

Per serving: 162 calories, 25 g protein, 11 g carbohydrates, 3 g total fat, 55 mg cholesterol, 121 mg sodium

Scallops & Shrimp in Béarnaise Cream

2 tablespoons butter or margarine
1 pound sea scallops, rinsed and cut in half horizontally
½ pound medium-large (30 to 35 per lb.) shrimp, shelled and deveined
⅓ cup finely chopped shallots
½ cup tarragon wine vinegar or white wine vinegar
¼ teaspoon dry tarragon
1 tablespoon Dijon mustard
½ cup whipping cream
Salt and ground white pepper

Combine butter, scallops, and shrimp in a 3-quart microwave-safe casserole. Cover and microwave on HIGH (100%) for 6 minutes, stirring once; let stand for

2 minutes. Using a slotted spoon, transfer seafood to a bowl, cover, and set aside.

To casserole add shallots, vinegar, tarragon, mustard, and cream. Microwave, uncovered, on HIGH (100%) for 10 to 12 minutes or until liquid is reduced to about ¾ cup. Stir in seafood and season to taste with salt and white pepper. Makes 4 servings.

Per serving: 306 calories, 30 g protein, 8 g carbohydrates, 17 g total fat, 157 mg cholesterol, 434 mg sodium

A Repertoire of Recipes

Seafood presentations for all occasions, from informal suppers to elegant company meals—and a selection of versatile sauces

Versatile fish and shellfish play many roles in today's meals, be they formal or impromptu in style, traditional or innovative in flavor. In the following collection of recipes, you'll find seafood dishes easily adaptable to any meal—and any taste. We include both classic preparations and some exciting updated versions that will expand your thinking about seafood.

When you prepare fish simply, using one of the basic cooking methods described in the previous chapter, you can add flair with one of the sauces or butters on pages 123–125. They can transform plain seafood into company appetizers, salads, or main dishes.

Use the following recipes in conjunction with the chart on pages 8–9 to determine which fish can be used in a recipe. If a recipe calls for fish in Group IIa, for example, you can probably use lingcod as successfully as rockfish—or any other fish listed in the same category on the chart. To double-check whether or not a particular fish is especially recommended for use in a recipe, look under "Suggested recipes" in the listing for that fish in the buyer's guide beginning on page 15.

Many of the appetizers, soups, and salads in this chapter can be used as main dishes if portion size is adjusted. For more main-dish and sauce recipes, turn to the "Basic Techniques" chapter (page 79).

Appetizers

Fish & Chard Pie

Preparation time: About 45 minutes
Baking time: 60 to 70 minutes
Cooling time: 15 minutes

Swiss Chard Filling (recipe follows)
1 package (17¾ oz.) frozen puff pastry
All-purpose flour
1 egg yolk beaten with 1 tablespoon water
1 pound boneless and skinless rockfish or cod fillets or other fillets from Group I, IIa, or IIb (pages 8–9)
¾ teaspoon black or yellow mustard seeds

Prepare Swiss Chard Filling. Set aside.

Thaw pastry according to package directions. Place a pastry sheet on a lightly floured board; cut remaining sheet into thirds. Place cut pastry pieces around 3 sides of uncut sheet, overlapping edges slightly. Roll and trim pastry into a 20-inch-diameter circle; discard scraps. Brush on some of the egg yolk mixture and fold into quarters. Nestle into a greased 9-inch spring-form pan; unfold evenly, letting extra pastry extend over rim.

Pat half the filling into pastry; top with fish in an even layer. Cover with remaining filling. Gather pastry over center, gently twisting to form a topknot. Brush with remaining egg yolk mixture; sprinkle with mustard seeds. Cut six 1½-inch slashes in top, 2 inches from rim. (At this point, you may cover and refrigerate until next day.)

Set pie on a rimmed baking sheet. Bake, uncovered, in a 375° oven until well browned (60 to 70 minutes). Let cool in pan on a wire rack for 15 minutes; remove pan sides. Serve slightly warm or at room temperature. Makes 8 to 10 appetizer servings.

■ **Swiss Chard Filling.** Rinse 3 pounds **Swiss chard;** trim and discard ends. Chop leaves coarsely. In a wide frying pan, combine ¼ cup **olive oil;** 2 small **fresh jalapeño chiles,** seeded and minced; 2 tablespoons minced **fresh ginger;** 1 medium-size **onion,** finely chopped; and 1 teaspoon *each* **ground nutmeg, ground cumin,** and **dry thyme leaves.** Cook over medium-high heat, stirring, until onion is soft (about 5 minutes).

Add chard, about a fourth at a time, and cook, stirring often, until wilted (10 to 12 minutes). Remove from heat and mix in 2 tablespoons **lemon juice;** season to taste with **salt.**

Per serving: 343 calories, 14 g protein, 24 g carbohydrates, 21 g total fat, 43 mg cholesterol, 535 mg sodium

Sea bass fillets poach to moist perfection in a tarragon-scented broth laden with vegetables. To make refreshingly light Fish Pot-au-Feu, turn to page 103.

Quenelles with Creamy Shallot Sauce

Preparation time: About 30 minutes
Chilling time: At least 3 hours
Cooking time: About 1 hour

8 to 10 slices soft white bread, crusts removed
1 pound boneless and skinless pike or salmon fillets or other fillets from Group I, IIa, or IIb (pages 8–9)
½ cup whipping cream
¼ cup sour cream
3 eggs
½ teaspoon salt
⅛ teaspoon *each* ground white pepper and ground nutmeg
All-purpose flour
Creamy Shallot Sauce (recipe follows)
Parsley or watercress sprigs

Place 8 bread slices in a food processor fitted with a metal blade; whirl, using short on-off bursts, to make fine crumbs (you should have 3 cups, lightly packed; if not, whirl 1 or 2 more slices). Set aside.

Rinse fish and pat dry. Process until smooth (10 to 15 seconds); transfer to a bowl and set aside.

In processor combine bread crumbs, whipping cream, and sour cream. Whirl until blended (about 5 seconds); add fish, eggs, salt, pepper, and nutmeg. Whirl until smooth (about 10 more seconds). Transfer to a bowl, cover, and refrigerate for at least 3 hours or until next day.

To cook, fill a 5- to 6-quart pan half-full with water, cover, and bring to a boil; adjust heat so water simmers. Meanwhile, place a rimmed heatproof platter in a 200° oven.

To shape quenelles, spoon about 2 tablespoons of the chilled fish mixture onto a lightly floured board; sprinkle with flour. Quickly and lightly roll mixture with palm of your hand into a 1-inch-thick cylinder about 3 inches long; or form ovals, tapering ends slightly. Place on wax paper and set aside. Repeat, shaping 5 or 6 at a time.

Toss each quenelle gently in palms of your hands to shake off excess flour. Drop into simmering water. Poach until firm in center (8 to 10 minutes). Lift out with a slotted spoon, drain, and place on warm platter. Cover with foil and

return to oven while shaping and poaching remaining quenelles.

Prepare Creamy Shallot Sauce. Pour over quenelles. If made ahead, cover loosely and keep warm for up to 1 hour. To serve, garnish with parsley. Makes about 24 quenelles, 8 to 12 appetizer servings.

■ Creamy Shallot Sauce. In a 1½- to 2-quart pan, melt ¼ cup **butter** or margarine over medium-high heat. Add 1 clove **garlic,** minced or pressed, and ¼ cup finely chopped **shallots.** Cook, stirring, until shallots are tender (2 to 3 minutes).

Blend in 3 tablespoons **all-purpose flour** and ⅛ teaspoon **ground nutmeg,** stirring until bubbly. Remove from heat and gradually blend in 1½ cups **regular-strength chicken broth;** return to heat and continue to cook, stirring, until sauce boils and thickens (about 10 minutes). Gradually stir in ½ cup **whipping cream** and cook for 5 more minutes; season to taste with **salt** and **pepper.** Stir in 1 tablespoon **dry sherry,** if desired.

Per serving: 221 calories, 11 g protein, 11 g carbohydrates, 14 g total fat, 122 mg cholesterol, 369 mg sodium

---

Pictured at right

Seviche with Kiwi Fruit

Preparation time: About 35 minutes
Chilling time: At least 10 hours

2 medium-size oranges
¾ cup lemon juice
1 pound boneless and skinless tilefish fillets or other deep-sea saltwater fish fillets from Group IIa or III (pages 8–9; also see page 13 for guidelines on using raw fish)
3 medium-size (about ¾ lb. *total*) firm-ripe kiwi fruit
1 small red onion
Jalapeño Vinaigrette (recipe follows)
About 2 cups watercress sprigs, washed and crisped
Salt

Cut oranges in half and squeeze or ream to make ¾ cup juice; reserve any extra fruit for other uses. Cut outer peel from 1 orange half into ¼-inch by 1-inch pieces. Combine orange juice, cut peel, and lemon juice in a deep bowl; set aside.

Rinse fish and pat dry. Cut into ¼-inch by 1-inch pieces; mix with juices. Cover and refrigerate, stirring every 3 to 4 hours, until fish is opaque when cut (at least 10 hours or up to a day).

Pare skin from kiwi fruit; cut crosswise ¼ inch thick. Thinly slice onion and separate into rings. Place fruit and onion in a bowl. With a slotted spoon, lift fish and peel from juices and add to kiwi mixture; reserve ¼ cup of the juices for Jalapeño Vinaigrette. Prepare dressing and add to kiwi mixture; mix gently.

Arrange watercress on 8 salad plates and add fish mixture with dressing. Season to taste with salt. Makes 8 appetizer servings.

■ Jalapeño Vinaigrette. Mix ¼ cup **reserved citrus juices,** 2 tablespoons **olive oil** or salad oil, 1 tablespoon drained **capers,** and 2 to 3 teaspoons minced **fresh jalapeño chile.**

Per serving: 114 calories, 11 g protein, 7 g carbohydrates, 4 g total fat, 20 mg cholesterol, 69 mg sodium

A symphony of fresh colors and flavors, Seviche with Kiwi Fruit (recipe at left) presents tilefish marinated in citrus juice.

Faux Salmon Terrine

Preparation time: About 10 minutes
Baking time: About 30 minutes
Chilling time: At least 6 hours

1¾ pounds boneless and skinless halibut fillets or other fillets from Group I, IIa, III, or IVa (pages 8–9)
2 eggs
1 small can (6 oz.) tomato paste
⅓ cup whipping cream
5 teaspoons drained green peppercorns
   Lemon Sauce (recipe follows)

Rinse fish, pat dry, and cut into chunks. In a food processor, whirl fish, eggs, tomato paste, and cream until smooth. Add peppercorns. Spoon purée into a deep, straight-sided 1-quart terrine or 4½- by 8½-inch loaf pan.

Cover and set in a larger pan; place in a 350° oven. Pour boiling water to a depth of 1 inch into larger pan. Bake until terrine feels firm when lightly pressed in center (about 30 minutes). Lift pan from water, uncover, and let cool. Then cover and refrigerate for at least 6 hours or until next day.

Prepare Lemon Sauce. Lift out ½-inch slices of terrine with a wide spatula. Offer with sauce. Makes 8 to 10 appetizer servings.

Per serving: 143 calories, 19 g protein, 4 g carbohydrates, 6 g total fat, 89 mg cholesterol, 194 mg sodium

■ **Lemon Sauce.** Mix 1 cup **mayonnaise**, 1 tablespoon *each* **lemon juice** and chopped **parsley**, and 2 teaspoons **Dijon mustard**. Makes about 1 cup.

Per tablespoon: 100 calories, 0 g protein, 1 g carbohydrates, 11 g total fat, 8 mg cholesterol, 98 mg sodium.

Garlic Mussels on the Half Shell

Preparation time: 35 minutes
Cooking time: About 10 minutes

1½ pounds mussels
1 cup dry white wine
¼ cup olive oil or salad oil
⅓ cup freshly grated Parmesan cheese
3 large cloves garlic, minced or pressed
1 tablespoon finely chopped parsley

Prepare mussels (page 44). In a large pan, combine mussels and wine. Cover and simmer over medium-high heat just until shells open (about 5 minutes). Remove from heat. Meanwhile, in a small bowl, mix oil, 3 tablespoons of the cheese, and garlic; set aside.

When cool enough to handle, remove mussels from shells, discarding any unopened shells. Pull shells apart; discard half. Arrange remaining shells in a single layer in a shallow baking dish or pan that can go under a broiler.

Put a mussel in each shell; drizzle with oil mixture. Broil 4 inches from heat just until cheese begins to melt (about 5 minutes). Sprinkle with parsley and remaining cheese. Serve with wooden picks. Makes about 3 dozen appetizers.

Per appetizer: 23 calories, 1 g protein, 0 g carbohydrates, 2 g total fat, 2 mg cholesterol, 33 mg sodium

■ **Garlic Clams on the Half Shell.** Follow directions for **Garlic Mussels on the Half Shell** (above), but substitute 3 dozen small **Atlantic or Pacific hard-shell clams,** suitable for steaming, scrubbed.

Spiced Shrimp Appetizer

Preparation time: About 20 minutes
Cooking time: 16 to 18 minutes
Chilling time: At least 2 hours

   Herb Seasoning Mixture (recipe follows)
1 pound medium-size (30 to 50 per lb.) shrimp in the shell
½ cup salad oil
4 large cloves garlic, minced or pressed
¼ cup lemon juice
1 tablespoon Dijon mustard
   Small butter lettuce leaves, washed and crisped

Prepare Herb Seasoning Mixture; set aside.

In a 4- to 5-quart pan, bring 1 quart water to a boil over high heat. Remove pan from heat and quickly add shrimp. Cover tightly and let stand until shrimp are opaque when cut (6 to 8 minutes). Drain; cool quickly in cold water. Shell and devein, reserving shells.

In a medium-size frying pan, combine shells, oil, garlic, and seasoning mixture. Stir over medium heat to flavor oil (about 10 minutes). Place shrimp in a bowl. Pour oil mixture through a strainer onto shrimp. Mix in lemon juice and mustard. Cover and refrigerate for at least 2 hours or until next day.

Place a shrimp on a lettuce leaf to eat. Makes 8 to 12 appetizer servings.

■ **Herb Seasoning Mixture.** Mix 1 tablespoon **mixed pickling spices;** 1 teaspoon *each* **dry basil leaves, dry oregano leaves,** and **dry tarragon;** ½ teaspoon **pepper;** and ¼ teaspoon **crushed red pepper.**

Per serving: 119 calories, 6 g protein, 1 g carbohydrates, 10 g total fat, 47 mg cholesterol, 84 mg sodium

Crabby Jack Quesadillas

Preparation time: About 45 minutes
Baking time: 7 to 9 minutes

¼ pound crabmeat
2 cups (8 oz.) shredded jack cheese
1 cup thinly sliced green onions (including tops)
10 flour tortillas (7 to 8 inches in diameter)
   Chile-Cilantro Sauce (recipe follows)
   Cilantro (coriander) sprigs

Flake crabmeat and mix lightly with cheese and onions. Place 5 of the tortillas in a single layer on 2 large baking sheets. Cover with crab mixture to within ¾ inch of edges. Top with remaining tortillas. (At this point, you may cover and refrigerate until next day.)

Shortly before serving, prepare Chile-Cilantro Sauce; keep warm.

Bake quesadillas in a 450° oven until cheese is melted and tortillas are lightly browned (7 to 9 minutes). Cut each into 6 wedges. Arrange on a platter and garnish with cilantro. Offer with sauce. Makes 10 appetizer servings.

Per serving: 194 calories, 11 g protein, 18 g carbohydrates, 9 g total fat, 31 mg cholesterol, 154 mg sodium

■ **Chile-Cilantro Sauce.** Place 4 medium-size **fresh Anaheim chiles** on a large baking sheet; broil 2 inches from

(Continued on next page)

Crabby Jack Quesadillas (cont'd)

heat, turning often, until browned and blistered on all sides (about 5 minutes). Let cool; pull off and discard skin, stems, and seeds. Chop chiles coarsely.

In a blender or food processor, whirl chiles; ¼ cup **dry white wine;** 1 medium-size **shallot,** chopped; and 1 tablespoon **lemon juice** until smooth. Pour into a 2- to 3-quart pan and boil over high heat, stirring, until reduced to ⅓ cup (5 to 10 minutes).

Return mixture to blender or food processor. Add 1 cup firmly packed **fresh cilantro** (coriander); whirl until smooth, scraping container sides often. With motor running, slowly add ¼ cup hot **melted butter** or margarine, whirling until blended; scrape sides once or twice. Serve warm. Makes ¾ cup.

Per tablespoon: 43 calories, .5 g protein, 2 g carbohydrates, 4 g total fat, 10 mg cholesterol, 41 mg sodium

Scallops with Shallot Butter

Preparation time: 15 minutes
Baking time: About 10 minutes

- 18   **sea scallops** (about 1 lb.)
- ⅓   cup **butter** or margarine, at room temperature
- ⅓   cup minced **shallots**
- 1   or 2 cloves **garlic,** minced or pressed
- 2   tablespoons minced **parsley**
    Salt and pepper
    Lemon wedges

Rinse scallops, pat dry, and divide evenly among 6 scallop shells or 5- to 6-inch shallow baking dishes. In a bowl, mix butter, shallots, garlic, and parsley. Dot scallops with butter mixture and sprinkle lightly with salt and pepper. Set shells in a shallow 10- by 15-inch baking pan. (At this point, you may cover and refrigerate for up to 6 hours.)

Bake, uncovered, on top rack of a 500° oven until scallops are opaque when cut (about 10 minutes). Garnish with lemon. Makes 6 appetizer servings.

Per serving: 163 calories, 13 g protein, 3 g carbohydrates, 11 g total fat, 52 mg cholesterol, 226 mg sodium

Soups & Stews

Pictured on facing page

Bourride

Preparation time: About 30 minutes
Cooking time: About 1 hour
Baking time: About 20 minutes

- 1   to 3 whole **fish** (about 4 lbs. *total*), such as rockfish, porgy, or other fish from Group IIa (pages 8–9)
- 2   quarts **water**
- 1   large **onion,** sliced
- 2   tablespoons packed fresh **thyme** sprigs or 2 teaspoons dry thyme leaves
- ½   teaspoon **fennel seeds**
- 2   **bay leaves**
- 12   whole **black peppercorns**
- 1   piece (1 by 7 inches) **orange peel** (orange part only)
    Rouille (recipe follows)
    Sourdough Toast (recipe follows)
    Salt and pepper
    Shredded Parmesan cheese

Fillet fish (page 80); save head, tail, and bones (discard entrails, gills, and skin). Cut fillets into 6 equal portions; rinse and pat dry. Cover and refrigerate.

In a 5- to 6-quart pan, combine fish trimmings, water, onion, thyme, fennel seeds, bay leaves, peppercorns, and orange peel. Bring to a boil over high heat; reduce heat, cover, and simmer for 45 minutes.

Pour broth through a fine strainer into a large bowl, pressing juice from trimmings and seasonings; discard residue. Return broth to pan. Prepare Rouille and Sourdough Toast; set aside.

Season broth to taste with salt and pepper; bring to a simmer over high heat. Add fish fillets; reduce heat, cover, and simmer until fish looks just slightly translucent or wet inside when cut in thickest part (about 5 minutes).

Place a toast slice in each of 6 wide soup bowls. Using a wide spatula, carefully lift fillets from broth and place each on a toast slice. Ladle on broth.

Pass Rouille and cheese to add to taste. Makes 6 servings.

■ **Rouille.** In a blender or food processor, combine 1 **egg yolk;** ½ medium-size **red bell pepper,** seeded and chopped; 1 clove **garlic,** minced or pressed; ¼ teaspoon **ground red pepper** (cayenne); ⅛ teaspoon **saffron threads;** 2 tablespoons **soft bread crumbs;** and 1 tablespoon of the strained **fish broth.** Whirl until fairly smooth. With motor running, gradually add ½ cup **olive oil.** Season to taste with **salt.** Makes about ¾ cup.

■ **Sourdough Toast.** Slice 1 **sourdough baguette** (1 lb.) diagonally ¾ inch thick. Using about ⅓ cup **olive oil,** lightly brush cut sides of bread with oil. Place in a single layer on a large baking sheet. Bake, uncovered, in a 375° oven until golden (about 20 minutes).

Per serving: 592 calories, 24 g protein, 46 g carbohydrates, 35 g total fat, 77 mg cholesterol, 497 mg sodium

Quick Colorful Chowder

Preparation time: About 15 minutes
Cooking time: About 40 minutes

- ¼   pound **salt pork**
- 1   large **onion,** chopped
- 2   large **red thin-skinned potatoes** (about 1 lb. *total*), peeled, if desired, and cut into ½-inch cubes
- 2   bottles (8 oz. *each*) **clam juice**
- 1   can (14½ oz.) **regular-strength chicken broth**
- 1   **bay leaf**
- 2   pounds boneless and skinless **cod** or catfish fillets or other fillets from Group IIa, IIb, or III (pages 8–9)
- 1   package (10 oz.) frozen **peas**
- 1   package (10 oz.) frozen **corn**
- 1½   cups **half-and-half** or milk
    Salt and pepper
    Chopped parsley

Dice pork, discarding rind, and place in a 4- to 5-quart pan. Cook over medium-high heat, stirring often, until browned and crisp; discard all but 2 tablespoons of the drippings. Add onion and cook, stirring occasionally, until onion is soft (about 5 minutes). Stir in potatoes, clam juice, broth, and bay leaf. Bring to a boil;

reduce heat, cover, and simmer until potatoes are tender when pierced (about 15 minutes).

Rinse fish and pat dry; cut into 1½-inch chunks. Add to broth with peas and corn. Bring to a boil over medium-high heat; reduce heat, cover, and simmer until fish looks just slightly translucent or wet inside when cut in thickest part (5 to 8 minutes). Stir in half-and-half and season to taste with salt and pepper. Heat just until steaming (do not boil). Sprinkle with parsley. Makes 6 to 8 servings.

Per serving: 522 calories, 38 g protein, 35 g carbohydrates, 26 g total fat, 91 mg cholesterol, 921 mg sodium

Puget Sound Salmon Gefillte Fish Soup

Preparation time: About 40 minutes
Cooking time: About 1½ hours

Vegetable Broth (recipe follows)
Horseradish Sauce (recipe follows)
¾ **pound chilled boneless and skinless salmon fillet**
¾ **pound chilled boneless and skinless lingcod or rockfish fillets or other fillets from Group IIa (pages 8–9)**
1 **medium-size onion, coarsely chopped**
2 **eggs**
About ⅓ cup matzo meal
1½ **teaspoons pepper**
½ **teaspoon salt**
Fresh dill sprigs (optional)

Prepare Vegetable Broth. Meanwhile, prepare Horseradish Sauce. Set both aside.

Rinse fish and pat dry; cut into 1-inch chunks. Whirl, a third at a time, in a food processor until very finely chopped (about 20 seconds; do not purée). As each batch is chopped, transfer to a large bowl. (Or grind fish using fine blade of a food chopper.) Cover fish and refrigerate.

Whirl onion and eggs in a food processor or blender until puréed. Add to fish with ⅓ cup of the matzo meal, pepper, and salt; stir until blended. Mixture should be just firm enough to hold its shape when formed into a ball with your hands; if too soft, stir in 2 to 3 more tablespoons matzo meal.

Pat fish mixture, 2 tablespoons at a time, into smooth balls. Rinse hands often in cool water to prevent sticking.

Bouillabaisse's country cousin, Bourride features gently poached fish enveloped in seasoned fish broth and a saffron-colored sauce (recipe on facing page).

Bring broth to a boil; adjust heat so broth simmers. Add fish balls in a single layer (without crowding). Simmer, uncovered, until opaque in center when cut (about 10 minutes). Lift out with a slotted spoon, drain on paper towels, and keep warm. Repeat until all fish balls are cooked.

Pour broth into a large bowl through a colander lined with several layers of dampened cheesecloth. Rinse and dry pan to remove any bits of fish. Return broth to pan, bring to a boil over high heat, and add fish balls; remove from heat, cover, and let stand until balls are hot (about 5 minutes).

Ladle into wide soup bowls and garnish with dill, if desired. Pass sauce to add to taste. Makes 4 to 6 servings.

■ **Vegetable Broth.** In a 5- to 6-quart pan, combine 1 large **onion,** quartered; 2 *each* large **carrots** and stalks **celery,** cut into 1-inch pieces; 1 tablespoon **whole black peppercorns;** 2 quarts **water;** and 3 **fish or chicken bouillon cubes.** Bring to a boil over high heat; reduce heat, cover, and simmer until vegetables are very soft (about 45 minutes). Pour broth through a strainer into a large bowl; discard vegetables.

Per serving: 208 calories, 25 g protein, 11 g carbohydrates, 6 g total fat, 152 mg cholesterol, 647 mg sodium

■ **Horseradish Sauce.** Stir together ¾ cup **sour cream,** ¼ cup **prepared horseradish,** and 1 tablespoon chopped **fresh**

dill or 1½ teaspoons dill weed. Cover and refrigerate for up to a day. Makes about 1 cup.

Per tablespoon: 25 calories, .4 g protein, 1 g carbohydrates, 2 g total fat, 5 mg cholesterol, 10 mg sodium

Pictured on page 98

Fish Pot-au-Feu

Preparation time: 12 minutes
Cooking time: 30 minutes

5 **cups regular-strength chicken broth or Fish Stock (page 93)**
1 **cup dry white wine; or 1 cup regular-strength chicken broth and 3 tablespoons white wine vinegar**
1 **tablespoon fresh tarragon leaves or ½ teaspoon dry tarragon**
4 **small red thin-skinned potatoes (1½ inches in diameter), unpeeled**
8 **baby carrots or 4 medium-size carrots, cut in half**
4 **medium-size leeks (about 2 lbs. *total*), roots and most of dark green tops trimmed**
1½ **pounds skinless cod or sea bass fillets or other fillets from Group IIa, III, or IVa (pages 8–9)**

In a 5- to 6-quart pan, combine broth, wine, and tarragon. Bring to a boil over high heat. Add potatoes and carrots and

(Continued on next page)

Fish Pot-au-Feu (cont'd)

return to a boil; reduce heat, cover, and boil gently for 10 minutes.

Meanwhile, split leeks lengthwise and rinse well. Add to pan, cover, and boil gently until leeks are tender when pierced (about 10 minutes). Lift out leeks and keep warm.

Rinse fish and pat dry; cut into 4 equal portions. Add to broth; cover and simmer until fish looks just slightly translucent or wet inside when cut in thickest part and vegetables are tender when pierced (7 to 10 minutes).

With a slotted spatula, carefully lift out fish and arrange in 4 wide soup bowls. Evenly distribute vegetables in bowls and ladle broth over all. Makes 4 servings.

Per serving: 304 calories, 36 g protein, 30 g carbohydrates, 5 g total fat, 89 mg cholesterol, 1,406 mg sodium

Tart with lime, hot with chiles, and fragrant with lemon grass, shellfish-laden Thai Seafood Firepot (recipe on facing page) boasts unexpected flavor contrasts.

Matelote of Eel

Preparation time: About 45 minutes
Cooking time: About 45 minutes

- 1½ **pounds skinned, dressed eel, cut into 2-inch lengths (page 32)**
- 1 **dozen small boiling onions**
- 2 **medium-size carrots, thinly sliced**
- 1½ **cups** *each* **dry white wine and regular-strength chicken broth**
- 1 **bay leaf**
- ½ **teaspoon dry thyme leaves**
- 1 **clove garlic, minced or pressed**
- 2 **tablespoons butter or margarine**
- 2 **tablespoons all-purpose flour**
- ½ **cup half-and-half**
  Salt and pepper
  Chopped parsley

Wipe fish with a damp cloth. In a large pan, combine onions, carrots, wine, broth, bay leaf, thyme, and garlic. Bring to a boil over high heat; reduce heat, cover, and simmer until onions are tender (about 10 minutes). Add fish; simmer until fish looks opaque when cut in thickest part (about 20 minutes for a 2-inch-thick fish).

Carefully lift out fish and vegetables, reserving liquid, and arrange in a deep 3- to 5-quart tureen or serving dish; cover and keep warm.

In a 2- to 3-quart pan, melt butter over medium-low heat. Stir in flour and cook until bubbly. Remove from heat and

gradually blend in half-and-half and reserved cooking liquid. Return to heat and cook, stirring constantly, until slightly thickened (10 to 15 minutes). Season to taste with salt and pepper. Pour over fish and sprinkle with parsley. Makes 4 servings.

Per serving: 462 calories, 34 g protein, 12 g carbohydrates, 30 g total fat, 241 mg cholesterol, 552 mg sodium

Fish Pil-Pil in Red Sauce

Preparation time: 10 minutes
Cooking time: About 25 minutes

- 2 **pounds (about 18) small hard-shell clams in shell, suitable for steaming, scrubbed**
- 2 **tablespoons dry white wine**
- 1 **tablespoon lemon juice**
- ½ **to 1 teaspoon crushed red pepper**
- ¾ **cup olive oil**
- 4 **cloves garlic, halved**
- 1 **small red bell pepper, seeded and cut into thin strips**
- 2 **pounds cod fillets or other steaks or skinless fillets (½ to 1 inch thick) from Group IIa or III (pages 8–9), cut into serving-size pieces**
  Salt

Steam clams (page 24). Remove from heat. Leaving a few clams in shells for garnish, if desired, remove clams from

remaining shells and set clams aside. If desired, cooking liquid may be used in place of wine in sauce.

Combine wine, lemon juice, and red pepper; set aside.

Heat oil in a wide frying pan over medium heat. When oil is hot, add garlic and bell pepper. Cook, stirring, until garlic is golden and pepper is soft (4 to 6 minutes); remove pan from heat. With a slotted spoon, lift out garlic and pepper; let drain separately on paper towels.

Rinse fish and pat dry. Add to pan and return to low heat. Gently shake pan to mix fish juices and oil. Keeping oil bubbling slowly, cook until bottom edges of fish turn white (2 to 4 minutes).

With a wide spatula, carefully turn fish. Add wine mixture and immediately begin to shake and swirl pan to blend sauce as fish cooks; adjust heat to maintain slow bubbles. Cook until fish looks just slightly translucent or wet inside when cut in thickest part (about 5 minutes).

Transfer fish to a warm platter and top with clams; keep warm if dish is to be served hot. Pour cooking sauce into a blender or food processor; add bell pepper and any juices from fish. Whirl until sauce is puréed and thickened. Season to taste with salt.

Pour sauce over fish and garnish with reserved garlic and any reserved clams in shell. Serve warm or at room temperature (within 2 hours). Makes 6 servings.

Per serving: 429 calories, 35 g protein, 2 g carbohydrates, 31 g total fat, 56 mg cholesterol, 96 mg sodium

Lobster Soup with Leeks

Preparation time: About 45 minutes
Cooking time: About 2¼ hours

1 **quart regular-strength chicken broth or Fish Stock (page 93)**
3 **cups dry white wine**
1 **live Maine lobster (1½ to 2 lbs.)**
3 **small oranges**
2 **medium-size leeks**
2 **large carrots, cut into 2-inch chunks**
2 **cloves garlic**
1 **bay leaf**
2 **tablespoons tomato paste**
½ **teaspoon dry thyme leaves**
1 **teaspoon whole black peppercorns**
2 **parsley sprigs**
¾ **cup whipping cream**

In an 8- to 10-quart pan, combine broth, wine, and 3 quarts water. Bring to a boil over high heat; plunge lobster, head first, into broth. Return to a boil; reduce heat, cover, and simmer for about 15 minutes. Lift out lobster and let cool, reserving broth.

Meanwhile, cut two 4-inch strips of peel (orange part only) from 1 orange. Ream enough of the oranges to make ½ cup juice. Add peel and juice to broth. Thinly slice remaining oranges and set aside.

Trim and discard root ends from leeks; cut off tough green tops, rinse well, and set aside. Split white part of leeks and rinse well; tie with string. Add to broth and simmer, uncovered, until tender when pierced (about 10 minutes). Lift out and set aside.

To broth add reserved leek tops, carrots, garlic, bay leaf, tomato paste, thyme, peppercorns, and parsley. Return to a boil over high heat and continue to boil, uncovered, while preparing lobster.

Remove lobster meat from shell (page 39), reserving meat, roe (if any), liver, and shells. (At this point, you may cover and refrigerate lobster meat and leeks until next day.)

Add shells to broth and continue to boil, uncovered, until reduced by about half (about 1½ hours). Pour broth through a strainer into a large bowl; discard vegetables and shells. Return broth to pan and boil over high heat, uncovered, until reduced to 3 cups.

Meanwhile, in a small bowl, mash reserved lobster roe with back of a spoon. Add to broth with cream and reserved liver. (At this point, you may cover and refrigerate until next day.)

Bring broth to a boil over high heat. Add leeks and lobster meat, reduce heat, and simmer just until hot. With a slotted spoon, remove leeks and cut crosswise into 1-inch lengths. Arrange leeks and lobster in 4 wide soup bowls. Ladle in hot broth without covering leeks and lobster completely. Garnish with orange slices. Pass any remaining broth. Makes 4 servings.

Per serving: 271 calories, 13 g protein, 20 g carbohydrates, 17 g total fat, 77 mg cholesterol, 1,259 mg sodium

Pictured on facing page

Thai Seafood Firepot

Preparation time: About 45 minutes
Cooking time: About 1 hour

3 **quarts regular-strength chicken broth or Fish Stock (page 93)**
3 **cups water**
1 **stalk (about 12 inches long) fresh lemon grass, sliced, ¼ cup sliced dried lemon grass, or yellow peel pared from 1 large lemon**
1 **or 2 fresh or pickled small (about 2½ inches long) hot chiles, thinly sliced**
1 **strip (about 8 inches long) pared lime peel, green part only**
18 **small hard-shell clams in shell, suitable for steaming, scrubbed**
1¼ **pounds large shrimp (under 30 per lb.), shelled and deveined**
1 **cooked large Dungeness crab (about 2 lbs.), cleaned and cracked (page 28)**
⅔ **cup lime juice**
½ **cup cilantro (coriander) sprigs**
3 **green onions (including tops), cut into 1-inch lengths**
  Lime wedges

In an 8- to 10-quart pan, combine broth and water. Loosely tie lemon grass, chile slices (reserve 4 to 6 for garnish), and lime peel in a piece of moistened cheesecloth; place in broth. Bring to a boil over high heat; reduce heat, cover,

and simmer for 45 minutes. Lift out wrapped spices and discard.

Add clams, shrimp, and crab. Cover and simmer until clams pop open and shrimp are opaque when cut (about 7 minutes). Stir in lime juice. Lift out seafood and place in a serving bowl. Pour in broth. Garnish with reserved chile slices, cilantro, and onions. Serve with lime wedges. Makes 4 to 6 servings.

Per serving: 221 calories, 32 g protein, 91 g carbohydrates, 7 g total fat, 153 mg cholesterol, 2,259 mg sodium

San Francisco-style Cioppino

Preparation time: About 30 minutes
Cooking time: About 50 minutes

¼ **cup olive oil or salad oil**
1 **large onion, chopped**
2 **cloves garlic, minced or pressed**
1 **large green bell pepper, seeded and chopped**
⅓ **cup chopped parsley**
1 **large can (15 oz.) tomato sauce**
1 **large can (28 oz.) tomatoes**
1 **cup dry red or white wine**
1 **bay leaf**
1 **teaspoon dry basil leaves**
½ **teaspoon dry oregano leaves**
12 **small hard-shell clams in shell, suitable for steaming, scrubbed**
1 **pound large shrimp (under 30 per lb.), shelled and deveined**
2 **cooked large Dungeness crabs (about 2 lbs. *each*), cleaned and cracked (page 28)**

In a 6- to 8-quart pan, combine oil, onion, garlic, bell pepper, and parsley; cook over medium heat, stirring often, until onion is soft (about 5 minutes). Stir in tomato sauce, tomatoes (break up with a spoon) and their liquid, wine, bay leaf, basil, and oregano. Bring to a boil. Reduce heat, cover, and simmer for 20 minutes.

Add clams, shrimp, and crabs. Cover and simmer until clams pop open and shrimp are opaque when cut (about 20 more minutes). Ladle broth and shellfish into 6 large soup bowls. Makes 6 servings.

Per serving: 328 calories, 38 g protein, 17 g carbohydrates, 12 g total fat, 168 mg cholesterol, 1,077 mg sodium

French Oyster Soup

Preparation time: About 10 minutes
Baking time: 35 to 40 minutes
Cooking time: About 5 minutes

- **2 tablespoons butter or margarine, at room temperature**
- **6 slices (about ½ inch thick) French bread**
- **3½ cups regular-strength chicken broth**
- **2 cups bottled clam juice**
- **½ cup whipping cream**
- **2 jars (8 to 10 oz. *each*) shucked oysters, chopped**
- **½ cup shredded Swiss cheese**

Butter both sides of bread slices and arrange in a single layer on a baking sheet. Bake in a 375° oven until richly browned and very hard (30 to 45 minutes; turn slices over after 20 minutes).

Meanwhile, in a 3- to 4-quart pan, combine broth, clam juice, and cream. Bring to a boil over high heat; stir in oysters and their liquid. Remove from heat.

Ladle soup into 6 ovenproof soup bowls. Mound cheese on toast slices and place a slice, cheese side up, in each bowl. Set bowls on 2 rimmed baking sheets. Bake in a 450° oven just until cheese is melted (about 5 minutes). Makes 6 servings.

Per serving: 326 calories, 17 g protein, 26 g carbohydrates, 17 g total fat, 94 mg cholesterol, 1,131 mg sodium

Tahoe Crayfish Bisque

Preparation time: About 1 hour
Cooking time: About 30 minutes

- **4 dozen live crayfish, rinsed**
- **1½ cups *each* milk and half-and-half**
- **2 tablespoons butter or margarine**
- **½ teaspoon curry powder**
- **¼ teaspoon paprika**
- **2 to 3 tablespoons brandy**
  Salt
- **½ to ⅔ cup freshly grated Parmesan cheese**

Remove sand vein from crayfish, if desired (page 30). In a 5- to 6-quart pan, bring 3 quarts water to a boil over high heat. Add crayfish and cook until tail meat is opaque throughout when tail is pulled off and cracked open (5 to 7 minutes). Drain. When cool enough to handle, remove meat from shells, reserving meat, any of the golden crayfish fat or orange eggs, and shells.

Return shells to pan. Add 3 cups water and bring to a boil over high heat; boil, uncovered, until reduced to about ½ cup. Pour through a fine strainer into a bowl, discarding shells. Rinse and dry pan to remove any bits of shell; return reduced liquid and boil, uncovered, until reduced to 2 to 3 tablespoons (watch carefully at end to avoid scorching). Add milk and half-and-half; heat just until scalding (do not boil).

Meanwhile, in a food processor or blender, purée half the crayfish meat with fat and eggs. Add to hot liquid and keep warm.

In an 8- to 10-inch frying pan, melt butter over medium heat; stir in curry powder and paprika and cook for about 1½ minutes. Stir in brandy and remaining crayfish. Set brandy mixture aflame (*not* beneath an exhaust fan or near flammable items). Shake pan for 30 to 40 seconds; then smother flames with lid. Gently mix into soup. Season to taste with salt and ladle into soup bowls. Pass cheese to add to taste. Makes 3 or 4 first-course servings.

Per serving: 316 calories, 18 g protein, 9 g carbohydrates, 23 g total fat, 128 mg cholesterol, 389 mg sodium

Steamed Clams with Linguisa & Pasta

Preparation time: 10 minutes
Cooking time: 25 minutes

- **2 tablespoons salad oil**
- **⅓ pound linguisa sausage, sliced ¼ inch thick**
- **1 medium-size onion, chopped**
- **1 large red bell pepper, seeded and diced**
- **3 cups water**
- **1½ cups regular-strength chicken broth**
- **¾ cup dry white wine**
- **¼ cup rice-shaped or other tiny pasta**
- **½ teaspoon dry basil leaves**
- **32 to 36 small hard-shell clams in shell, suitable for steaming, scrubbed**
  Minced parsley

In a 5- to 6-quart pan, combine oil and sausage; cook over medium-high heat, stirring, until sausage is lightly browned. Add onion and bell pepper; cook, stirring, until onion is limp (2 to 3 minutes). Add water, broth, wine, pasta, and basil. Cover and boil gently until pasta is just tender to bite (8 to 10 minutes).

Skim off and discard fat. Add clams. Cover and bring to a boil; reduce heat and simmer until clams pop open (about 5 minutes).

Lift out clams and distribute equally in 4 wide soup bowls. Ladle broth over clams. Lightly sprinkle with parsley. Makes 4 servings.

Per serving: 306 calories, 26 g protein, 17 g carbohydrates, 14 g total fat, 76 mg cholesterol, 732 mg sodium

Hearty Clam Chowder

Preparation time: 45 minutes
Cooking time: About 25 minutes

- **4 slices bacon, diced**
- **⅓ cup chopped green onions (including tops)**
- **5 medium-size potatoes, peeled and cut into ½-inch cubes**
- **2 tablespoons finely chopped green bell pepper**
- **1 stalk celery, thinly sliced**
- **1 medium-size carrot, thinly sliced**
- **1 clove garlic, minced or pressed**
- **2 cups water**
- **1 teaspoon salt**
- **½ teaspoon ground white pepper**
- **1 teaspoon Worcestershire**
- **4 drops liquid hot pepper seasoning**
- **2 cups fresh or frozen chopped or minced raw clams, with their nectar (to clean and shuck live clams, see page 23; finely chop meat or put through a food chopper fitted with a medium blade)**
- **2 cups half-and-half**

In a large, deep pan, cook bacon over medium heat, stirring occasionally, until crisp. Add onions, potatoes, bell pepper, celery, carrot, garlic, water, salt, white pepper, Worcestershire, and hot pepper seasoning. Bring to a boil; reduce heat, cover, and boil gently until potatoes are tender (about 15 minutes), adding clams during last 3 minutes.

Stir in half-and-half. Heat just until steaming (do not boil). Serve immediately. Makes 4 servings.

Per serving: 492 calories, 23 g protein, 37 g carbohydrates, 28 g total fat, 98 mg cholesterol, 859 mg sodium

Salads

Salmon Salad with Tarragon Vinaigrette

Preparation time: About 25 minutes
Cooking time: About 25 minutes

4   **salmon steaks (about ½ lb. and 1 inch thick *each*)**
    Tarragon Vinaigrette Dressing (recipe follows)
2   **medium-size heads Belgian endive (about 4 oz. *each*), leaves separated**
4   **cups lightly packed curly endive leaves, washed and crisped**
2   **cups lightly packed watercress sprigs, tough stems removed, washed and crisped**
½   ***each* medium-size red and green bell peppers, seeded and thinly sliced crosswise**

Poach salmon steaks the classic way (page 93), using one-half recipe Poaching Liquid. Let cool. (At this point, you may cover and refrigerate for up to 8 hours.)

Prepare Tarragon Vinaigrette Dressing.

Place a salmon steak on each of 4 dinner plates. Arrange Belgian and curly endive, watercress, and bell peppers around salmon. Pass dressing to add to taste. Makes 4 servings.

Per serving: 308 calories, 41 g protein, 5 g carbohydrates, 13 g total fat, 110 mg cholesterol, 113 mg sodium

▪ Tarragon Vinaigrette Dressing.
Combine ⅓ cup **white wine vinegar,** 1 tablespoon **Dijon mustard,** 1½ tablespoons minced **fresh tarragon** or 1 teaspoon dry tarragon, and 1 teaspoon **sugar.** Whisking rapidly, gradually add ⅔ cup **salad oil.** Makes about 1 cup.

Per tablespoon: 84 calories, .02 g protein, .58 g carbohydrates, 9 g total fat, 0 mg cholesterol, 28 mg sodium

Piquant flavors permeate two Latin-influenced salads, Veracruz Fish Salad (at left) and, at right, Chile, Shrimp & Corn Salad (recipes below and on page 108). Offer tortilla chips with salsa to complete a seafood salad buffet.

Pictured above

Veracruz Fish Salad

Preparation time: 40 minutes
Chilling time: At least 2 hours

2½ **pounds orange roughy fillets or other skinless fillets from Group IIa, IIb, or III (pages 8–9)**
3   **large tomatoes, coarsely diced**
⅔   **cup lime juice**
3   **cloves garlic, minced or pressed**
1   **cup sliced pimento-stuffed green olives**
⅓   **cup drained capers**
½   **cup thinly sliced green onions (including tops)**
    Salt and pepper
    About 8 large iceberg lettuce leaves, washed and crisped
2   **limes, cut into wedges**

Rinse fish and pat dry. Place in a 9- by 13-inch baking dish, overlapping fillets slightly. Cover and bake in a 400° oven just until slightly translucent or wet inside when cut in thickest part (12 to 15 minutes). Let cool; then cover and refrigerate for at least 2 hours or for up to a day.

Lift out fish, discarding pan juices. Pull out and discard any bones. Break fish into bite-size chunks.

In a large bowl, combine tomatoes, lime juice, garlic, olives, capers, onions, and fish; mix gently. Season to taste with salt and pepper. Line a serving bowl with lettuce leaves; spoon in salad. Garnish with lime wedges. Makes 6 to 8 servings.

Per serving: 179 calories, 28 g protein, 7 g carbohydrates, 5 g total fat, 50 mg cholesterol, 648 mg sodium

A potent dipping sauce transforms traditional crab salad into Red Chile Louis (recipe on facing page).

Seviche Salad

Preparation time: About 20 minutes
Chilling time: At least 3 hours

1½ **pounds boneless and skinless tilefish fillets or other deep-sea saltwater fish fillets from Group IIa or III (pages 8–9; also see page 13 for guidelines on using raw fish)**
¾ **cup lemon or lime juice**
1 **small red onion, chopped (cut off 1 or 2 rings and reserve for garnish)**
⅓ **cup fresh cilantro (coriander) leaves**
1 **ripe avocado**
Romaine lettuce leaves, washed and crisped

Rinse fish and pat dry. Finely dice and place in a large bowl. Add lemon juice, chopped onion, and ¼ cup of the cilantro; mix lightly.

Pit, peel, and dice avocado; place over fish mixture and spoon on some of the lemon juice to prevent darkening. Garnish with reserved onion rings and remaining cilantro. Cover and chill until fish is opaque when cut (at least 3 hours or for up to a day).

Spoon salad mixture into romaine leaves to eat. Makes 6 servings.

Per serving: 166 calories, 22 g protein, 5 g carbohydrates, 7 g total fat, 54 mg cholesterol, 102 mg sodium

Thai Fish & Watercress Salad

Preparation time: About 45 minutes
Cooking time: About 10 minutes

4 **cups lightly packed watercress sprigs, tough stems removed, washed and crisped**
1 **pound swordfish or tuna or other boned and skinned fish from Group III or IV (pages 8–9), sliced ½ to 1 inch thick**
¼ **cup sliced almonds**
3 **tablespoons salad oil**
2 **tablespoons minced fresh ginger**
3 **cloves garlic, minced or pressed**
2 **or 3 fresh jalapeño chiles, seeded and thinly sliced crosswise**
1 **tablespoon Oriental bean paste (optional)**
1 **tablespoon Oriental fish sauce or soy sauce**
¼ **pound large shrimp (under 30 per lb.), shelled and deveined, cut in half lengthwise**
Lemon wedges

Arrange watercress on 4 salad plates; refrigerate while preparing salad.

Rinse fish and pat dry. If fish is 1 inch thick, cut in half horizontally. Cut fish into strips about ½ inch wide and 3 inches long; set aside.

In a wok or wide frying pan, stir almonds over high heat until golden (2 to 3 minutes). Remove and set aside.

Mix oil, ginger, garlic, and chiles; add to wok and cook, stirring, for 1 minute. Add bean paste, if desired, fish sauce, fish strips, and shrimp. Cook, stirring gently, until fish looks just slightly translucent or wet inside and shrimp are opaque when cut (2 to 3 minutes).

Evenly spoon seafood mixture over watercress. Sprinkle with almonds and accompany with lemon wedges. Makes 4 servings.

Per serving: 304 calories, 30 g protein, 5 g carbohydrates, 18 g total fat, 79 mg cholesterol, 668 mg sodium

Pictured on page 107
Chile, Shrimp & Corn Salad

Preparation time: 45 minutes
Chilling time: At least 1 hour

3 **small dried hot red chiles**
¼ **cup olive oil or salad oil**
½ **teaspoon pepper**
2 **cups corn cut from cob or 1 package (10 oz.) frozen whole-kernel corn, thawed and drained**
1 **medium-size red bell pepper, seeded and finely chopped**
1 **pound medium-size raw shrimp (30 to 50 per lb.), shelled and deveined**
1 **tablespoon soy sauce**
⅔ **cup cider vinegar**
1 **pound spinach, stems removed, washed and crisped**
1 **pound green leaf lettuce, washed and crisped**

In a wide frying pan, combine chiles and oil over medium heat; cook, stirring, until chiles are lightly browned (about 4 minutes). Add pepper, corn, and bell pepper. Increase heat to high and cook, stirring constantly, until vegetables are tender to bite (about 3 minutes). Add shrimp and cook, stirring, just until shrimp are opaque when cut (about 3 minutes).

Remove pan from heat. Stir in soy sauce and vinegar; spoon shrimp mixture into a bowl. Let cool; then cover and refrigerate for at least 1 hour or for up to 4 hours.

Meanwhile, tear spinach and lettuce into bite-size pieces (you should have about 4 quarts total, lightly packed). Place greens in a large salad bowl; spoon shrimp mixture over greens (lift out chiles and use for garnish, or discard). Mix lightly. Makes 6 to 8 servings.

Per serving: 174 calories, 13 g protein, 14 g carbohydrates, 9 g total fat, 70 mg cholesterol, 241 mg sodium

Pictured on facing page

Red Chile Louis

Preparation time: About 1 hour
Cooking time: 25 to 45 minutes
Chilling time: At least 2 hours

2 or 3 live or cooked Dungeness crabs in shell (4 to 5 lbs. *total*) or ¾ to 1 pound crabmeat
    Red Chile Sauce (recipe follows)
½ cup mayonnaise
2 tablespoons lime juice
¼ to ½ teaspoon coarsely ground black pepper
2 large oranges
1 medium-size mild red onion
    Romaine lettuce leaves, washed and crisped
    Cilantro (coriander) sprigs
    Lime wedges

Cook, crack, and clean crabs (page 29). Cover and refrigerate for at least 2 hours or for up to 8 hours.

Prepare Red Chile Sauce. In a medium-size bowl, combine mayonnaise, lime juice, pepper, and ½ to ⅔ cups of the sauce. Mix until well blended; set aside.

Cut peel and white membrane from oranges; separate into segments. Thinly slice onion and separate into rings.

Line 4 plates with lettuce. Arrange crab, orange segments, and onion rings on each plate. Garnish with cilantro and lime. Pass sauce for dipping at the table. Makes 4 servings.

Per serving: 364 calories, 21 g protein, 19 g carbohydrates, 24 g total fat, 80 mg cholesterol, 480 mg sodium

■ **Red Chile Sauce.** Rinse and pat dry 1 ounce dried whole **New Mexico or California chiles** (3 to 4 chiles). Place in a single layer on a baking sheet. Bake in a 450° oven just until chiles smell toasted (2 to 3 minutes). Let cool. Break off and discard stems; shake out and discard seeds.

In a 1½- to 2-quart pan, combine chiles, ¾ cup **water**, ⅓ cup chopped **onion**, and 1 small clove **garlic**. Bring to a boil over high heat; reduce heat, cover, and simmer until chiles are very soft when pierced (about 20 minutes). Let cool slightly.

Purée chile mixture in a blender until very smooth; or drain chile mixture,

reserving liquid, and purée solids in a food processor, adding back liquid. Rub purée firmly through a strainer; discard residue. Season to taste with **salt.** If made ahead, cover and refrigerate for up to 1 week; freeze for longer storage. Makes ⅔ to ¾ cup.

Per tablespoon: 9 calories, .34 g protein, 2 g carbohydrates, .41 g total fat, 0 mg cholesterol, .8 mg sodium

Mussel & Potato Salad

Preparation time: About 25 minutes
Cooking time: About 25 minutes
Chilling time: At least 30 minutes

1½ pounds small (1½ inches in diameter or less) red thin-skinned potatoes
    Basil Vinaigrette Dressing (recipe follows)
2 pounds mussels in shells
1 jar (7 oz.) roasted red peppers, drained and cut into ¼-inch strips
    Fresh basil sprigs

Place potatoes in a 3- to 4-quart pan; add enough water to cover potatoes by 1 inch. Bring to a boil over high heat; cover and boil gently until tender when pierced (about 25 minutes); drain.

Meanwhile, prepare Basil Vinaigrette Dressing; set aside.

Cut warm potatoes in half, place in a large bowl, and mix lightly with dressing. Let stand while cooking mussels.

Prepare and steam mussels (page 44). When cool enough to handle, remove mussels from shells and add to potatoes; discard shells.

Add peppers to potato mixture, mixing gently. Cover and refrigerate for at least 30 minutes or for up to a day. Spoon salad into a serving bowl and garnish with basil sprigs. Makes 5 or 6 servings.

■ **Basil Vinaigrette Dressing.** Combine ⅓ cup **seasoned rice vinegar** (or ⅓ cup white wine vinegar and 1 teaspoon sugar), ⅓ cup finely chopped **fresh basil leaves**, 2 tablespoons **olive oil** or salad oil, 1 tablespoon **Dijon mustard**, ½ teaspoon **pepper**, and 1 clove **garlic**, minced or pressed. Mix until well blended.

Per serving: 189 calories, 8 g protein, 26 g carbohydrates, 6 g total fat, 12 mg cholesterol, 218 mg sodium

Stir-fried Scallops & Asparagus on Cool Pasta

Preparation time: 10 minutes
Cooking time: About 20 minutes

8 ounces dry capellini or coil vermicelli
1 pound asparagus
3 tablespoons salad oil
3 tablespoons water
1 clove garlic, minced or pressed
1 tablespoon minced fresh ginger
½ pound bay scallops or sea scallops, cut into ½-inch chunks, rinsed and drained
½ cup rice vinegar; or ½ cup white wine vinegar and 1 teaspoon sugar
2 tablespoons sugar
1 teaspoon *each* soy sauce and Oriental sesame oil

In a 5- to 6-quart pan, cook pasta in 3 quarts boiling water just until barely tender to bite (3 to 5 minutes). Or cook according to package directions. Drain and rinse with cold water until cool; drain well. Place in a shallow dish.

Snap off and discard tough ends of asparagus. Cut diagonally into ¼-inch-thick slices 1½ to 2 inches long.

Place a wok or wide frying pan over high heat. Add 1 tablespoon of the salad oil and asparagus; stir to coat with oil. Add water; cover and cook just until tender-crisp (2 to 3 minutes). Lift out asparagus and spoon over pasta.

To wok add remaining 2 tablespoons salad oil, garlic, ginger, and scallops. Cook, stirring, until scallops are opaque when cut (2 to 3 minutes). Add rice vinegar, sugar, soy sauce, and sesame oil; cook, stirring, just until sugar is dissolved. Pour over pasta mixture.

If made ahead, cover and refrigerate for up to 4 hours. Makes 4 to 6 servings.

Per serving: 272 calories, 12 g protein, 37 g carbohydrates, 8 g total fat, 12 mg cholesterol, 120 mg sodium

Mexican-style Squid Salad

Preparation time: About 30 minutes
Cooking time: About 5 minutes

2 **pounds cleaned squid tubes (mantles), cut into 1-inch rings (page 67); or 2 pounds large shrimp (under 30 per lb.), shelled and deveined**
Chile Dressing (recipe follows)
1 **small red bell pepper, seeded and thinly sliced into bite-size strips**
¾ **cup cooked corn kernels**
1 **small can (8¾ oz.) kidney beans, drained**
Romaine lettuce leaves, washed and crisped
Salt and pepper

In a 4- to 5-quart pan, bring 1½ inches water to a boil over high heat. Add squid rings; cook until squid is opaque (about 30 seconds); or cook shrimp until opaque when cut (about 2 minutes). Drain, rinse with cold water, and pat dry. Prepare Chile Dressing.

In a bowl, mix squid, dressing, bell pepper, corn, and beans. Arrange lettuce on salad plates; top with squid mixture. Season to taste with salt and pepper. Makes 4 to 6 servings.

■ **Chile Dressing.** Mix ½ cup **salad oil**, ⅓ cup **lemon juice**, 1½ teaspoons *each* **dry oregano leaves** and **ground cumin**, and 1 or 2 **jalapeño or serrano chiles**, seeded and finely chopped.

Per serving: 365 calories, 27 g protein, 18 g carbohydrates, 21 g total fat, 353 mg cholesterol, 218 mg sodium

Main Dishes

Pictured at right

Sole-wrapped Belgian Endive Rolls

Preparation time: 10 minutes
Cooking time: About 20 minutes
Baking time: 10 to 15 minutes

1 **tablespoon butter or margarine**
8 **heads Belgian endive (2 oz. *each*)**
¼ **cup water**
8 **thin sole fillets (2 to 3 oz. *each*)**
Salt and ground white pepper
⅓ **cup finely chopped shallots**
¼ **teaspoon dry tarragon**
1 **cup *each* dry white wine and regular-strength chicken broth**
½ **cup whipping cream**

In a wide frying pan, melt butter over medium heat. Add endive and water. Cover and cook, turning often, until endive is tender when pierced (15 to 20 minutes); set aside.

Rinse fish and pat dry. Season to taste with salt and pepper. Lay an endive head on one end of each fillet; roll up. Set rolls, seam sides down, in a greased shallow 2- to 2½-quart baking dish. Cover and bake in a 400° oven until fish looks just slightly translucent or wet inside when cut in thickest part (10 to 15 minutes).

Meanwhile, in pan used to cook endive, combine shallots, tarragon, wine, and broth. Boil, uncovered, over high heat until reduced by half (about 10 minutes). When fish is done, drain juices from baking dish into wine mixture; add cream. Boil until reduced to ¾ cup. Spoon over fish. Makes 4 servings.

Per serving: 253 calories, 24 g protein, 8 g carbohydrates, 14 g total fat, 96 mg cholesterol, 395 mg sodium

A creamy tarragon and shallot sauce embellishes Sole-wrapped Belgian Endive Rolls (recipe at left).

Sole with Mushroom Velvet

Preparation time: About 15 minutes
Cooking time: 12 to 15 minutes

⅓ **pound mushrooms, finely chopped**
2 **tablespoons thinly sliced green onion (including top)**
3 **or 4 whole allspice**
1 **pound sole fillets (¼ to ½ inch thick)**
4 **to 6 thin lemon slices**
1 **cup dry white wine**
½ **cup whipping cream**
¼ **to ½ cup butter or margarine**

Spread mushrooms and onion in a wide frying pan; add allspice. Rinse fish and pat dry; lay on vegetables, overlapping as little as possible. Cover with lemon slices and pour in wine.

Bring to a boil over high heat; reduce heat, cover, and simmer until fish looks just slightly translucent or wet inside when cut in thickest part (3 to 5 minutes).

With a wide spatula, carefully transfer fish and lemon to a warm platter and keep warm. Boil pan juices, uncovered, until reduced by half. Add cream and any accumulated juices from fish. Boil until reduced by half again. Reduce heat to low. Add butter in one chunk and stir constantly until blended. Pour over fish. Makes 4 servings.

Per serving: 306 calories, 23 g protein, 4 g carbohydrates, 22 g total fat, 119 mg cholesterol, 224 mg sodium

Fish Fillets with Sherry-Mushroom Sauce

Preparation time: 15 to 20 minutes
Cooking time: About 20 minutes

  2 **tablespoons olive oil or butter**
  ¼ **pound mushrooms, thinly sliced**
1½ **pounds cod, sea bass, or other fillets (¾ inch thick) from Group IIa or III (pages 8–9)**
  1 **teaspoon cornstarch**
  ⅓ **cup water**
  ¼ **cup dry sherry**
  1 **tablespoon soy sauce**
  2 **cloves garlic, minced or pressed**
  2 **teaspoons minced fresh ginger**
  ½ **cup sliced green onions (including tops)**

Heat 1½ tablespoons of the oil in a wide frying pan over medium heat. When oil is hot, add mushrooms and cook, stirring, until lightly browned (about 8 minutes). Lift out and set aside.

Rinse fish and pat dry. Heat remaining ½ tablespoon oil in pan over medium-high heat. When oil is hot, add fish in a

single layer. Cover and cook until just slightly translucent or wet inside when cut in thickest part (about 8 minutes). With a wide spatula, lift out fish and transfer to a warm platter; keep warm.

Stir together cornstarch, water, sherry, soy sauce, garlic, and ginger. Pour into pan; add mushrooms and stir to loosen brown bits. Cook over high heat, stirring, until mixture comes to a boil. Add onions; pour over fish. Makes 4 or 5 servings.

Per serving: 244 calories, 33 g protein, 5 g carbohydrates, 9.5 g total fat, 60 mg cholesterol, 363 mg sodium

Pan-fried Catfish with Jicama Salad

Preparation time: About 35 minutes
Cooking time: About 10 minutes

     Jicama Salad (recipe follows)
  4 **to 6 catfish fillets (4 to 5 oz. *each*)**
  ¼ **cup all-purpose flour**
  2 **eggs**
  ¾ **cup dehydrated masa flour (corn tortilla flour)**
     Salad oil
     Salt and pepper
  2 **or 3 limes, cut into wedges**

Prepare Jicama Salad; set aside.

Rinse fish and pat dry. Coat with flour; shake off excess. Beat eggs in a shallow dish until blended. Dip fillets in eggs, lift out, and drain briefly; roll in masa to coat.

Pour oil to a depth of ⅛ inch into a wide frying pan. Place over medium-high heat and heat until oil ripples when pan is tilted. Place fillets (without crowding) in pan and cook, turning once, until browned and just slightly translucent or wet inside when cut (8 to 10 minutes). As fillets cook, transfer to a warm platter. Season to taste with salt and pepper.

Serve with salad; offer lime wedges to squeeze over fish and salad. Makes 4 to 6 servings.

Per serving fish: 251 calories, 18 g protein, 17 g carbohydrates, 13 g total fat, 135 mg cholesterol, 72 mg sodium

▪ **Jicama Salad.** Peel 1 **jicama** (1 to 1¼ lbs.) and cut into sticks ⅛ by 1½ inches (you should have about 4 cups).

Combine jicama; 2 **green onions** (including tops), finely chopped; 2 tablespoons *each* minced **fresh cilantro** (coriander) and **salad oil;** and 1 or 2 **small fresh hot chiles,** such as jalapeño or serrano, seeded and finely chopped to make about 1 tablespoon. (At this point, you may cover and refrigerate until next day.)

Peel 2 **small bananas;** cut into ¼-inch cubes. Add to jicama mixture with 3 to 4 tablespoons **lime juice;** mix gently. Makes about 6 cups.

Per serving salad: 101 calories, 1 g protein, 14 g carbohydrates, 5 g total fat, 0 mg cholesterol, 6 mg sodium

Five-Spice Fish

Preparation time: About 15 minutes
Chilling time: At least 4 hours
Broiling time: About 10 minutes

1½ **to 2 pounds boneless and skinless fish fillets, such as orange roughy, or other fillets (¾ to 1 inch thick) from Group IIb, IIc, or IVb (pages 8–9)**
  3 **green onions (including tops), cut into 2-inch lengths, crushed**
  8 **thin slices (about 1 inch in diameter) fresh ginger, crushed**
  ⅓ **cup soy sauce**
  2 **tablespoons rice wine or dry sherry**
  2 **tablespoons sugar**
  1 **tablespoon Oriental sesame oil**
  ½ **teaspoon Chinese five-spice or ⅛ teaspoon *each* ground cinnamon, ground allspice, ground cloves, and crushed anise seeds**

Rinse fish and pat dry. Cut into 1½- by 2½-inch pieces. Combine with onions, ginger, soy sauce, wine, sugar, sesame oil, and five-spice. Cover and refrigerate for at least 4 hours or for up to a day.

Lift fish from marinade and set slightly apart on a greased rack in a broiler pan. Broil about 4 inches from heat, turning once, until just slightly translucent or wet inside when cut in thickest part (8 to 10 minutes total). Makes 8 servings.

Per serving: 104 calories, 17 g protein, 3 g carbohydrates, 2 g total fat, 30 mg cholesterol, 952 mg sodium

Orange Roughy Maître d'Hôtel

Preparation time: 10 minutes
Baking time: 8 to 10 minutes

- ¼ **cup butter or margarine**
- 2 **tablespoons** *each* **lemon juice, chopped parsley, and snipped chives**
- 1 **teaspoon dill weed**
- 2 **dashes ground red pepper (cayenne)**
- 1 **pound orange roughy fillets or other fillets (½ to ¾ inch thick) from Group IIa or IIb (pages 8–9)**
  Salt

In a small pan, melt butter over medium heat. Stir in lemon juice, parsley, chives, dill weed, and red pepper; set aside.

Rinse fish and pat dry. Arrange in a single layer, overlapping slightly if necessary, in a 9-inch square baking pan. Pour butter mixture over fish.

Bake, uncovered, in a 400° oven until fish looks just slightly translucent or wet inside when cut in thickest part (8 to 10 minutes). With a wide spatula, transfer fish to a warm platter and keep warm. Boil juices in pan over high heat, stirring occasionally, until reduced to about ¼ cup. Drain any accumulated juices from fish into sauce, stir, and pour over fish. Season to taste with salt. Makes 2 or 3 servings.

Per serving: 331 calories, 23 g protein, 1 g carbohydrates, 26 g total fat, 72 mg cholesterol, 255 mg sodium

Mackerel with Tart Onion Sauce

Preparation time: About 5 minutes
Cooking time: 18 to 20 minutes
Standing time: 15 to 30 minutes

- 4 **medium-size (¾ to 1 lb.** *each***) or 2 large (1¼ to 1½ lbs.** *each***) mackerel or bluefish, cut into fillets (page 80)**
  About ⅓ cup all-purpose flour
- 3 **to 4 tablespoons olive oil or salad oil**
  Salt and pepper
- 1 **medium-large onion, thinly sliced**
- 3 **tablespoons red wine vinegar**

Rinse fish and pat dry. Dredge in flour to coat; shake off excess.

Pan-fry fillets (page 90), substituting 2 tablespoons of the olive oil for salad oil and butter. Lift out fish and transfer to a heatproof serving plate. Season to taste with salt and pepper; place in a 250° oven to keep warm.

Heat 1 more tablespoon of the oil in pan over medium heat; add onion and cook, stirring often, until lightly browned (about 10 minutes). Add vinegar and cook for 1 more minute. Spoon onion mixture over fish. Let stand in warm oven for 15 to 30 minutes to blend flavors. Makes 4 servings.

Per serving: 366 calories, 22 g protein, 10 g carbohydrates, 26 g total fat, 79 mg cholesterol, 102 mg sodium

Baked Fish & Ratatouille

Preparation time: 15 to 20 minutes
Baking time: About 1 hour

- 1 **medium-size zucchini, sliced**
- 1 **small eggplant (about ¾ lb.), cut into ½-inch cubes**
- 1 *each* **medium-size yellow and red bell peppers, seeded and cut into thin strips**
- 1 **tablespoon dry basil leaves**
- 1 **teaspoon dry oregano leaves**
- 2 **tablespoons olive oil**
- 10 **to 16 ounces individually frozen fish fillets, such as cod, orange roughy, or other frozen fillets from Group IIa, IIb, or IIc (pages 8–9)**
  Salt and pepper
- ¾ **cup shredded Havarti cheese (optional)**

In a shallow 3-quart baking dish, combine zucchini, eggplant, bell peppers, basil, oregano, and oil. Cover and bake in a 425° oven for 40 minutes. Stir vegetables and push to sides of dish. Lay frozen fish in center, layering if necessary. Cover and continue to bake until fish looks just slightly translucent or wet inside when cut in thickest part (about 20 minutes).

Season to taste with salt and pepper. If desired, sprinkle fish with cheese, cover, and continue to bake just until cheese is melted (2 to 3 minutes). Makes 3 or 4 servings.

Per serving: 159 calories, 15 g protein, 9 g carbohydrates, 8 g total fat, 30 mg cholesterol, 44 mg sodium

Braised Sablefish

Preparation time: About 10 minutes
Chilling time: At least 1 hour
Cooking time: 6 to 8 minutes

- ½ **cup thinly sliced green onions (including tops)**
- ¼ **cup** *each* **soy sauce and dry sherry**
- 1 **large clove garlic, minced or pressed**
- ½ **teaspoon grated fresh ginger**
- 1½ **pounds sablefish, Greenland turbot (halibut), or Chilean sea bass fillets or steaks (about ¾ inch thick)**
- 1 **tablespoon salad oil**
- 1 **teaspoon Oriental sesame oil**
  Hot boiled small potatoes

Mix onions, soy sauce, sherry, garlic, and ginger. Rinse fish and pat dry. Add to marinade, turning to coat all sides. Cover and refrigerate, turning once or twice, for at least 1 hour or for up to 1½ hours.

Place a wide frying pan over medium-high heat. When pan is hot, add salad oil. Lift fish from marinade and drain, reserving marinade. Add fish to pan and cook, uncovered, carefully turning once with a wide spatula, until browned on both sides (about 5 minutes total). Stir sesame oil into reserved marinade and pour over fish. Cook, uncovered, until marinade has almost evaporated. Serve fish with pan juices and potatoes. Makes 3 servings.

Per serving: 525 calories, 32 g protein, 6 g carbohydrates, 41 g total fat, 111 mg cholesterol, 1,501 mg sodium

Steamed Salmon with Sorrel

Preparation time: 15 minutes
Cooking time: 15 to 20 minutes

- 3 **cups lightly packed sorrel leaves, stems removed**
- 2 **skinless salmon fillets or steaks (6 to 8 oz.** *each***; ¾ to 1 inch thick)**
  About ¼ cup regular-strength chicken broth
- 2 **tablespoons butter or margarine**
- 1 **tablespoon chopped fresh mint leaves or sorrel leaves**

Spread whole sorrel leaves evenly in an 8- to 9-inch-diameter rimmed heatproof plate or shallow pan. Rinse fish and pat dry. Place on sorrel. Drape foil over plate and place in a steamer basket or on a rack set over 1 inch boiling water in a wok or deep, wide pan. Cover and steam over high heat until fish looks just slightly translucent or wet inside when cut in thickest part (10 to 15 minutes).

Holding fish on plate with a wide spatula, carefully pour pan juices into a measuring cup; keep fish warm. Add broth to juices to make ½ cup. Pour into a medium-size frying pan and boil, uncovered, over high heat until reduced to ¼ cup. Reduce heat to medium; add butter and mint. Cook, swirling pan, until butter is melted and sauce is smooth. Pour over fish. Makes 2 servings.

Per serving: 359 calories, 35 g protein, 3 g carbohydrates, 23 g total fat, 125 mg cholesterol, 320 mg sodium

Pictured above right

Grilled Salmon on Wilted Chicory Salad

Crisp greens provide dramatic contrast for thyme-accented fish in Grilled Salmon on Wilted Chicory Salad (recipe at left).

Preparation time: 20 to 25 minutes
Cooking time: 20 to 25 minutes

- **8 tablespoons extra-virgin olive oil**
- **½ pound chanterelles or button mushrooms, cut into ½-inch pieces**
- **¼ cup thinly sliced green onions (including tops)**
- **2 tablespoons red wine vinegar**
- **4 cloves garlic, minced or pressed**
- **⅓ cup minced fresh thyme leaves or 2 tablespoons dry thyme leaves**
- **6 skinless salmon fillets or steaks (6 to 8 oz. each)**
- **9 cups bite-size pieces chicory (curly endive), washed and crisped**
  Salt and pepper

In a wide frying pan, combine 2 tablespoons of the oil and chanterelles; cook over high heat, stirring occasionally, until mushrooms are lightly browned (10 to 12 minutes). Meanwhile, in a small bowl, stir together 4 more tablespoons of the oil, onions, vinegar, garlic, and half the thyme; set aside. Rinse fish and pat dry. Coat both sides with remaining oil and sprinkle with remaining thyme; set aside.

Add oil-vinegar dressing to mushrooms; remove from heat. Add chicory, mixing lightly to coat with dressing.

Distribute salad on individual plates or arrange on a large platter.

Barbecue fish using direct heat (page 86) or broil using dry-heat method (page 88), turning once (omit basting), until fish looks just slightly translucent or wet inside when cut in thickest part (8 to 10 minutes). Place fish on salad. Season to taste with salt and pepper. Makes 6 servings.

Per serving: 482 calories, 39 g protein, 16 g carbohydrates, 31 g total fat, 94 mg cholesterol, 199 mg sodium

Baby Salmon with Sautéed Leeks

Preparation time: About 20 minutes
Baking time: About 10 minutes

- **About 1½ pounds leeks**
- **4 tablespoons butter or margarine**
- **½ teaspoon dry thyme leaves**
- **2 tablespoons lemon juice**
  Salt and ground white pepper
- **6 boned baby salmon or trout (about 8 oz. each), heads removed**
  Lemon wedges

Trim and discard root ends and tough green tops from leeks; remove tough outer leaves. Split leeks in half lengthwise and rinse well; thinly slice (you should have about 3 cups). In a wide frying pan, melt 2 tablespoons of the butter over medium heat. Add leeks and cook, stirring, until soft (8 to 10 minutes). Stir in thyme and lemon juice; season to taste with salt and pepper.

Spread fish open and place, skin sides down, in a single layer in a greased shallow baking pan. Spoon leek mixture evenly down center of each fish. Melt remaining 2 tablespoons butter and drizzle over fish.

Bake, uncovered, in a 400° oven until fish looks just slightly translucent or wet inside when cut in thickest part (about 10 minutes). With a wide spatula, carefully transfer to a serving platter. Garnish with lemon wedges. Makes 6 servings.

Per serving: 341 calories, 35 g protein, 7 g carbohydrates, 19 g total fat, 114 mg cholesterol, 164 mg sodium

Trout with Leeks & Vinegar

Preparation time: 15 to 20 minutes
Cooking time: About 15 minutes

- **1 pound leeks**
- **2 bottles (8 oz. *each*) clam juice**
- **⅓ cup (2 oz.) diced cooked ham, fat trimmed**
- **⅓ cup white wine vinegar**
- **4 cleaned whole trout (6 to 8 oz. *each*)**
  All-purpose flour
- **½ to 2 tablespoons butter or margarine**
- **½ to 2 tablespoons salad oil**
  Pepper

Trim and discard root ends and tough green tops from leeks; remove tough outer leaves. Split leeks in half lengthwise and rinse well. Cut lengthwise ½ inch thick. Divide into 8 equal portions; securely tie each bundle with string.

In a wide frying pan, combine clam juice, ham, and leeks. Bring to a boil over high heat; reduce heat, cover, and simmer until leeks are tender when pierced (about 5 minutes).

Stir vinegar into leek mixture. Lift out leeks, place on a warm rimmed platter, and keep warm. Increase heat to high and boil liquid, uncovered, until reduced to 1 cup (8 to 10 minutes).

Meanwhile, rinse fish and pat dry. Trim and discard fins. Coat lightly with flour; shake off excess. Pan-fry in butter and oil (page 90).

Place trout on platter, arranging bundles of leeks between them. Remove strings. Spoon ham and liquid over all. Season to taste with pepper. Makes 4 servings.

Per serving: 403 calories, 40 g protein, 11 g carbohydrates, 21 g total fat, 130 mg cholesterol, 657 mg sodium

Calico Stuffed Trout

Preparation time: 30 minutes
Baking time: 10 to 12 minutes

- **About 2½ tablespoons salad oil**
- **½ cup *each* finely chopped green and red bell peppers, onion, celery, and carrot**
- **1 clove garlic, minced or pressed**
- **½ teaspoon *each* dry basil leaves and dry oregano leaves**
- **¼ teaspoon *each* salt and pepper**
- **2 tablespoons *each* dry white wine and white wine vinegar**
- **6 cleaned whole trout (¾ to 1 lb. *each*)**
  Lemon wedges

Heat 2 tablespoons of the oil in a medium-size frying pan over medium heat; add bell peppers, onion, celery, carrot, garlic, basil, and oregano. Cook, stirring often, until onion is soft but not browned (8 to 10 minutes). Stir in salt, pepper, wine, and vinegar; continue to cook, stirring, until most of the liquid has evaporated. Remove from heat.

Rinse fish and pat dry. Spoon vegetable mixture evenly into cavity of each trout. Place trout, slightly apart, in a greased shallow baking pan. Brush tops of fish with oil.

Bake, uncovered, in a 400° oven until fish looks just slightly translucent or wet inside when cut in thickest part (10 to 12 minutes). Serve with lemon wedges. Makes 6 servings.

Per serving: 245 calories, 25 g protein, 4 g carbohydrates, 14 g total fat, 188 mg cholesterol, 166 mg sodium

Pictured at left

Mr. Zhu's Steamed Fish

Preparation time: About 15 minutes
Cooking time: 8 to 10 minutes

- **1 scaled and cleaned whole rockfish (1½ to 2½ lbs.) or other fish of comparable size from Group IIa (pages 8–9), or 1½ pounds skinless and boneless fillets from Group IIa or IIb**
  Salt
- **3 tablespoons slivered fresh ginger**
- **3 green onions (including tops), thinly sliced**
- **1 slice bacon, cut into ½-inch pieces**
- **1 dried hot red chile (about 3 inches long)**
- **1 tablespoon rice vinegar or wine vinegar**
- **1 tablespoon soy sauce**
  Cilantro (coriander) sprigs

Rinse fish and pat dry. Remove head from whole fish, if desired (page 79). Make 3 diagonal slashes across body on each side. Place fish in a wide bowl or rimmed plate that will fit inside a steamer basket, wok, or deep, wide pan. If fish is too long, cut in half crosswise and place halves side by side. (Or arrange fillets on plate, overlapping thin edges.)

Moist heat intensifies distinctive flavors of fresh ginger, hot chile, and soy sauce in Mr. Zhu's Steamed Fish (recipe at right).

Sprinkle fish lightly, inside and out, with salt. Place half the ginger, onions, and bacon inside fish cavity; put remainder on top (or put all on top of fillets). Set chile on fish. Pour vinegar and soy sauce over top.

Drape foil over bowl and place in a steamer basket or on a rack set over 1 inch boiling water in pan. Cover and steam over high heat until fish looks just slightly translucent or wet inside when cut in thickest part (8 to 10 minutes for each inch of thickness). Remove from steamer. If necessary, reassemble halves; garnish with cilantro. Makes 4 to 6 servings.

Per serving: 137 calories, 22 g protein, 2 g carbohydrates, 4 g total fat, 42 mg cholesterol, 267 mg sodium

Pine Cone Fish

Preparation time: 20 to 25 minutes
Cooking time: About 10 minutes

¼ **cup pine nuts or slivered almonds**
    Sweet & Sour Sauce (recipe follows)
1   **scaled and cleaned whole rockfish or snapper (about 4 lbs.), with head and tail**
    About 2 tablespoons dry sherry
    Ground white pepper
    About ½ cup cornstarch
    Salad oil
1   **cup lightly packed cilantro (coriander) sprigs**

Place pine nuts in a shallow baking pan and toast in a 350° oven, shaking pan several times, until golden (about 6 minutes); set aside. Prepare Sweet & Sour Sauce; set aside.

Rinse fish and pat dry. Cut fish behind collarbone down to backbone. Turn knife parallel and cut along backbone to within 3 inches of tail; extend belly cavity to 3 inches above tail. Grasp fish

(as cut free) at collarbone. Cut closely along rib bones to within 3 inches of tail; as you cut, pull fillet back to provide tension. Repeat on other side. Fold both fillets back away from bone; tap knife with a mallet to cut through bone 3 inches above tail. Discard head and bones. (You will now have 2 fillets connected at tail.)

Lay fillets, skin sides down, on a board. Score flesh in a crisscross pattern, cutting just to skin and forming ½-inch diamonds. Sprinkle with sherry, rubbing it into crevices; sprinkle lightly with white pepper. Coat scored flesh with cornstarch, patting and rubbing it into crevices. Shake off excess.

Half-fill a wok or deep, wide frying pan with oil and heat to 375° F on a deep-frying thermometer. Twist fillets so skin sides touch and tail is exposed. Grasp ends of fillets with one hand, tail with the other. Slowly immerse fish in hot oil. Cook until richly browned (about 5 minutes); if fish is not completely submerged, gently spoon oil over fish as it cooks.

With a large wire skimmer or 2 slotted spatulas, lift fish from oil, drain briefly, and place on a heatproof rimmed platter. Keep warm, if desired, in a 150° oven for up to 15 minutes.

Bring sauce to a boil; pour over fish. Sprinkle with nuts and garnish with cilantro. To serve, cut into chunks, spooning sauce over each serving. Makes 4 servings.

Per serving fish: 269 calories, 26 g protein, 12 g carbohydrates, 13 g total fat, 44 mg cholesterol, 79 mg sodium

Sweet & Sour Sauce. Heat ¼ cup **salad oil** in a 2- to 3-quart pan over medium-high heat. Add ⅓ cup *each* diced **carrot** and thinly sliced **green onions** (including tops) and 3 cloves **garlic,** minced or pressed. Cook, stirring, for 1 minute.

Add 1¼ cups **regular-strength chicken broth;** 6 tablespoons *each* **soy sauce, red wine vinegar,** and **sugar;** and 2½ tablespoons **cornstarch** mixed with 2½ tablespoons **water.** Cook, stirring, until sauce boils and thickens. If made ahead, cover and let stand for up to 4 hours. Makes 2¾ cups.

Per tablespoon sauce: 22 calories, .2 g protein, 3 g carbohydrates, 1 g total fat, 0 mg cholesterol, 169 mg sodium

Monkfish Scaloppine with Shallots

Preparation time: About 20 minutes
Cooking time: About 10 minutes

1   **large monkfish fillet (1 to 1½ lbs.)**
    All-purpose flour
2   **to 3 tablespoons butter or margarine**
1   **to 2 tablespoons salad oil**
    Salt and ground white pepper
¾ **cup finely chopped shallots**
½ **cup *each* dry vermouth and regular-strength chicken broth**
1   **tablespoon lemon juice**
1   **teaspoon minced fresh thyme leaves or ¼ teaspoon dry thyme leaves**
    Fresh thyme sprigs (optional)

Prepare monkfish for scaloppine (page 42). Coat with flour; shake off excess. Lay pieces in a single layer on wax paper.

Place a wide frying pan over medium-high heat. Add 1 tablespoon each of the butter and oil. When butter is melted, lay as many fish pieces in pan as will fit without crowding. Cook, turning once, until fish looks opaque when cut in center (1½ to 2 minutes total). Lift out and transfer to a warm platter; keep warm. Repeat for remaining fish, adding up to 1 more tablespoon each of the butter and oil as needed. Season to taste with salt and pepper.

In same pan, melt 1 more tablespoon of the butter over medium heat. Add shallots and cook, stirring, until limp (3 to 4 minutes). Add vermouth, broth, lemon juice, and minced thyme. Increase heat to high and boil, uncovered, until reduced by half. Spoon sauce over fish. Garnish with thyme sprigs, if desired. Makes 4 servings.

Per serving: 223 calories, 18 g protein, 12 g carbohydrates, 11 g total fat, 44 mg cholesterol, 212 mg sodium

Quick Ways with Smoked Seafood

Smoked seafood—both fish and shellfish—is prized for its special flavor, but too often it's reserved just for special-occasion buffet tables. You can enliven any meal by incorporating smoked seafood into a first course, salad, or main course. Because most smoked seafood is already cooked, the final dish can be prepared quickly.

You can either smoke your own fish as directed on page 84 or purchase the smoked product. Many kinds of fish and shellfish are available smoked—look for them in specialty delicatessens or fish markets. Some can be found in supermarket delis as well.

You can purchase smoked seafood fresh-smoked, frozen, vacuum-packed, or canned. Remember that smoked seafood, except when canned, is perishable and must be refrigerated or frozen.

Spoilage time in the refrigerator varies from 5 days to 3 months (for such hard-smoked products as fish jerky), but, to be on the safe side, consume any purchased smoked seafood within a few days of opening. Frozen products can be kept for up to 6 months in the freezer; they should not be thawed and refrozen.

Most smoked seafood can be eaten either cold or gently heated. Some products that are lightly smoked or smoke flavored but not cooked, such as finnan haddie (cod or haddock), must be cooked before serving.

Offer smoked seafood with crackers or bread and lemon wedges as an appetizer, or sliver it into quiche, egg dishes, or pasta sauces. For a salad, slice or flake smoked fish onto romaine lettuce leaves, sprinkle with toasted sliced almonds, and drizzle with Dijon Vinaigrette Dressing (page 124). Or try one of the following recipes.

Steamed Smoked Fish with Dill Butter

4 to 6 small red thin-skinned potatoes
2 pieces (6 to 8 oz. *each*) smoked sablefish (black cod)
¼ cup unsalted butter or margarine, at room temperature
1 tablespoon chopped fresh dill or 1 teaspoon dill weed
Fresh dill sprigs (optional)

Using a vegetable peeler, remove a thin strip of skin around center of each potato. Arrange potatoes on a steamer rack in a 5- to 6-quart pan. Cover and steam over boiling water until tender when pierced (about 25 minutes).

Remove and discard skin and bones from fish, if necessary. When potatoes are done, add fish to steamer rack; cover and steam until fish is hot (about 5 minutes).

Meanwhile, mix butter and chopped dill.

Arrange fish and potatoes on 2 plates; garnish with dill sprigs, if desired. Spoon butter on potatoes and fish. Makes 2 servings.

Smoked Salmon Mousse

3 ounces smoked salmon (or lox), coarsely chopped
1 egg yolk
1½ tablespoons lemon juice
3 tablespoons salad oil
2 cucumbers, thinly sliced
Red onion slivers
Watercress sprigs
Thin lemon wedges

In a blender or food processor, combine salmon, egg yolk, and lemon juice; whirl until puréed. With motor on high, add oil, a few drops at a time at first and then increasing to a slow, steady stream about 1⁄16 inch wide. Cover and refrigerate for at least 1 hour or for up to a day.

On 4 salad plates, arrange equal portions of cucumber, overlapping slices slightly. Mound a spoonful of the salmon mousse on each plate. Garnish each with a few slivers of onion, 2 or 3 watercress sprigs, and a lemon wedge. Makes 4 first-course servings.

Pictured at left

Smoked Mussels with Lemon-Garlic Mayonnaise

½ cup Lemon-Garlic Mayonnaise (recipe follows)
18 smoked mussels, clams, or oysters

Prepare Lemon-Garlic Mayonnaise. Arrange mussels on a platter with a small bowl of mayonnaise. Skewer mussels with a small fork or wooden pick and dip into mayonnaise. Makes 3 or 4 appetizer servings.

■ **Lemon-Garlic Mayonnaise.** In a blender or food processor, combine 2 tablespoons **lemon juice,** 2 cloves **garlic,** 1 large **egg,** and ⅛ teaspoon **paprika.** Whirl until blended. With motor on high, add 1 cup **salad oil,** a few drops at a time at first and then increasing to a slow, steady stream about 1⁄16 inch wide. Season to taste with **salt** and **pepper.**

If made ahead, cover and refrigerate for up to 2 days. Makes 1¼ cups.

For a delightful appetizer, offer Smoked Mussels with Lemon-Garlic Mayonnaise (recipe at right).

Grilled Tuna with Teriyaki Fruit Sauce

Preparation time: 15 to 20 minutes
Grilling time: 3 to 4 minutes

- ¼ cup *each* soy sauce and sugar
- 6 tablespoons sake or dry sherry
- 3 thin slices fresh ginger or ¼ teaspoon ground ginger
- 1 pound boneless and skinless tuna fillets or steaks (about 1 inch thick), cut into 4 equal pieces
  Olive oil or salad oil
- 8 to 12 thin slices peeled, seeded papaya
- 2 teaspoons finely chopped candied or crystallized ginger
- 1 medium-size green bell pepper, seeded and cut into long slivers

In a 2-quart pan, combine soy sauce, sugar, sake, and ginger slices; bring to a boil over high heat and cook, stirring, until sugar is dissolved. Continue to boil until reduced to ⅓ cup; discard ginger slices. Keep warm.

Rinse fish and pat dry. Brush both sides with oil. Barbecue over direct heat (page 86), placing fish directly on grill and turning once (omit basting), until just slightly translucent or wet inside when cut in thickest part (3 to 4 minutes total).

Place tuna on individual plates. Evenly top with soy sauce mixture, papaya slices, and candied ginger; arrange bell pepper alongside. Makes 4 servings.

Per serving: 263 calories, 28 g protein, 24 g carbohydrates, 6 g total fat, 43 mg cholesterol, 1,078 mg sodium

Pan-fried Skate with Cucumbers & Capers (recipe below) hails the increasing popularity of this delicate, sweet-tasting fish.

Pictured above

Pan-fried Skate with Cucumbers & Capers

Preparation time: 15 to 20 minutes
Cooking time: 10 to 15 minutes

- 1 European-style cucumber (about 1 lb.)
- 1 pound skate fillets or 1¼ pounds unfilleted skate, cut into 4 equal pieces
  About ¼ cup all-purpose flour
- 3 tablespoons salad oil
- ⅓ cup minced Italian or regular parsley
- 3 tablespoons lemon juice
- 2 tablespoons drained capers
  Italian parsley sprigs
  Salt and pepper

Peel cucumber, halve lengthwise, and scoop out and discard seeds. Slice crosswise about ⅓ inch thick; set aside.

Rinse fish and pat dry. Prepare skate (page 64). Dredge in flour to coat; shake off excess. Pan-fry (page 90), using 2 tablespoons of the oil and omitting butter; keep warm.

Heat remaining 1 tablespoon oil in a wide frying pan over medium-high heat. When oil is hot, add cucumber and cook, stirring often, until slightly limp (about 3 minutes). Remove from heat and stir in minced parsley, lemon juice, and capers. Spoon over skate. Garnish with parsley sprigs. Season to taste with salt and pepper. Makes 4 servings.

Per serving: 247 calories, 26 g protein, 10 g carbohydrates, 11 g total fat, 62 mg cholesterol, 200 mg sodium

Swordfish Steaks with Mushrooms

Preparation time: About 10 minutes
Standing time: 30 minutes
Cooking time: 10 to 13 minutes

- 2 pounds swordfish steaks or other steaks (about 1 inch thick) from Group IVb (pages 8–9)
- 3 tablespoons lemon juice
- ¼ cup dry white wine or water
- 1 clove garlic, minced or pressed
- ½ teaspoon *each* dry oregano leaves, salt, and pepper
- ¼ teaspoon fennel seeds, crushed
- 2 tablespoons olive oil or salad oil
- ½ pound mushrooms, sliced
- 2 or 3 green onions (including tops), thinly sliced

Rinse fish and pat dry. In a 9- by 13-inch dish, combine lemon juice, wine, garlic, oregano, salt, pepper, and fennel seeds.

(Continued on next page)

Add fish and let stand, turning occasionally, for 30 minutes.

With a slotted spatula, lift out fish and drain briefly, reserving marinade. Broil as directed for dry-heat broiling (page 88).

Meanwhile, heat oil in a small frying pan over medium-high heat; add mushrooms and cook, stirring occasionally, until soft and lightly browned. Stir in reserved marinade and boil gently for about 2 minutes.

Transfer fish to a warm platter; top with mushroom sauce and sprinkle with onions. Makes 4 to 6 servings.

Per serving: 217 calories, 28 g protein, 3 g carbohydrates, 10 g total fat, 53 mg cholesterol, 308 mg sodium

Skewered Fish, Northwest Style

Preparation time: 20 minutes
Chilling time: At least 10 minutes
Broiling time: About 8 minutes

- ¼ cup *each* Worcestershire, soy sauce, and dry white wine
- 2 tablespoons olive oil or salad oil
- ½ pound boneless Pacific (northern) or Atlantic halibut or other firm fish from Group IV (pages 8–9)
- ½ pound sea scallops, rinsed and drained
- 15 small (about 1 inch in diameter) mushrooms
- 1 medium-size green bell pepper, seeded and cut into 1-inch squares

Mix Worcestershire, soy sauce, wine, and oil. Rinse fish and pat dry; cut into 1-inch cubes. Add halibut and scallops to soy mixture; mix lightly. Cover and refrigerate, stirring occasionally, for at least 10 minutes or for up to 1 hour.

Celebrate summer's bounty with Grilled Scallops with Red Pepper Sauce (recipe below), yellow summer squash, and tender young green beans.

Thread halibut, scallops, mushrooms, and bell pepper onto 5 thin skewers, alternating ingredients and dividing equally; reserve marinade.

Arrange skewers slightly apart on a greased rack in a broiler pan. Broil about 3 inches from heat, turning once and brushing with reserved marinade, until fish looks just slightly translucent or wet inside when cut and scallops are opaque (about 8 minutes total). Makes 5 servings.

Per serving: 165 calories, 19 g protein, 6 g carbohydrates, 7 g total fat, 30 mg cholesterol, 1,054 mg sodium

Pictured above

Grilled Scallops with Red Pepper Sauce

Preparation time: About 1 hour
Cooking time: 10 minutes
Grilling time: 5 to 8 minutes

- 2 small red bell peppers
- ½ cup regular-strength chicken broth
- ¼ cup dry white wine
- ¼ teaspoon dry basil leaves
- ½ cup (¼ lb.) butter or margarine
- 1½ pounds sea scallops (1 to 1½ inches in diameter), rinsed and drained
  Melted butter or margarine or salad oil

Place peppers in a shallow baking pan. Bake on lowest rack in a 450° oven, turning often, until skins blister and blacken (about 35 minutes). Cover pan with foil and let stand until peppers are cool enough to handle. Peel and discard skins; remove and discard stems and seeds.

Whirl peppers, broth, and wine in a blender or food processor until smooth. Pour mixture into a wide frying pan. Add basil. Bring to a boil over high heat; continue to boil, stirring often, until mixture is reduced to about ¾ cup. Reduce heat to medium. Add the ½ cup butter in one chunk and stir constantly until blended.

To keep sauce warm for up to 4 hours, pour into top of a double boiler or measuring cup and set in water that is just hot to touch; stir occasionally, replacing hot water as needed. Do not reheat or sauce will separate.

Thread scallops on 4 to 6 skewers and barbecue as directed for Fish or Shellfish Kebabs (page 86), omitting vegetables; baste with butter. Pour sauce into a warm rimmed serving platter or individual plates. Place skewers on top. Makes 4 to 6 servings.

Per serving: 243 calories, 20 g protein, 4 g carbohydrates, 16 g total fat, 79 mg cholesterol, 424 mg sodium

Sesame-Ginger Steamed Mussels

Preparation time: 25 minutes
Cooking time: About 15 minutes

2 tablespoons Oriental sesame oil
1½ tablespoons minced fresh ginger
3 cloves garlic, minced or pressed
2 green onions (including tops), thinly sliced
1 tablespoon soy sauce
1 cup dry white wine or water
1 cup regular-strength chicken broth
2 pounds mussels in shells
1 tablespoon *each* cornstarch and water
¼ cup chopped fresh cilantro (coriander)

In a 4- to 5-quart pan, combine oil, ginger, and garlic. Cook over medium-high heat, stirring, for 1 minute. Remove from heat; add onions, soy sauce, wine, and broth.

Prepare mussels (page 44) and add to broth mixture. Cover and bring to a boil; reduce heat and simmer until shells open (about 5 minutes). With a slotted spoon, transfer mussels to a large serving bowl, discarding any unopened shells; keep warm.

Combine cornstarch and water and stir into broth mixture. Bring to a boil over high heat, stirring; mix in cilantro. Pour over mussels. Makes 3 servings.

Per serving: 377 calories, 38 g protein, 17 g carbohydrates, 17 g total fat, 85 mg cholesterol, 1,549 mg sodium

Seafood Linguine

Preparation time: About 45 minutes
Cooking time: About 20 minutes

2 pounds mussels or small Atlantic or Pacific hard-shell clams in shells, suitable for steaming
1 bottle (8 oz.) clam juice
4 tablespoons butter or margarine
¾ cup sliced green onions (including tops)
2 large cloves garlic, minced or pressed
½ cup dry white wine
1 pound medium-size shrimp (30 to 50 per lb.), shelled and deveined
12 ounces fresh linguine or dry tagliarini
½ cup chopped parsley
1 cup (about 5 oz.) grated Parmesan cheese (optional)

Prepare and steam mussels (page 44), using clam juice as liquid. (Or prepare and steam clams as directed on pages 23–24.) Drain, reserving liquid; keep shellfish warm. Strain cooking liquid to remove any grit; measure and reserve 1 cup of the liquid.

In a 12- to 14-inch frying pan, melt 2 tablespoons of the butter over medium heat. Add onions and garlic; cook, stirring often, until onions are soft (about 5 minutes). Mix in wine and reserved cooking liquid. Increase heat to high and bring to a boil; cook until reduced by about half. Stir in remaining 2 tablespoons butter; then add shrimp. Immediately cover pan and remove from heat; let stand, covered, until shrimp are opaque when cut (6 to 8 minutes).

Meanwhile, in an 8- to 10-quart pan, cook linguine in 6 quarts boiling water just until tender to bite (2 to 3 minutes). Or cook according to package directions. Drain well and add to shrimp mixture along with parsley. Lifting with 2 forks, mix lightly.

Mound linguine mixture on a warm platter. Sprinkle with cheese, if desired. Set mussels (in shells) around edge of platter. Makes 6 servings.

Per serving: 388 calories, 25 g protein, 46 g carbohydrates, 10 g total fat, 126 mg cholesterol, 385 mg sodium

Seafood Brochettes with Champagne Sauce

Preparation time: About 40 minutes
Broiling time: About 10 minutes
Cooking time: About 5 minutes

16 extra-jumbo shrimp (16 to 20 per lb.), shelled and deveined
16 sea scallops (1¼ to 1½ inches in diameter), rinsed and drained
1 small onion, thinly sliced
6 tablespoons butter or margarine
1 teaspoon minced fresh thyme leaves or ½ teaspoon dry thyme leaves
⅛ teaspoon *each* ground turmeric and ground white pepper
½ cup dry champagne or dry white wine
2 teaspoons fine dry bread crumbs
2 large firm-ripe tomatoes, cut into ¾-inch-thick wedges
½ cup lightly packed fresh basil leaves or 2 tablespoons dry basil leaves
½ teaspoon sugar
2 cloves garlic, minced or pressed
Salt
Basil sprigs

Insert an 8- to 12-inch skewer through tail of a shrimp. Slide a scallop on skewer so it lies flat; then let shrimp curve around scallop and skewer head end. Repeat with remaining shrimp and scallops, placing 3 or 4 pairs on each skewer.

Scatter onion evenly in a shallow rimmed baking pan. Place skewers on onion. Melt 2 tablespoons of the butter; mix in thyme, turmeric, and pepper. Brush tops of shrimp and scallops with half the butter mixture. Pour champagne into pan.

Broil 4 inches from heat until tops of shrimp are pink (4 to 5 minutes). Turn brochettes over and brush with remain-

(Continued on next page)

ing butter mixture. Sprinkle evenly with bread crumbs. Continue to broil until tops begin to brown and shrimp and scallops are opaque when cut (4 to 6 more minutes). Set brochettes aside and keep warm.

Pour pan juices through a fine strainer into a wide frying pan; discard onion. To juices add tomatoes, basil leaves, sugar, and garlic. Cook over high heat, gently turning tomatoes occasionally, until hot (about 1 minute). Reduce heat to medium. Add remaining 4 tablespoons butter in one chunk and stir constantly until blended. Season to taste with salt.

Spoon sauce and tomatoes onto a warm serving platter or individual plates. Place brochettes on top. Garnish with basil sprigs. Makes 4 or 5 servings.

Per serving: 285 calories, 28 g protein, 8 g carbohydrates, 16 g total fat, 172 mg cholesterol, 372 mg sodium

Shrimp with Green Onions

Preparation time: About 20 minutes
Cooking time: About 5 minutes

1   **pound medium-large shrimp (30 to 35 per lb.), shelled, if desired, and deveined**
    Salt
1   **tablespoon rice wine or dry sherry**
1   **tablespoon cornstarch**
2   **tablespoons salad oil**
4   **green onions (including tops), thinly sliced**

Mix shrimp with about 1 tablespoon salt and let stand for 5 minutes. Rinse well and drain. Mix with wine and cornstarch.

Place a wok or wide frying pan over high heat. When pan is hot, add oil and swirl to coat. Add shrimp and cook, stirring, until pink (2 to 3 minutes). Add onions and cook, stirring, until shrimp are opaque when cut (about 1 more minute). Season to taste with salt. Makes 3 servings.

Per serving: 227 calories, 25 g protein, 5 g carbohydrates, 11 g total fat, 186 mg cholesterol, 183 mg sodium

Pictured on facing page

Orange Risotto with Shrimp

Preparation time: About 20 minutes
Cooking time: About 1 hour

5   **tablespoons butter or margarine**
1   **medium-size onion, finely chopped**
1½   **cups short-grain (pearl) rice**
1   **teaspoon grated orange peel**
1   **cup orange juice**
1¾   **cups dry white wine**
2   **cups regular-strength chicken broth**
1¼   **teaspoons dry thyme leaves**
1   **pound shelled and deveined medium-size shrimp (30 to 50 per lb.)**
3   **tablespoons Marsala, Madeira, or medium-dry sherry**
      Orange slices
      Italian parsley sprigs

In a 4- to 5-quart pan, melt 3 tablespoons of the butter over medium heat. Add onion and cook, stirring often, until slightly golden (about 6 minutes). Add rice and orange peel; cook, stirring often, until most of the rice is opaque (about 4 minutes).

Add orange juice, 1 cup of the wine, and broth; bring to a boil over high heat. Reduce heat and simmer, uncovered, stirring occasionally at first and then more often to prevent scorching as liquid is absorbed, until rice is tender to bite (about 40 minutes). Spoon onto a warm platter and keep warm.

In same pan, combine remaining 2 tablespoons butter, remaining ¾ cup wine, and thyme. Bring to a boil over high heat. Add shrimp and cook, stirring often, until opaque when cut (about 2 minutes).

With a slotted spoon, lift out shrimp and arrange on risotto; keep warm. Add Marsala to pan juices. Boil, uncovered, over high heat until slightly syrupy and reduced to about ¼ cup. Pour over shrimp. Garnish with orange slices and parsley. Makes 4 servings.

Per serving: 581 calories, 30 g protein, 73 g carbohydrates, 18 g total fat, 211 mg cholesterol, 828 mg sodium

Pan-fried Soft-shell Crab with Ginger or Cayenne Sauce

Preparation time: About 40 minutes
Cooking time: About 30 minutes

6   **soft-shell blue crabs (about 2 oz. each), prepared and pan-fried (pages 29–30)**
    Ginger Sauce or Cayenne Sauce (recipes follow)
    Fresh chives
    Lemon wedges

Keep cooked crabs warm until all are browned. Meanwhile, prepare either Ginger Sauce or Cayenne Sauce.

Serve Ginger Sauce spooned over crab or as a dip; or pour a pool of Cayenne Sauce onto serving plates and top with 2 or 3 cooked crabs. Garnish with chives and lemon wedges. Makes 2 or 3 servings.

Per serving: 318 calories, 23 g protein, 13 g carbohydrates, 19 g total fat, 128 mg cholesterol, 559 mg sodium

■ **Ginger Sauce.** Stir together ⅓ cup **rice wine vinegar**, 1 to 2 tablespoons sliced **green onion** (including top), 1½ tablespoons minced **fresh ginger**, and 1 teaspoon **sugar**. Makes about ¾ cup.

Per tablespoon: 3 calories, .01 g protein, .7 g carbohydrates, 0 g total fat, 0 mg cholesterol, 1 mg sodium

■ **Cayenne Sauce.** In a small frying pan, combine ¼ cup **dry white wine**, 3 tablespoons chopped **shallots**, 2 tablespoons **red wine vinegar**, and ¼ to ½ teaspoon **ground red pepper** (cayenne). Bring to a boil over high heat; boil, uncovered, until reduced to about 1 tablespoon.

Scrape mixture into a blender; add 2 **egg yolks.** Whirl until blended; with motor running, slowly add ¾ cup hot melted **butter** or margarine. Serve hot or at room temperature; do not reheat. Makes 1¼ cups.

Per tablespoon: 69 calories, .37 g protein, .33 g carbohydrates, 7 g total fat, 46 mg cholesterol, 71 mg sodium

Sweet tang of citrus permeates rice in elegant Orange Risotto with Shrimp (recipe on facing page), finished with a glistening Marsala wine sauce.

crumbled dry basil leaves; and ½ teaspoon crumbled **dry rosemary.** Season to taste with **salt** and **pepper.** Cook over low heat, stirring often, until crisp and golden (about 30 minutes). Keep warm. Makes about 1½ cups.

Per serving: 924 calories, 42 g protein, 92 g carbohydrates, 45 g total fat, 86 mg cholesterol, 1,198 mg sodium

Crab Lace Patties on Lettuce

Preparation time: 15 minutes
Cooking time: 6 to 10 minutes

- ¾ **pound cooked crabmeat**
- ¾ **cup grated Parmesan cheese**
- 2 **tablespoons minced parsley**
- ½ **teaspoon dry oregano leaves**
- 2 **cloves garlic, minced or pressed**
- ¼ **cup fine dry bread crumbs**
- 2 **green onions (including tops), thinly sliced**
- 1 **egg, beaten**
- ¼ **cup whipping cream**
  About 1 tablespoon olive oil or salad oil
- 1 **large avocado**
- 8 **to 12 large butter lettuce leaves, washed and crisped**

Break crabmeat into flakes. Combine with cheese, parsley, oregano, garlic, bread crumbs, onions, egg, and cream; mix lightly.

Heat 2 teaspoons of the oil in a wide frying pan over medium heat. For each patty, mound 3 tablespoons of the crab mixture in pan, spreading to make a 3-inch cake. Cook until bottom is lightly browned (about 2 minutes). Turn and cook until other side is very lightly browned (about 1 more minute); keep warm. Repeat until all patties are cooked, adding more oil as needed.

Pit, peel, and slice avocado. Line individual plates with lettuce. Arrange avocado slices and crab patties on each plate. Makes 4 servings.

Per serving: 381 calories, 28 g protein, 12 g carbohydrates, 25 g total fat, 182 mg cholesterol, 594 mg sodium

Laurita-style Crab & Pasta

Preparation time: About 30 minutes
Baking time: 15 to 20 minutes
Cooking time: About 1 hour

Seasoned Crumbs (recipe follows)
- ¾ **cup olive oil or salad oil**
- ¼ **cup minced garlic**
- 2 **cups lightly packed minced parsley**
- 3 **large cans (28 oz. *each*) tomatoes**
- 4 **cooked large Dungeness crabs (about 2 lbs. *each*), cleaned and cracked (page 28)**
- 1 **cup lightly packed chopped fresh basil leaves or ¼ cup dry basil leaves**
  Salt and pepper
- 1 **pound dry linguine**
  Lemon wedges

Prepare Seasoned Crumbs.

Meanwhile, in an 8- to 10-quart pan, combine oil, garlic, and parsley; cook over medium heat, stirring often, until garlic is soft (about 5 minutes). Add tomatoes (break up with a spoon) and their liquid. Cook, uncovered, stirring occasionally, until reduced to 8 cups (about 40 minutes).

Add crab pieces; reduce heat, cover, and simmer, stirring occasionally, until hot (15 to 20 minutes). Stir in basil; season to taste with salt and pepper.

Meanwhile, in a 5- to 6-quart pan, cook pasta in 3 quarts boiling water just until tender to bite (about 10 minutes). Or cook according to package directions. Drain; spoon pasta onto a warm platter or individual plates and at once top with crab and sauce. Sprinkle with crumbs and garnish with lemon wedges. Makes 6 to 8 servings.

■ **Seasoned Crumbs.** Place ¼ pound (about 5 slices) sliced **French bread** on a baking sheet. Bake in a 350° oven until golden and firm (15 to 20 minutes).

Break bread into chunks and whirl in a blender or food processor until fine crumbs form. In a wide frying pan, combine crumbs; ⅓ cup minced **parsley;** 6 tablespoons **olive oil;** 2 cloves **garlic,** minced or pressed; 1 tablespoon minced **fresh basil leaves** or 1 teaspoon

Mushroom-stuffed Calamari

Preparation time: 30 minutes to 1 hour
Cooking time: About 30 minutes

- ⅓ **cup olive oil**
- ¼ **pound mushrooms, sliced**
- ¼ **cup finely chopped onion**
- 1 **teaspoon chopped fresh oregano leaves or ½ teaspoon dry oregano leaves**
- ½ **teaspoon *each* ground cinnamon and freshly ground pepper**
- 2 **large cloves garlic, minced or pressed**
- 1½ **cups salted soda cracker crumbs**
- 1¼ **cups white retsina or dry white wine**
- ¼ **pound feta cheese, crumbled**
- 2 **pounds small whole squid, cleaned (page 67), or 1 pound cleaned tubes (mantles) and tentacles or tubes only**
- 2 **medium-size tomatoes, chopped**
- 2 **to 3 cups hot cooked rice Fresh oregano, thyme, mint, or parsley sprigs**

Heat oil in a wide frying pan over medium heat. Add mushrooms, onion, chopped oregano, cinnamon, pepper, and half the garlic. Cook, stirring often, until onion is soft and liquid from mushrooms has evaporated (about 8 minutes). Remove from heat and stir in cracker crumbs, ¼ cup of the wine, and cheese.

With your fingers or a small spoon, loosely stuff squid tubes with mushroom mixture to within ½ inch of opening (do not pack stuffing or tubes may burst during cooking). Press open end of each tube together to seal loosely.

Place stuffed tubes in a wide frying pan. Add tentacles (if used), tomatoes, remaining garlic, and remaining 1 cup wine; bring to a boil over medium-high heat. Reduce heat to keep liquid just below a simmer. Cover and cook until squid is tender when pierced (about 15 minutes).

Spoon rice onto a warm platter. With a slotted spoon, lift tubes from pan and place over rice; top with tomatoes. Arrange tentacles (if used) at sides; keep warm. Bring liquid in pan to a boil over high heat. Cook, uncovered, stirring occasionally, until reduced to ¼ cup. Pour over squid and garnish with oregano sprigs. Makes 6 servings with tentacles, 4 servings without.

Per serving with tentacles: 435 calories, 25 g protein, 38 g carbohydrates, 20 g total fat, 292 mg cholesterol, 462 mg sodium

Hangtown Fry

Preparation time: About 5 minutes
Standing time: About 30 minutes
Cooking time: 8 to 10 minutes

- 5 **eggs**
- 2 **tablespoons whipping cream**
- ¼ **pound shucked oysters (if large, cut into bite-size pieces) All-purpose flour**
- 3 **tablespoons cracker crumbs**
- 3 **tablespoons butter or margarine Salt and pepper**

Combine eggs and cream; beat with a wire whisk until well combined. Set aside.

Coat oysters with flour; shake off excess. Dip oysters in beaten egg mixture; drain briefly. Then roll in cracker crumbs. Set slightly apart on a wire rack and let stand until coating is set (about 30 minutes).

In a 10- to 12-inch frying pan, melt 2 tablespoons of the butter over medium-high heat. Add oysters, placing them slightly apart. Cook, turning once, until golden on both sides (about 2 minutes total). Lift out with a spatula; drain on paper towels and keep warm.

Add remaining 1 tablespoon butter to pan; reduce heat to medium-low. Pour in remaining egg mixture. When just set on bottom, lift cooked portions so uncooked egg can flow underneath; cook until eggs are firm but still moist. Slide out of pan onto a warm platter; top with oysters. Season to taste with salt and pepper. Makes 2 servings.

Per serving: 499 calories, 21 g protein, 19 g carbohydrates, 37 g total fat, 19 mg cholesterol, 417 mg sodium

Garlic Oyster Sandwiches

Preparation time: About 10 minutes
Baking time: About 25 minutes
Cooking time: 6 to 8 minutes

- ½ **cup (¼ lb.) butter or margarine**
- 1 **clove garlic, minced or pressed**
- 6 **slices (½ inch thick) sourdough French bread from a long 1-pound loaf**
- 2 **jars (8 to 10 oz. *each*) small shucked oysters**
- ½ **pound jack cheese, thinly sliced**
- 2 **to 3 tablespoons chopped parsley**

In a wide frying pan, melt ¼ cup of the butter over medium heat. Add garlic and cook, stirring, until slightly softened (1 to 2 minutes). Brush garlic butter over one side of each bread slice; arrange, butter sides up, in a shallow rimmed baking pan. Bake, uncovered, in a 350° oven until bread is toasted (about 20 minutes). Set aside.

In same frying pan, melt remaining ¼ cup butter over medium-high heat. Add oysters and cook, turning once, until edges curl (4 to 5 minutes).

With a slotted spoon, lift out oysters and place on toast slices; reserve juices in pan. Cover oysters evenly with cheese. Bake just until cheese is melted (about 5 minutes). Sprinkle with parsley. Pass juices to spoon onto sandwiches. Eat with a knife and fork. Makes 6 servings.

Per serving: 456 calories, 22 g protein, 25 g carbohydrates, 30 g total fat, 128 mg cholesterol, 663 mg sodium

Sauces & Butters

Homemade Mayonnaise

Preparation time: About 5 minutes

1 **large whole egg or 3 egg yolks**
1 **teaspoon Dijon mustard**
1 **tablespoon white wine vinegar or lemon juice**
1 **cup salad oil**
 Salt (optional)

In a blender or food processor, combine egg, mustard, and vinegar. Whirl until well blended (3 to 5 seconds). With motor on high, add oil, a few drops at a time at first and then increasing to a slow, steady stream about 1⁄16 inch wide. Season to taste with salt, if desired. If made ahead, cover and refrigerate for up to 2 weeks.

Serve with any cold poached fish or cold shellfish, or use in salad. Makes about 1½ cups.

Per tablespoon: 84 calories, .25 g protein, .07 g carbohydrates, 9 g total fat, 11 mg cholesterol, 9 mg sodium

■ **Lemon Mayonnaise.** Follow directions for **Homemade Mayonnaise** (above), adding 2 teaspoons grated **lemon peel** to blender or processor with egg and mustard; omit vinegar and use 2 tablespoons **lemon juice.**

Serve with mild-flavored hot or cold fish or with any shellfish. Makes about 1½ cups.

■ **Remoulade Sauce.** Prepare **Homemade Mayonnaise** (above). Stir in 2 tablespoons finely chopped **parsley,** a pinch

of **ground red pepper** (cayenne), 1 teaspoon **anchovy paste,** ¼ cup finely chopped **dill pickles,** 1 tablespoon drained chopped **capers,** and 2 **hard-cooked eggs,** chopped.

Serve with cold shrimp or cold poached fish. Makes about 2 cups.

■ **Tartar Sauce.** Prepare **Homemade Mayonnaise** (at left). Combine ½ cup of the mayonnaise or ¼ cup *each* mayonnaise and sour cream; ¼ cup **sweet pickle relish,** well drained; 1 tablespoon finely chopped **green onion** (including top); ¼ teaspoon **Worcestershire;** 4 drops **liquid hot pepper seasoning;** and ½ teaspoon **lemon juice.** Mix well. Cover and refrigerate for at least 30 minutes to blend flavors.

Serve with hot fried or barbecued fish or shellfish or with cold poached fish. Makes about ¾ cup.

■ **Creamy Horseradish Sauce.** Prepare **Homemade Mayonnaise** (at left). Combine ¼ cup of the mayonnaise, ½ cup **sour cream,** ¼ cup **prepared horseradish,** and 1 tablespoon chopped **fresh dill** or 1 teaspoon dill weed.

Serve with rich-flavored hot or cold fish or with shrimp. Makes about 1 cup.

Aïoli

Preparation time: 8 to 10 minutes

2 **egg yolks**
1 **tablespoon Dijon mustard**
4 **teaspoons lemon juice**
3 **tablespoons chopped chives**
2 **to 4 large cloves garlic, minced or pressed**
½ **cup** *each* **olive oil and salad oil**

In a blender or food processor, combine egg yolks, mustard, lemon juice, chives, and garlic. Whirl until well blended (about 5 seconds). With motor on high, add olive oil and salad oil, a few drops at a time at first and then increasing to a slow, steady stream about 1⁄16 inch wide. If made ahead, cover and refrigerate for up to 2 weeks.

Serve with hot barbecued fish, cold poached fish, or cold shellfish. Makes about 1⅓ cups.

Per tablespoon: 99 calories, .29 g protein, .28 g carbohydrates, 11 g total fat, 26 mg cholesterol, 22 mg sodium

Stingy on calories but generous in flavor, Radish Tartar Sauce (recipe below) transforms a simply poached lingcod steak into a splendid salad supper.

Pictured above

Radish Tartar Sauce

Preparation time: About 20 minutes

¾ **cup** *each* **plain yogurt and sour cream**
1 **cup chopped radishes**
½ **cup thinly sliced green onions (including tops)**
3 **tablespoons drained capers**
1½ **tablespoons prepared horseradish**
 Salt

Combine yogurt, sour cream, radishes, onions, capers, and horseradish; mix until blended. Season to taste with salt. If made ahead, cover and refrigerate until next day. Stir before using.

Serve with cold poached fish steaks or fillets. Makes about 2½ cups.

Per tablespoon: 13 calories, .38 g protein, .68 g carbohydrates, .97 g total fat, 2 mg cholesterol, 23 mg sodium

Dijon Vinaigrette Dressing

Preparation time: 8 to 10 minutes

¼ **cup Dijon mustard**
3 **large cloves garlic, minced or pressed**
⅔ **cup wine vinegar**
¼ **cup olive oil**
½ **cup salad oil**

Combine mustard, garlic, vinegar, olive oil, and salad oil; mix until blended. If made ahead, cover and refrigerate for up to 1 week. Shake well before using.

Use in fish salads or drizzle over cold poached fish or cold shellfish. Makes about 1¾ cups.

Per tablespoon: 58 calories, .02 g protein, .64 g carbohydrate, 6 g total fat, 0 mg cholesterol, 68 mg sodium

Cocktail Sauce

Preparation time: About 5 minutes

½ **cup catsup**
¼ **cup *each* tomato-based chili sauce and grapefruit juice**
2 **tablespoons lemon juice**
1 **tablespoon thinly sliced green onion (including top)**
1 **teaspoon *each* prepared horseradish and Worcestershire**
2 **or 3 drops liquid hot pepper seasoning**

Combine catsup, chili sauce, grapefruit juice, lemon juice, onion, horseradish, Worcestershire, and hot pepper seasoning; mix until blended. If made ahead, cover and refrigerate for up to 3 days.

Serve with raw oysters, cold poached fish, or cold shellfish. Makes about 1 cup.

Per tablespoon: 16 calories, .30 g protein, 4 g carbohydrates, .04 g total fat, 0 mg cholesterol, 150 mg sodium

Tomato-Caper Sauce

Preparation time: 8 to 10 minutes
Cooking time: 15 to 20 minutes

¼ **cup butter or margarine**
1 **medium-size onion, chopped**
1 **clove garlic, minced or pressed**
2 **teaspoons capers**
1 **can (about 14 oz.) pear-shaped tomatoes**
1 **tablespoon lemon juice**
2 **tablespoons minced parsley**

In a 9- to 10-inch frying pan, melt butter over medium heat. Add onion and garlic; cook, stirring often, until onion is soft (about 5 minutes). Add capers and tomatoes (break up with a spoon) and their liquid. Bring to a gentle boil. Cook, uncovered, stirring often, until thickened (about 10 minutes). Stir in lemon juice and parsley.

Spoon over hot cooked fish. Makes about 2 cups.

Per tablespoon: 16 calories, .14 g protein, 1 g carbohydrate, 1 g total fat, 4 mg cholesterol, 40 mg sodium

Hollandaise Sauce

Preparation time: 8 to 10 minutes

1 **egg or 3 egg yolks**
1 **teaspoon Dijon mustard**
1 **tablespoon lemon juice or wine vinegar**
1 **cup (½ lb.) butter or margarine, melted and hot**

In a blender or food processor, combine egg, mustard, and lemon juice; whirl until well blended. With motor on high, add butter, a few drops at a time at first and then increasing to a slow, steady stream about 1/16 inch wide.

To keep sauce warm for up to 3 hours, pour into top of a double boiler or measuring cup and set in water that is just hot to touch; stir sauce occasionally, replacing hot water as needed. Do not reheat or sauce will separate.

Serve with hot poached, barbecued, or broiled fish steaks or fillets. Makes 1 to 1½ cups.

Per tablespoon: 71 calories, .33 g protein, .08 g carbohydrates, 8 g total fat, 32 mg cholesterol, 87 mg sodium

■ **Mousseline Sauce.** Prepare **Hollandaise Sauce** (below left) and set aside. Beat ½ cup **whipping cream** until stiff peaks form. Fold into sauce (hot or at room temperature) and serve at once. Serve as for Hollandaise. Makes about 2 cups.

■ **Béarnaise Sauce.** In a small pan, combine 1 tablespoon minced **shallot** or onion, ½ teaspoon **dry tarragon,** and 2 tablespoons **wine vinegar.** Cook over medium heat, stirring constantly, until only a few drops of liquid remain. Transfer mixture to a blender or food processor; following directions for **Hollandaise Sauce** (below left), add egg, mustard, lemon juice, and butter. Serve as for Hollandaise. Makes 1 to 1½ cups.

Mornay Sauce

Preparation time: About 5 minutes
Cooking time: About 5 minutes

2 **tablespoons butter or margarine**
2 **tablespoons all-purpose flour**
½ **cup regular-strength chicken broth**
½ **cup half-and-half**
2 **tablespoons shredded Gruyère or Swiss cheese**
2 **tablespoons grated Parmesan cheese**
 Salt and ground red pepper (cayenne)

In a small pan, melt butter over medium heat. Add flour and cook, stirring, until light golden.

Remove from heat and stir in broth and half-and-half. Increase heat to high and bring to a boil, stirring constantly. Reduce heat and stir Gruyère and Parmesan cheeses into simmering sauce.

Remove from heat and season to taste with salt and red pepper. If made ahead, cover and refrigerate until next day; to reheat, stir over medium-low heat.

Use as a base for fish and shellfish casseroles or spoon over hot cooked seafood. Makes about 1 cup.

Per tablespoon: 34 calories, .9 g protein, 1 g carbohydrates, 3 g total fat, 8 mg cholesterol, 64 mg sodium

Citrus Beurre Blanc

Preparation time: 8 to 10 minutes
Cooking time: 5 to 8 minutes

- 1 strip (1 inch long) thin outer peel of 1 *each* lemon, lime, orange, and grapefruit
- 3 tablespoons finely chopped shallots
- 1 tablespoon *each* lemon juice and lime juice
- ¼ cup *each* orange juice and grapefruit juice
- ½ cup (¼ lb.) butter or margarine

Cut citrus peels into thin julienne strips to make ¼ teaspoon of each. Set aside.

In a wide frying pan, combine shallots and lemon, lime, orange, and grapefruit juices. Bring to a boil over high heat; continue to boil, uncovered, until mixture is reduced to about ⅓ cup. Reduce heat to low. Add butter in one chunk and heat, stirring, until butter is melted and sauce is smooth. Stir in peels.

To keep sauce warm for up to 4 hours, pour into top of a double boiler or measuring cup and set in water that is just hot to touch; stir sauce occasionally, replacing hot water as needed. Do not reheat or sauce will separate.

Serve with any hot cooked fish. Makes about ¾ cup.

Per tablespoon: 75 calories, .19 g protein, 2 g carbohydrates, 8 g total fat, 21 mg cholesterol, 79 mg sodium

Warm Garlic Butter

Preparation time: 5 minutes
Heating time: 3 to 5 minutes

- ½ cup (¼ lb.) butter or margarine
- ½ cup olive oil
- 3 cloves garlic, minced or pressed
- 3 tablespoons finely chopped parsley

In a 1- to 1½-quart pan, combine butter, oil, garlic, and parsley. Heat over medium-high heat, stirring occasionally, until bubbly.

Serve as a dip for hot cooked shellfish. Makes about 1 cup.

Per tablespoon: 112 calories, .1 g protein, .22 g carbohydrates, 12 g total fat, 16 mg cholesterol, 59 mg sodium

Provençale Butter. Follow directions for **Warm Garlic Butter** (above),

Fanciful cutouts of sliced Basil Garlic Butter (recipe below) melt flavorfully into grilled halibut steak.

adding 1 teaspoon **herbes de Provence** or ¼ teaspoon *each* dry basil, oregano, thyme, and marjoram leaves.

Serve with barbecued fish or shellfish. Makes about 1 cup.

Garlic-Lemon Butter. Follow directions for **Warm Garlic Butter** (at left), but omit olive oil and parsley. Increase butter to 1 cup; decrease garlic to 2 cloves, minced or pressed. Add 1 tablespoon **lemon juice.**

Serve with hot barbecued or broiled fish or shellfish. Makes about 1 cup.

Pictured above

Basil Garlic Butter

Preparation time: About 10 minutes
Chilling time: At least 1 hour

- 1 cup loosely packed fresh basil leaves, rinsed and patted dry; or ¾ cup fresh parsley and 3 tablespoons dry basil leaves
- 4 or 5 cloves garlic
- 1 cup (½ lb.) butter or margarine, at room temperature
   Pepper

In a food processor or with a knife, mince basil and garlic. Add butter and mix until well combined. Season to taste with pepper.

On plastic wrap, shape butter into a log about 2 inches in diameter. Wrap snugly; refrigerate or freeze until firm (at least 1 hour). If made ahead, refrigerate for up to 1 week or freeze for up to 1 month.

To serve, slice about ½ inch thick. If desired, use hors d'oeuvre cutters to

make fancy shapes. Place slices atop hot barbecued or broiled fish. Makes about 1¼ cups.

Per tablespoon: 85 calories, .25 g protein, .75 g carbohydrates, 9 g total fat, 25 mg cholesterol, 95 mg sodium

Diable Butter

Preparation time: About 10 minutes
Chilling time: At least 1 hour

- ⅓ cup butter or margarine, at room temperature
- 2 tablespoons lemon juice
- 2 teaspoons Dijon mustard
- ⅛ teaspoon ground red pepper (cayenne)
- 1 tablespoon finely chopped parsley

Beat butter until creamy; gradually beat in lemon juice until mixture is fluffy. Beat in mustard, red pepper, and parsley.

On plastic wrap, shape butter into a log 1 to 1½ inches in diameter. Wrap snugly; refrigerate or freeze until firm (at least 1 hour). If made ahead, refrigerate for up to 1 week or freeze for up to 1 month.

To serve, slice about ¼ inch thick. Place slices atop hot barbecued, broiled, or poached fish. Makes about ½ cup.

Per tablespoon: 70 calories, .09 g protein, .44 g carbohydrates, 8 g total fat, 20 mg cholesterol, 116 mg sodium

Index

Abalone, 15
  suggested recipes, 15
Aïoli, 123
Alaska pollock, 26
Albacore (tuna), 74
Alewife (herring), 35
Almond or filbert browned butter, 92
Almond–rice stuffing, 83
Almond–wild rice stuffing, 83
Ama'ama (mullet), 43
Amberjack, 35
American lobster, 38
Anatomy, fish forms &, 6, 7, 10
Angler (monkfish), 42
Antarctic whiting (cod), 26
Appetizers, 99–102
  caviar pie, 19
  crabby jack quesadillas, 101
  faux salmon terrine, 101
  fish & chard pie, 99
  garlic clams on the half shell, 101
  garlic mussels on the half shell, 101
  quenelles with creamy shallot
    sauce, 100
  scallops with shallot butter, 102
  seviche with kiwi fruit, 100
  smoked mussels with lemon-
    garlic mayonnaise, 116
  smoked salmon mousse, 116
  spiced shrimp, 101
Arctic char, 72
Arrowtooth flounder, 33
Asparagus, stir-fried scallops &,
  on cool pasta, 109
Atlantic butterfish, 20
Atlantic cod, 26
Atlantic croaker, 31
Atlantic halibut, 34
Atlantic hard-shell clams, 22
Atlantic mackerel, 40
Atlantic ocean perch (rockfish), 51
Atlantic oysters, 48
Atlantic pollock, 26
Atlantic salmon, 53
Atlantic soft-shell clams, 22

Baby salmon with sautéed leeks, 113
Baked fish & ratatouille, 112
Baked fish with a creamy topping,
  85
Baked large whole fish, 85
Baked stuffed fish, 83
Baking, 82
Baquetta (grouper), 58
Barbecue, smoking fish on the, 84
Barbecuing, 86
Barracuda, 16
  suggested recipes, 16
Basic techniques, 79–97
Basil
  garlic butter, 125
  -Parmesan marinade, 87
  vinaigrette dressing, 109
Bass, 16. See also Sea bass
  suggested recipes, 17
Bastes, 87
Batters, 90
Bay scallops, 56
Béarnaise
  cream, scallops & shrimp in, 97
  sauce, 124
Beer batter, British, 90
Belgian endive rolls, sole-
  wrapped, 110
Beurre blanc, citrus, 125
Bigeye (tuna), 75
Bighead carp, 20
Bisque, Tahoe crayfish, 106
Blackback flounder, 33
Black cod (sablefish), 52
Black drum, 31
Blackfish (tautog), 70
Black grouper, 57
Blackline tilefish, 71
Black mullet, 43
Black sea bass, 57

Blacktip (shark), 61
Blue crab, 27
Bluefin (tuna), 74
Bluefish, 17
  suggested recipes, 18
Blue mussels, 43
Bluenose sea bass, 57
Blue runner (jack), 35
Bocaccio rockfish, 51
Bones and fins, 80
Bonito (shark), 61
Bonito (tuna), 75
Bouillon, court, 93
Bourride, 102
Braised sablefish, 112
Braised salt cod, 25
British beer batter, 90
Broiled fish or oysters with crumb
  coating, 89
Broiled seafood, 88
Broth, vegetable, 103
Browned butter sauces, quick, 92
Brown shrimp, 62
Buffalo, 18
  suggested recipes, 18
Burmese fish with sweet onions, 96
Butterfish, 20
  suggested recipes, 20
Butterfish (sablefish), 52
Butters, 92, 125
Buyer's guide to seafood, 15–77

Calamari. See also Squid
  mushroom-stuffed, 122
Calico scallops, 56
Calico stuffed trout, 114
California barracuda, 16
California halibut (flounder), 33
California pompano (butterfish), 20
Canary rockfish, 51
Candlefish (smelt), 65
Cape blackfish (tautog), 70
Caper(s)
  butter, 92
  cucumbers &, pan-fried skate
    with, 117
  sauce, tomato-, 124
Carp, 20
  suggested recipes, 21
Catfish, 21
  pan-fried, with jicama salad, 111
  suggested recipes, 22
Caviar, 19
Cayenne sauce, ginger or, pan-
  fried soft-shell crab with, 120
Cero mackerel, 40
Champagne sauce, seafood
  brochettes with, 119
Chard pie, fish &, 99
Cheddar topping, sour cream-, 85
Cheese-crumb coating, 85
Chicory salad, wilted, grilled
  salmon on, 113
Chile
  -cilantro sauce, 101
  red, Louis, 109
  shrimp & corn salad, 108
Chilean sea bass, 57
Chilipepper rockfish, 51
China rockfish, 51
Chinese-style steamed fish, 94
Chinook (king) salmon, 53
Chowders
  hearty clam, 106
  quick colorful, 102
Chub (cisco), 76
Chum salmon, 53
Ciguatera poisoning, 13
Cilantro sauce, chile-, 101
Cioppino, San Francisco-style, 105
Cisco, 76
Citrus beurre blanc, 125
Clam(s), 22
  barbecuing, 87
  chowder, hearty, 106
  garlic, on the half shell, 101
  microwaving, 97
  shucking, 23
  steamed, with linguisa & pasta,
    106
  suggested recipes, 24
Classic poached fish, 92

Cleaning fish, 79
Coatings, 92
Cobia, 24
  suggested recipes, 24
Cockles, 22
Cocktail sauce, 124
Cod, 26
  black. See Sablefish
  braised salt, 25
  suggested recipes, 27
Coho (silver) salmon, 53
Common thresher (shark), 61
Cooking characteristics of fish, 8
Cooking methods, 82–97
Corbina (weakfish), 59
Corn salad, chile, shrimp &, 108
Corvina (weakfish), 59
Corvina (white sea bass), 57
Court bouillon, 93
Crab, 27
  crabby jack quesadillas, 101
  lace patties on lettuce, 121
  pan-fried soft-shell, with ginger
    or cayenne sauce, 120
  & pasta, Laurita-style, 121
  suggested recipes, 30
Crabby jack quesadillas, 101
Crabeater (cobia), 24
Crawfish (crayfish), 30
Crawfish (lobster), 38
Crayfish, 30. See also Lobster
  bisque, Tahoe, 106
  suggested recipes, 30
Creamy horseradish sauce, 123
Creamy shallot sauce, 100
Creamy vegetable topping, 85
Croaker, 31. See also Drum
  suggested recipes, 31
Crumb coating, broiled fish or
  oysters with, 89
Cucumbers & capers, pan-fried
  skate with, 117
Curing fish, 84
Curry cream, seafood in, 69
Cusk, 26
Cusk eel (kingklip), 36
Cuts, fish, 10

Dab (flounder), 33
Daurade (sea bream), 58
Deep-fried fish or shrimp, 89
Deep-fried squid, 89
Deep-frying, 89
Dentex (sea bream), 58
Diable butter, 125
Dijon vinaigrette dressing, 124
Dill butter, steamed smoked fish
  with, 116
Dollarfish (butterfish), 20
Dolphin (mahi mahi), 41
Doneness, judging, 82
Dorado (mahi mahi), 41
Dover sole, 33
Drum, 31. See also Croaker;
  Seatrout; White sea bass
  suggested recipes, 32
Dungeness crab, 27

Eel, 32
  matelote of, 104
  suggested recipes, 32
English sole, 33
Eulachon (smelt), 65
European flat oysters, 48

Fat content, 8, 12
Faux salmon terrine, 101
Filbert browned butter, almond or,
  92
Filleting, 80, 81
Fillets
  with dill and tangerine, fish, 91
  forms, 6, 10
  with sherry-mushroom sauce, 111
  sole, with peas and sesame oil, 91
Fins, 80
Firepot, Thai seafood, 105
Fish
  Burmese, with sweet onions, 96
  & chard pie, 99

Fish (cont'd)
  cooking methods, 82–97
  fillets with dill and tangerine, 91
  fillets with sherry-mushroom
    sauce, 111
  five-spice, 110
  forms & anatomy, 6, 7, 10
  groups, 8–9
  judging freshness, 7
  Mr. Zhu's steamed, 114
  nutrition, 12
  pil-pil in red sauce, 104
  pine cone, 115
  pot-au-feu, 103
  & ratatouille, baked, 112
  raw, using, 13
  safety, 13
  salad, Veracruz, 107
  skewered, Northwest style, 118
  steamed smoked, with dill
    butter, 116
  stock, 93
  storing, 10
  & watercress salad, Thai, 108
Five-spice fish, 111
Flatfish
  anatomy, 6, 7
  filleting, 81
Florida pompano, 50
Flounder, 32
  suggested recipes, 34
Flour coating, 92
Fluke (flounder), 33
Foil-steamed fish, 94
Forms & anatomy, fish, 6, 7, 10
Freezing seafood, 11
French oyster soup, 106
Freshness, judging, 7
Freshwater drum, 31
Freshwater shrimp, 62
Fruit sauce, teriyaki, grilled tuna
  with, 117

Gafftopsail pompano, 50
Garlic
  butter, basil, 125
  butter, warm, 125
  clams on the half shell, 101
  -lemon butter, 125
  mayonnaise, lemon-, smoked
    mussels with, 116
  mussels on the half shell, 101
  oyster sandwiches, 122
Gaspergau (drum), 31
Gefilite fish soup, Puget Sound
  salmon, 103
Geoducks, 22
Giant squid, 66
Ginger
  or cayenne sauce, pan-fried
    soft-shell crab with, 120
  sauce, 120
  sauce, hot, 94
  -soy marinade, 87
  steamed mussels, sesame-, 119
Golden croaker, 31
Golden egg wash, 92
Golden tilefish, 71
Goosefish (monkfish), 42
Grass carp, 20
Gravlax plus, 47
Gray snapper, 65
Gray sole, 33
Gray tilefish, 71
Gray trout, 73
Gray weakfish, 59
Great barracuda, 16
Greenland turbot, 34
Greenling (lingcod), 37
Green mussels, 43
Green onions, shrimp with, 120
Green sturgeon, 68
Grilled salmon on wilted chicory
  salad, 113
Grilled scallops with red pepper
  sauce, 118
Grilled tuna with teriyaki fruit
  sauce, 117
Grouper, 57
  suggested recipes, 58
Groups, fish, 8–9
Grunion (smelt), 65

Haddock, 26
Hake, 26
Halibut, 34
    California (flounder), 33
    suggested recipes, 35
Hangtown fry, 122
Hapu'upu'u (sea bass), 57
Hardhead croaker, 31
Harvestfish (butterfish), 20
Health, seafood &, 12
Hearty clam chowder, 106
Heavy crumb coating, 92
Herb seasoning mixture, 101
Herring, 35
    suggested recipes, 35
Hoki (cod), 26
Hollandaise sauce, 124
Homemade mayonnaise, 123
Horse mackerel, 40
Horseradish sauce, 103
    creamy, 123
Humpback (pink) salmon, 53

Ikijima tai (sea bream), 58
Italian-style marinade, 87

Jack, 35
    mackerel, Pacific, 40
    suggested recipes, 36
Jack quesadillas, crabby, 101
Jalapeño vinaigrette, 100
Japanese tempura batter, 90
Japanese yellowtail (jack), 36
Jicama salad, pan-fried catfish
    with, 111
John Dory, 36
Jonah crab, 28
Jumping mullet, 43

Kahala (jack), 35
Kaku (barracuda), 16
Kebabs, fish or shellfish, 86
Keta (chum) salmon, 53
King crab, 27
Kingklip, 36
    suggested recipes, 37
King mackerel, 40
King salmon, 53
Kiwi fruit, seviche with, 100
Kumamoto oysters, 48

Lake trout, 73
Lake whitefish, 76
Langosta (lobster), 38
Langostino (lobster), 38
Langousto (lobster), 38
Laurita-style crab & pasta, 121
Leeks
    lobster soup with, 105
    sautéed, baby salmon with, 113
    & vinegar, trout with, 114
Lemon batter, 90
Lemon butter, garlic-, 125
Lemon-butter baste, 87
Lemonfish (cobia), 24
Lemon-garlic mayonnaise,
    smoked mussels with, 116
Lemon mayonnaise, 123
Lemon sauce, 101
Lemon sole, 33
Lettuce
    crab lace patties on, 121
    & peas, steamed trout with, 96
Light crumb coating, 92
Ling (cobia), 24
Lingcod, 37
    suggested recipes, 37
Ling (kingklip), 36
Linguine, seafood, 119
Linguisa & pasta, steamed clams
    with, 106
Lobster, 38
    soup with leeks, 105
    suggested recipes, 40
Longfin squid, 66
Lotte (monkfish), 42
Loup de mer (wolffish), 77
Lumpfish caviar, 19

Mackerel, 40
    suggested recipes, 41
    with tart onion sauce, 112
Mahi mahi, 41
    suggested recipes, 41
Main dishes, 110–122
    baby salmon with sautéed leeks,
        113
    baked fish with a creamy
        topping, 85
    baked fish & ratatouille, 112
    baked large whole fish, 85
    baked stuffed fish, 83
    barbecued seafood, 85
    braised salt cod, 25
    braised sablefish, 112
    broiled fish or oysters with
        crumb coating, 89
    broiled seafood, 88
    Burmese fish with sweet onions,
        96
    calico stuffed trout, 114
    Chinese-style steamed fish, 94
    classic poached fish, 93
    crab lace patties on lettuce, 121
    deep-fried fish or shrimp, 89
    deep-fried squid, 89
    fish baked in sauce, 82
    fish fillets with sherry-mushroom
        sauce, 111
    five-spice fish, 111
    foil-steamed fish, 94
    garlic oyster sandwiches, 122
    grilled salmon on wilted chicory
        salad, 113
    grilled scallops with red pepper
        sauce, 118
    grilled tuna with teriyaki fruit
        sauce, 117
    Hangtown fry, 122
    Laurita-style crab & pasta, 121
    mackerel with tart onion sauce,
        112
    maki sushi, 54
    Mr. Zhu's steamed fish, 114
    monkfish scaloppine with
        shallots, 115
    mushroom-stuffed calamari, 122
    orange risotto with shrimp, 120
    orange roughy maître d'hôtel, 112
    oven-browned fish, 85
    pan-fried catfish with jicama
        salad, 111
    pan-fried fish, 90
    pan-fried skate with cucumbers
        & capers, 117
    pan-fried soft-shell crab with
        ginger or cayenne sauce,
        120
    pan-poached fish, 92
    pine cone fish, 115
    prebrowned fish, 92
    scallops & shrimp in béarnaise
        cream, 97
    seafood baked in parchment, 91
    seafood brochettes with
        champagne sauce, 119
    seafood in curry cream, 69
    seafood linguine, 119
    sesame-ginger steamed
        mussels, 119
    shrimp with green onions, 120
    skewered fish, Northwest style,
        118
    snapper Florentine, 96
    sole with mushroom velvet, 110
    sole-wrapped Belgian endive
        rolls, 110
    steamed salmon with sorrel, 112
    steamed smoked fish with dill
        butter, 116
    steamed trout with lettuce &
        peas, 96
    steeped fish, 94
    stir-fried fish or shellfish with
        peas, 95
    swordfish steaks with
        mushrooms, 117
    temaki sushi, 55
    trout with leeks & vinegar, 114
Maki sushi (rolled sushi), 54
Mako (shark), 61
Marinades, 87

Matelote of eel, 104
Mayonnaise, 123
    lemon-garlic, smoked mussels
        with, 116
Mexican-style squid salad, 110
Microwaving, 96
Mr. Zhu's steamed fish, 114
Monkfish, 42
    scaloppine with shallots, 115
    suggested recipes, 43
Monterey (California) squid, 66
Moonfish (opah), 45
Mornay sauce, 124
Mousse, smoked salmon, 116
Mousseline sauce, 124
Mullet, 43
    suggested recipes, 43
Mushroom(s)
    sauce, sherry-, fish fillets with, 111
    -stuffed calamari, 122
    swordfish steaks with, 117
    velvet, sole with, 110
Mussel(s), 43
    barbecuing, 87
    garlic, on the half shell, 101
    microwaving, 97
    & potato salad, 109
    sesame-ginger, steamed, 119
    suggested recipes, 44
Mustard
    eggs, 19
    sauce, 47
Mutton snapper, 65

Nassau grouper, 58
New Zealand groper (grouper), 58
New Zealand snapper (sea
    bream), 59
Northern pike, 50
Northern pink shrimp, 62
Nutrition, 12
Nutritional data, 13

Ocean catfish (wolffish), 77
Ocean perch (rockfish), 51
Ocean pink shrimp, 62
Ocean pout, 44
    suggested recipes, 45
Octopus, 45
    suggested recipes, 45
Oil and vinegar dressing, 19
Olympia oysters, 48
Onaga (snapper), 65
Onion(s)
    green, shrimp with, 120
    sauce, tart, mackerel with, 112
    sweet, Burmese fish with, 96
Ono (wahoo), 40
Opah, 45
    suggested recipes, 46
Opakapaka (snapper), 65
Orange risotto with shrimp, 120
Orange roughy, 46
    maître d'hôtel, 112
    suggested recipes, 46
Oven-browned fish, 85
Oyster(s), 48
    barbecuing, 87
    broiled fish or, with crumb
        coating, 89
    Hangtown fry, 122
    microwaving, 97
    sandwiches, garlic, 122
    soup, French, 106
    suggested recipes, 49

Pacific barracuda, 16
Pacific butterfish, 20
Pacific cod, 26
Pacific halibut, 34
Pacific hard-shell clams, 22
Pacific jack mackerel, 40
Pacific mackerel, 40
Pacific ocean perch (rockfish), 51
Pacific oysters, 48
Pacific red snapper. See Rockfish
Pacific sanddab (flounder), 33
Paloma. See Pompano
Palometa. See Pompano

Pan-fried catfish with jicama salad,
    111
Pan-fried fresh fish, 90
Pan-fried frozen fish, 90
Pan-fried skate with cucumbers &
    capers, 117
Pan-fried soft-shell crab with
    ginger or cayenne sauce, 120
Pan-frying, 90
Pan-poached fish, 92
Papio (jack), 36
Paralytic shellfish poisoning, 13
Parchment packets of flavor, 91
Parmesan marinade, basil-, 87
Pasta
    cool, stir-fried scallops &
        asparagus on, 109
    Laurita-style crab &, 121
    seafood linguine, 119
    steamed clams with linguisa &,
        106
Peas
    steamed trout with lettuce &, 96
    stir-fried fish or shellfish with, 95
Pepper sauce, red, grilled
    scallops with, 118
Perch, 49
    ocean (rockfish), 51
    suggested recipes, 50
Permit. See Pompano
Petrale sole, 33
Pickerel (pike), 50
Pike, 50
    suggested recipes, 50
Pine cone fish, 115
Pink salmon, 53
Pink shrimp, 62
Piquant vegetable sauce, 82
Plaice, American (flounder), 33
Poaching, 92
Polenta, hot cooked, 25
Pollock, 26
Pompano, 50
    California (butterfish), 20
    suggested recipes, 51
Porgy, 58
    suggested recipes, 59
Potato salad
    with caviar, 19
    mussel &, 109
Pot-au-feu, fish, 103
Prawns. See Shrimp
Prebrowned fish, 92
Provencale butter, 125
Puget Sound salmon gefillte fish
    soup, 103
Pumpkin-seed (butterfish), 20

Quenelles with creamy shallot
    sauce, 100
Quesadillas, crabby jack, 101
Quick browned butter sauces, 92
Quick colorful chowder, 102
Quillback rockfish, 51

Radish tartar sauce, 123
Rainbow runner (jack), 35
Rainbow smelt, 65
Rainbow trout, 72
Ratatouille, baked fish &, 112
Raw fish, using, 13
Ray (skate), 64
Razor clams, 22
Red chile Louis, 109
Red chile sauce, 109
Red crab, 29
Red drum, 31
Redfish (drum), 31
Redfish (rockfish), 51
Red grouper, 57
Red pepper sauce, grilled
    scallops with, 118
Red sauce, fish pil-pil in, 104
Red snapper, 65. See also
    Rockfish
Red (sockeye) salmon, 53
Remoulade sauce, 123
Rex sole, 33

Rice
  stuffing, almond-, 83
  sushi, 55
  wild, stuffing, almond-, 83
Risotto, orange, with shrimp, 120
Rock crab, 28
Rockfish, 51
  Florentine, 96
  suggested recipes, 52
Rock lobster, 38
Rock shrimp, 62
Roe, shad &, 60. *See also* Caviar
Rouille, 102
Round fish
  anatomy, 6, 7
  filleting, 80
Rusty flounder, 33

Sablefish, 52
  braised, 112
  suggested recipes, 52
Safety, seafood, 13
St. Pierre (John Dory), 36
Salad(s), 107–110
  chile, shrimp & corn, 108
  grilled salmon on wilted chicory, 113
  jicama, pan-fried catfish with, 111
  Mexican-style squid, 110
  mussel & potato, 109
  potato, with caviar, 19
  red chile Louis, 109
  salmon with tarragon vinaigrette, 107
  seviche, 108
  stir-fried scallops & asparagus on cool pasta, 109
  Thai fish & watercress, 108
  Veracruz fish, 107
Salmon, 53
  baby, with sautéed leeks, 113
  gefilte fish soup, Puget Sound, 103
  gravlax plus, 47
  grilled, on wilted chicory salad, 113
  mousse, smoked, 116
  salad with tarragon vinaigrette, 107
  steamed, with sorrel, 112
  suggested recipes, 56
  terrine, faux, 101
Salt cod, 25
Sandbar (shark), 61
Sanddab (flounder), 33
Sand sole, 33
Sandwiches, garlic oyster, 122
San Francisco-style cioppino, 105
Sardine, 35
  suggested recipes, 35
Sauces. *See also* Butters
  aïoli, 123
  béarnaise, 124
  cayenne, 120
  chile-cilantro, 101
  cocktail, 124
  creamy horseradish, 123
  creamy shallot, 100
  ginger, 120
  hollandaise, 124
  homemade mayonnaise, 123
  horseradish, 103
  hot ginger, 94
  lemon, 101
  lemon-garlic mayonnaise, 116
  lemon mayonnaise, 123
  mornay, 124
  mousseline, 124
  mustard, 47
  piquant vegetable, 82
  quick browned butter, 92
  radish tartar, 123
  red chile, 109
  remoulade, 123
  rouille, 102
  sesame, 55
  sweet & sour, 115
  tartar, 123
  tempura dipping, 89
  tomato-caper, 124
  watercress cream, 94

Scaling, 79
Scallops, 56
  & asparagus, sitr-fried, on cool pasta, 109
  grilled, with red pepper sauce, 118
  microwaving, 97
  with shallot butter, 102
  shrimp or, and pesto, 91
  & shrimp in béarnaise cream, 97
  suggested recipes, 57
Scampi (lobster), 38
Scombroid poisoning, 13
Scorpionfish (rockfish), 51
Scup, 58
Sea bass, 57. *See also* Bass
  suggested recipes, 58
Sea bream, 58
  suggested recipes, 59
Sea cat (wolffish), 77
Seafood
  baked in parchment, 91
  brochettes with champagne sauce, 119
  in curry cream, 69
  firepot, Thai, 105
  linguine, 119
  nutrition, 12
  nutritional data, 13
  safety, 13
  shopping for, 7
  storing, 10
Sea scallops, 56
Seatrout, 59. *See also* Drum; White sea bass
  suggested recipes, 60
Sergeant fish (cobia), 24
Sesame
  -ginger steamed mussels, 119
  sauce, 55
  seeds, toasted, 55
  -soy baste, 87
Seviche
  with kiwi fruit, 100
  salad, 108
Shad & roe, 60
  suggested recipes, 61
Shallot(s)
  butter, scallops with, 102
  monkfish scaloppine with, 115
  sauce, creamy quenelles with, 100
Shark, 61
  suggested recipes, 62
Sheepshead (drum), 31
Sheepshead (sea bream), 59
  suggested recipes, 59
Shellfish
  choosing, 7
  kebabs, fish or, 86
  look-alikes, surimi, 69
  nutrition, 12
  safety, 13
  stir-fried fish or, with peas, 95
  storing, 10
Sherry-mushroom sauce, fish fillets with, 111
Shopping for seafood, 7
Shortfin squid, 66
Shrimp, 62
  & corn salad, chile, 108
  deep-fried fish or, 89
  with green onions, 120
  microwaving, 97
  orange risotto with, 120
  scallops &, in béarnaise cream, 97
  or scallops and pesto, 91
  spiced, appetizer, 101
  suggested recipes, 63
Sidestripe shrimp, 62
Silk snapper, 65
Silverbrite (chum) salmon, 53
Silver dollar (butterfish), 20
Silver salmon, 53
Skate, 64
  pan-fried, with cucumbers & capers, 117
  suggested recipes, 64
Skewered fish, Northwest style, 118
Slipper lobsters, 38
Smelt, 65
  suggested recipes, 65

Smoked mussels with lemon-garlic mayonnaise, 116
Smoked salmon mousse, 116
Smoked seafood, 116
Smoking fish on the barbecue, 84
Snapper, 65
  Florentine, 96
  New Zealand (sea bream), 58
  Pacific red (rockfish), 51
  suggested recipes, 66
Snook, 66
Snow crab, 27
Sockeye salmon, 53
Soft-shell crab, pan-fried, with ginger or cayenne sauce, 120
Sole (flounder), 32
  fillets with peas and sesame oil, 91
  with mushroom velvet, 110
  suggested recipes, 34
  -wrapped Belgian endive rolls, 110
Sorrel, steamed salmon with, 112
Soupfin (shark), 61
Soups & stews, 102–106
  bourride, 102
  fish pil-pil in red sauce, 104
  fish pot-au-feu, 103
  French oyster soup, 106
  hearty clam chowder, 106
  lobster soup with leeks, 105
  matelote of eel, 104
  Puget Sound salmon gefilte fish soup, 103
  quick colorful chowder, 102
  San Francisco-style cioppino, 105
  steamed clams with linguisa & pasta, 106
  Tahoe crayfish bisque, 106
  Thai seafood firepot, 105
Sour cream-Cheddar topping, 85
Sourdough toast, 102
Southern flounder, 33
Spanish mackerel, 40
Spiced shrimp appetizer, 101
Spinach-mushroom stuffing, 83
Spiny lobster, 38
Spot (croaker), 31
Spot shrimp, 62
Spotted seatrout, 59
Squid, 66
  deep-fried, 89
  salad, Mexican-style, 110
  suggested recipes, 68
Starry flounder, 33
Steaks
  cutting, 80
  forms, 6, 10
Steamed clams with linguisa & pasta, 106
Steamed fish, Mr. Zhu's, 114
Steamed mussels, sesame-ginger, 119
Steamed salmon with sorrel, 112
Steamed smoked fish with dill butter, 116
Steamed trout with lettuce & peas, 96
Steaming, 94
Steelhead trout, 72
Steeping, 94
Stir-fried fish or shellfish with peas, 95
Stir-fried scallops & asparagus on cool pasta, 109
Stir-frying, 95
Stone crab, 28
Storing seafood, 10
Striped bass, 16
Striped mullet, 43
Stuffed trout, calico, 114
Stuffings, 83
Sturgeon, 68
  caviar, 19
  suggested recipes, 68
Summer flounder, 33
Surf smelt, 65
Surimi, 69
Sushi, 54
Sweet & sour sauce, 115
Swiss chard filling, 99
Swordfish, 70
  steaks with mushrooms, 117
  suggested recipes, 70

Ta'ape (snapper), 65
Tahoe crayfish bisque, 106
Tarragon vinaigrette dressing, 107
Tartar sauce, 123
  radish, 123
Tart onion sauce, mackerel with, 112
Tautog, 70
  suggested recipes, 71
Techniques, basic, 79–97
Temaki sushi (hand-rolled sushi), 55
Tempura
  batter, Japanese, 90
  dipping sauce, 89
Teriyaki fruit sauce, grilled tuna with, 117
Terrine, faux salmon, 101
Thai fish & watercress salad, 108
Thai seafood firepot, 105
Thresher, common (shark), 61
Tilapia, 71
  suggested recipes, 71
Tilefish, 71
  suggested recipes, 72
Toasted bread cube stuffing, 83
Togue (trout), 73
Tomato-caper sauce, 124
Trout, 72
  calico stuffed, 114
  with leeks & vinegar, 114
  steamed, with lettuce & peas, 96
  suggested recipes, 74
Tuna, 74
  anatomy, 6
  grilled, with teriyaki fruit sauce, 117
  suggested recipes, 76
Turbot, Greenland, 34. *See also* Flounder

Uku (snapper), 65
Ulva (jack), 36

Vegetable(s)
  broth, 103
  prepared, 55
  sauce, piquant, 82
  topping, creamy, 85
Veracruz fish salad, 107
Vermilion rockfish, 51
Vermilion snapper, 65
Vinegar, leeks &, trout with, 114

Wahoo (mackerel), 40
Walleye (perch), 49
Warm garlic butter, 125
Warsaw grouper, 58
Wasabi paste, 55
Watercress
  cream, 94
  salad, Thai fish &, 108
Weakfish, 59
  suggested recipes, 60
Weathervane scallops, 56
White bass, 17
Whitefish, 76
  caviar, 19
  suggested recipes, 77
White sea bass, 57. *See also* Drum
White shrimp, 62
White sturgeon, 68
Whiting, 26
Widow rockfish, 51
Wilted chicory salad, grilled salmon on, 113
Winter flounder, 33
Witch flounder, 33
Wolffish, 77
  suggested recipes, 77

Yelloweye rockfish, 51
Yellowfin grouper, 58
Yellowfin tuna, 75
Yellow perch, 49
Yellowtail (jack), 36
Yellowtail flounder, 33
Yellowtail snapper, 65